Who Pays for Student Diversity?

TWELFTH ANNUAL YEARBOOK
OF THE AMERICAN EDUCATION FINANCE ASSOCIATION
1991

Who Pays for Student Diversity?

Population Changes and Educational Policy

edited by
James Gordon Ward
Patricia Anthony

CORWIN PRESS, INC.
A Sage Publications Company
Newbury Park, California

To Lynn Elizabeth Ward

For information address:

Corwin Press
A Sage Publications Company
2455 Teller Road
Newbury Park, California 91320

SAGE Publications Ltd.
6 Bonhill Street
London EC2A 4PU
United Kingdom

SAGE Publications India Pvt. Ltd.
M-32 Market
Greater Kailash I
New Delhi 110 048 India

Printed in the United States of America

Library of Congress Cataloging-in-Publication Data

Main entry under title:

Who pays for student diversity? : population changes and educational policy/ edited by James Gordon Ward, Patricia Anthony.
    p.   cm.—(Annual yearbook of the American Education Finance Association; 12th)
    ISBN 0-8039-4019-X
    1. Public Schools—United States—Finance.   2. Education—Demographic aspects—United States.   I. Ward, James G. (James Gordon), 1944- . II. Anthony, Patricia, 1948- . III. Series.
LB2826.W43   1992
379.2'0973—dc20   91-35594
                                                                        CIP

92 93 94 95 10 9 8 7 6 5 4 3 2 1

Corwin Press Production Editor: Tara S. Mead

Contents

Preface

There are those who claim that demography is destiny. To be sure, demographic trends have a profound effect on public schools and the way they are financed and governed. We need only look at the major dislocations caused by the national enrollment decline that began in 1972 to see this. Recent demographic data indicate that the public schools of the United States will see increasing numbers of African American, Hispanic, immigrant, limited-English-speaking, and poor children. Because education will provide the competitive edge in a global economy, recognizing demographic changes and restructuring public education to meet these new challenges become critical. Issues of finance undergird all education policy decisions, and demographic changes have clear financial impact.

This volume presents some of the best thinking about the effects of demography on financing public schools. It explores these issues from a variety of perspectives and looks at what has been happening in selected states. It is not meant to be comprehensive or exhaustive but is designed to provide a "peak at reality" from a number of views. Its purpose is not so much to describe as to interpret. It is no accident that this yearbook of the American Education Finance Association follows one that explored concepts in social justice and discussed

the impact of those concepts and ideas on public school finance. It is critical that the field consider normative issues as
well as issues of technical efficiency and productivity.

These are issues that have not been addressed before in an
edited volume representing multiple perspectives. This book
should be useful to everyone concerned about the financing
of our public schools. It should be especially useful to federal
and state policymakers and school finance researchers as they
confront the many problems of sorting out the meaning of
changing populations and financing public schools. Students
in education will find the volume a valuable supplementary
text that will enrich their understandings of the intricacies of
school finance. The historical treatment in many of the chapters provides context that should help the development of
public policy in the states.

Overview of Contents

The book begins with an introductory chapter by the senior
editor on recent demographic trends in the United States and
their effects on schools. This topic has been painted with a
broad brush, looking at the increasing diversity of the U.S.
population, the maturation of America, changing family
structures, shifting income distributions, and regional variations in population change. The chapter concludes with recommendations for sweeping changes in school organization,
curricula, governance, and financing to meet the challenges
our nation faces. In Chapter 2 Cibulka takes a penetrating
look at the demographics of urban life in the United States
and the condition of urban school districts. He argues that a
renaissance for urban schools will need to be based on major
investments in all urban social institutions and public services, not just schools. He calls for vision and creativity in
solving a worsening problem and concludes that the solutions
to urban school problems are political rather than technical.
Haller and Monk in Chapter 3 turn to rural America and
show that demographic factors are just as important there in

achieving understanding of social and economic changes. They examine the role of the rural school as both a possible cause and a victim of the out-migration of the young adult population in rural areas. They use impressive empirical data to conclude that schools have little effect on the migration of rural youth.

In Chapter 4 Verstegen examines the mismatch in federal policy toward children and the needs of children in the decade of the 1980s. She surveys the recent demographic and economic changes in the country in an international context and looks at their effects on children. She makes a compelling point about the need for coordinated social services for children and argues for justice and fairness for all children as a basis for public policy decisions. She concludes by predicting that the failure to eradicate poverty among children will have an adverse effect on all of society. Thompson turns attention in Chapter 5 to state policy decisions and terms today's children a "generation at risk." He portrays a complex and disheartening picture of demographic changes in a number of major states and shows how state education and school finance policies have not kept up with social and economic conditions. He supports Verstegen's arguments and feels that the lack of economic and social opportunities for many children will become a national tragedy. Chapter 6 focuses on the needs of Hispanic children in American schools. Hyland discusses the results of a national study of how public schools will need to change to meet the needs of one of the fastest growing segments of the public school population. She finds a high degree of consensus among experts about what changes will be beneficial, but she raises questions about the ability and willingness of states and communities to finance these changes.

In the beginning of a series of chapters on the effects of demographic changes on education and school finance in several states, Sparkman and Campbell (Chapter 7) intertwine the changing demography of Texas with the saga of school finance reform in that state. They raise questions about the ability of court-mandated reform to be sufficiently sensitive to the needs of minority populations. Like a number of the other authors, they suggest that vision and political courage may be the missing ingredients in bringing about positive change. In Chapter 8 Wood and Honeyman move our attention to Florida and chronicle the complex changes that have occurred over time in the Florida school finance system in an attempt to accommodate the needs of a changing school population. They argue that other state infrastructure needs may curtail funding for public schools and do not offer an optimistic prognosis for progress in school finance in Florida.

Koppich (Chapter 9), in considering demographic changes in California, argues that traditional school finance notions may need to be altered if states are to meet the needs of all children. She suggests that a wider variety of elements embracing many social attributes of children will need to be factored into school finance formulas and systems. Positing that California is the social laboratory of the nation, she calls for viewing "school finance" as "education finance," with a view of education that encompasses a broad array of social services for children. In Chapter 10 Hess provides a contrast by discussing conditions in Illinois, a state not experiencing the rapid growth in school enrollments of Texas, Florida, and California. He demonstrates through a rich array of statistical data how the internal shifts within Illinois are presenting new problems, and he offers a variety of policy options for their solution.

Eaton (Chapter 11) provides a historical perspective and distinguishes inequity from inequality in financing public schools. He discusses how private problems become public policy issues and raises questions about new judicial routes to social justice. Like many of the other chapter authors, he is encouraged by trends that focus on the needs of children and the coordination of a variety of social services for children.

Finally, the concluding chapter by the senior editor considers the effects of class and race on power relationships in public education and speculates on their ultimate effect on social justice in the Untied States. In particular, I note the failure of current policy mechanisms to bring about fundamental fairness in our system of financing public schools and suggest that some more radical approaches may be necessary.

Acknowledgments

I owe a major intellectual debt to Michael Kirst and the late Walter I. Garms for first stimulating my thinking about the complex relationships among social, economic, and political factors and the public schools. M. David Alexander, Richard G. Salmon, and Kern Alexander sharpened my views on equity, social justice, and the financing of public schools. Richard A. Rossmiller and John A. Rohr have more to do with the way I think about schools, social justice, and public policy than they probably realize. Finally, my friend and professional collaborator William E. Sparkman deserves credit for his support, intellectual stimulation, and much appreciated humor at times when all were needed.

My wife, Lynn, and my children, Heather, Jay, and Audrey, have all suffered with me as I have suffered through the normal travails of compiling an edited volume. For too long they have only seen the back of my head as I toil over the keyboard. As I emerge a more multifaceted person, I hope they like what they see.

As I write these words on a Memorial Day weekend, I want to pay homage to my grandparents, William J. and Frances Ingalls Ward and Marion J. and Alice Jennings Wooster, all now deceased. They bear responsibility for my parents, Gordon J. and Alice A. Ward, who taught me right from wrong.

JAMES GORDON WARD

About the Contributors

Patricia Anthony is Assistant Professor of Educational Administration at the University of Massachusetts at Amherst. Prior to entering higher education, she was a special education teacher and curriculum specialist. From 1985 to 1989, she was editor of the *Journal of Education Finance*, for which she now serves as a member of the Editorial Advisory Board. She received her doctorate from the University of Florida. Her primary research interests are in the interrelationship of law and finance in producing public policy relevant to the use of public funds for private schools and in the funding of programs for special needs students. She has published widely in the fields of school law and school finance.

Trudy A. Campbell is Assistant Professor of Education at Texas Tech University, where she teaches graduate courses in educational administration. Her Ph.D. degree is from the University of Illinois at Urbana-Champaign, where she specialized in bilingual education and educating multicultural populations. She has been a public school administrator and a foreign language teacher. Her research interests center on ethnic and gender issues in school leadership.

James G. Cibulka is Professor of Administrative Leadership and Director of the Ph.D. Program in Urban Education at the University of Wisconsin-Milwaukee. He received his Ph.D.

from the University of Chicago, where he concentrated on educational administration and political science. He is past president of the Politics of Education Association. His research interests focus on the politics of urban education. He has written numerous articles and books, including the forthcoming *The Politics of Urban Education in the United States,* coedited with Rodney J. Reed and Kenneth K. Wong.

William Edward Eaton is Professor and Chair of the Department of Educational Administration and Higher Education at Southern Illinois University at Carbondale. He received his Ph.D. from Washington University in St. Louis with a specialization in the history and philosophy of education. His research concentrates on the history of American education, with a special interest in teacher unions and reconstructionism. He has recently turned his attention to the history of American school administration.

Emil J. Haller is Professor in the Department of Education at Cornell University, where his primary interests are in educational administration. His research interests are in the areas of social class, race and ability grouping, and rural education. Recent works include *The Ethics of School Administration* (1988) and *An Introduction to Educational Administration* (1986).

G. Alfred Hess, Jr., is Executive Director of the Chicago Panel on Public School Policy and Finance. He received his Ph.D. in anthropology from Northwestern University. He has been instrumental in providing public scrutiny of the finance and budgeting processes of the Chicago public schools and has been a key participant in school reform in Chicago. His most recent publication, *School Restructuring, Chicago Style* (1991), is in the area of urban education reform.

David S. Honeyman is Associate Professor of Educational Leadership at the University of Florida, where he is also Co-Director of the University Council of Educational Administration's Center for Education Finance. He has also served on the faculties of Lehigh University and Kansas State University, and he has been a building-level school administrator and teacher. He earned his doctorate at the University of

Virginia. His research has been focused on education finance equity and adequacy. He is currently involved in school finance litigation in several states.

Concetta Raimondi Hyland is Principal, Longfellow Junior High School, Indianapolis, Indiana. She has been a secondary English teacher, guidance counselor, coordinator of pupil personnel, and administrator in public school districts in both Illinois and Indiana. She received her Ed.D. degree from the University of Illinois at Urbana-Champaign in educational administration. She has research interests and has published in the areas of the education of minority children and Hispanic education.

Julia E. Koppich is Deputy Director of Policy Analysis for California Education (PACE). She received her Ph.D. in educational administration and policy analysis from the University of California, Berkeley. She worked on the staff of the California legislature, taught high school government in the San Francisco area, and served as Staff Director for the San Francisco Federation of Teachers (AFT). She has also served as Assistant Editor of *Educational Evaluation and Policy Analysis*. Her research interests include the politics of education, public sector labor relations, integrated services for children, and reform of educational systems.

David H. Monk is Professor of Educational Administration at Cornell University. He received his Ph.D. from the University of Chicago. He has taught at the University of Rochester and several universities abroad. His research interests are in the economic aspects of educational administration and resource allocation practices at multiple levels of educational systems. He is a senior research fellow with the Finance Center of the Consortium for Policy Research in Education. He has written *Educational Finance: An Economic Approach* and is President-Elect of the American Education Finance Association.

William E. Sparkman is Associate Dean for Graduate Education and Research and Professor of Education at Texas Tech University. He teaches graduate courses in school law and school finance. He received his Ph.D. degree from the University of Florida and is a past president of the American Education Finance Association. His research interests are in the areas of school finance litigation, education finance, and school law.

David C. Thompson is Associate Professor of Educational Administration at Kansas State University and is Co-Director of the University Council for Educational Administration's (UCEA) Center for Education Finance. He holds an Ed.D. from Oklahoma State University. He served as a public school teacher, principal, and superintendent for 15 years before joining the University. His research specialties focus on school finance litigation and state school finance policy, including service to plaintiffs and defendants in numerous lawsuits throughout the nation.

Deborah Verstegen is currently Assistant Professor of Education Policy and Finance in the Curry School of Education at the University of Virginia. She serves on the Board of Directors of the American Education Finance Association (AEFA), the Advisory Board for the U.S. Department of Education's National Center for Education Statistics Technical Panel, and the Finance Center of the University Council for Education Administration (UCEA). She is also the editor of the *Journal of Education Finance*. She has received a distinguished service award from AEFA and UCEA and has served as expert witness in state school finance litigation. She is active in school finance cases currently before state courts. Her research focus is on equity in education finance and the fiscal aspects of education policy. She has authored or coauthored more than 80 publications, most recent of which is her collaboration with James Ward on *Spheres of Justice in Education* (1991).

James Gordon Ward is Associate Dean of Education, and Associate Professor of Educational Administration, of Curriculum and Instruction, and of Government and Public Affairs, at the University of Illinois at Urbana-Champaign. He is a past president of the American Education Finance Association. He is a former teacher as well as educational policy analyst and served for eight years as Director of Research for the American Federation of Teachers. He received his Ed.D. from

Virginia Polytechnic Institute and State University. His research interests include the political and legal aspects of state school finance policy, school organization and leadership, and political theory. He has an emerging interest in the institutional relationships among school finance, curriculum, and school quality.

R. Craig Wood is Chair and Professor, Department of Educational Leadership, University of Florida. He is also Co-Director of the University Council of Educational Administration's Center for Education Finance. He received his Ed.D. from Virginia Polytechnic Institute and State University. He has served as an assistant superintendent of schools for finance and served on the faculty of Purdue University. His research interests involve school finance litigation, educational equity, and school business management. He currently is involved in school finance litigation in several states. He is editor of *Principles of School Business Management*.

ONE

The Power of Demographic Change
IMPACT OF POPULATION
TRENDS ON SCHOOLS

JAMES GORDON WARD

E. A. Wrigley (1969, p. 8) began his classic *Population and History* with the words, "When Kant wished to illustrate the notion that even historical events whose occurrence seems quite random and unpredictable may in the mass show notable regularities, he turned to population." This is not to say that demography is destiny, but it does suggest that there are strong social forces, like demographic change, that have a tremendous impact on other events and regularities in society. This is a fact recognized by sociologists, by historians, and even occasionally by economists as well as by demographers. Amatai Etzioni, Fernand Braudel, and Kenneth Boulding especially come to mind as scholars who acknowledge population trends and social forces as powerful determiners of historic events and trends. Populations, their fluctuations, and their characteristics are important to our understanding of many social institutions, including U.S. public schools and their finance and governance.

It is important to talk openly about demographic changes and their effects on schools and schooling, because, as Heifetz and Sinder (1988, p. 179) remind us, "Prevailing ideas about what is good for society often determine how problems are posed, which actions are taken, and by whom." Public discourse can be a powerful factor in determining how issues are framed on the public policy agenda. Education policymakers need to recognize social trends and understand how they may pose problems for the functioning of schools. The way those problems are defined, and hence solved, will be determined on the basis of how we understand them. For example, if we do not understand the root causes of increasing numbers of public school students who are limited English proficient and who come from poor families, we may not understand why the numbers of such children are likely to grow and why some school districts, and not others, without large numbers of such children, may be likely to see their numbers increase. To be able to extrapolate recent trends into the future will help us construct school finance systems that will not be outmoded before the signature is dry on the legislation enacting them.

This chapter will examine some changes in U.S. public education during the last few decades, will discuss some recent demographic trends in the United States and projections for the near future, will examine demographic trends affecting public schooling, and will suggest how the most powerful of these trends could affect public school finance. Later chapters will explore specific aspects of population change as well as investige the effects of population trends on education in specific states. The book will conclude with an exploration of some of the normative aspects of demographic change.

American Public Education Since 1960

A Statistical Profile

In the more than three decades since 1960, there have been some major changes in the U.S. public schools and many of them are the result of population changes. These characteristics and changes set the stage for understanding future changes in schools. (All data in this section are from the *Digest of Education Statistics 1990* of the National Center for Education Statistics [NCES]; U.S. Department of Education, 1991.)

School-age youth were a larger proportion of the total population in 1960 than today. In 1959-1960 the U.S. population aged 5-17 years were 24.5% of the total population, but this figure had declined to 18.6% in 1987-1988. The youth-dominated U.S. society of the late 1950s and early 1960s has become a society dominated by middle age in the 1990s with the maturation of the "baby boom" generation. Enrollment in public elementary and secondary schools increased from about 36 million in 1959-1960 to more than 45 million in the early 1970s before falling back to 40 million in the late 1980s. Enrollment in kindergarten and grades 1 through 8 increased slightly from 27.6 million in 1959-1960 to 27.9 million in 1987-1988 but increased in grades 9-12 from 8.5 million to 12.1 million. The number of high school graduates increased from 1.6 million in 1960 to 2.5 million in 1988. A dramatic increase has been seen in instructional staff, who numbered 1.4 million in 1959-1960 but had burgeoned to 2.4 million in 1987-1988. This increase in staff has affected school costs per pupil in a dramatic fashion.

In constant 1986-1987 dollars, current expenditure per average daily attendance (ADA) increased from $1,862 in 1959-1960 to $4,642 in 1987-1988. During the same period the average salary of instructional staff increased from about $20,400 to about $29,177. In 1959-1960 the average instructional staff salary represented 95% of the average personal income of all labor force members but had fallen slightly to 94% in 1987-1988. For the most part then, public school instructional staff maintained their position in spending power of slightly below the income of the average worker.

In 1959-1960, revenues for public elementary and secondary schools came primarily from local sources (56.5%), with 39.1% coming from state sources. The federal government provided 4.4% of public school funds. By 1987-1988 the local and state roles had reversed, with 49.5% of revenues coming from state sources and 44.1% from local sources. Federal revenues accounted for 6.3% of all revenues.

Public school expenditures for current operations were 79.0% of total expenditures in 1959-1960 because rampant school construction to accommodate a growing student population (capital outlay and debt service) consumed 20.1% of all public school expenditures that year. By 1987-1988 current operations accounted for 91.2% of total expenditures and capital construction and debt service only 8.8%.

The median years of school completed by persons age 25 and over was 10.5 in 1960, but there were large differences by race. White adults had achieved a median education of 10.8 years in 1960, but nonwhites had only 8.2 years of schooling. By 1988 the national average median years of schooling for those 25 and older was 12.7, a gain of 2.2 years in a 28-year span. Whites had gained 1.9 years to 12.7, but nonwhites gained 4.3 years to a median of 12.5 years of schooling in 1988. Schools became a critical factor in the quest for social justice in the United States.

Trends in American Schooling

In addition to the trends identified by the quantitative data above, there have been other notable differences in U.S. schooling during the last three decades. This is not the place to discuss them all, but some are particularly notable for the purposes of this chapter.

The civil rights movement and greater emphasis on equal educational opportunity for all children had a profound effect on schools, expanding the opportunities of African Americans, handicapped children, and children whose native language is not English. The school finance reform movement, beginning in the late 1960s and extending in a number of phases through the early 1990s, is a direct manifestation of the civil rights movement.

A cultural revolution in the United States in the 1960s and 1970s saw many barriers to individual autonomy and freedom of expression for all. Student and teacher rights blossomed, and traditional approaches to curriculum and instruction fell. Some argue that discipline left the schools also. Drug and alcohol abuse became more prominent problems, and social problems entered the schools with a vengeance.

This period also saw the rise of collective bargaining in public schools and the transformation of both the National Education Association and the American Federation of Teachers, and their state and local affiliates, into major labor unions. Power relationships within school districts and schools were altered, and state politics of education were greatly changed. Although this has not been recognized by some scholars and some school administrators, teachers became a major force in school governance. School district programs and practices became controlled by the triumvirate of state statute, school board policy, and the collective bargaining contract. Between 1960 and 1990 the "most prominent American educator title" probably passed from James B. Conant to Albert Shanker, with the nation's governors collectively challenging for the title now.

States became far more important in education policy issues. This has been seen not only in school finance but in curriculum issues, in testing and accountability, in teacher education and certification, and in myriad other areas of education. State reforms in the 1980s, spurred on by various national reports, shifted attention away from issues of equity toward new emphases on *excellence*, a word never adequately defined. School finance suits in many states have shifted from a basis in equal protection to a new dependence on the wording of the state constitution's education clause or article.

The latter part of this period saw many new faces in public schools, many of them Asian and Hispanic. Many city schools became almost exclusively African American in student enrollment. Just as the family of Mom and Dad and the two kids living in the middle-class white suburban development was no longer the social norm, Dick and Jane became an outdated and false caricature of the U.S. public school. These changes provided new opportunities for schools as well as presenting new challenges.

The more things changed, the more they changed. Population trends and social forces transformed U.S. society and its schools with it. Our interactions with science and technology have taught us that change is not steady but is constantly accelerating. Recent population trends in the United States will set the stage for our immediate future.

Recent Population Trends in the United States

Volumes of population data on the United States exist, but the difficult chore is to make sense out of the numbers. After all, data and information are two very different things. Analysts need to discern patterns, to strive for understanding of the discovered patterns, and to give those understandings meaning for public policymakers and administrators. Various students of population trends have provided some of the patterns. These patterns are broader than just student enrollment statistics and pertain to the wider social context of public schooling. They relate to the labor force, social institutions, economic growth and development, family issues, and the spatial array of Americans as well as other factors in our lives.

More Diverse Population

The population of the United States is becoming more racially, ethnically, and culturally diverse. The United States is an anomaly in most of the rest of the world because the majority population of the nation is not of color (Usdan, 1984). Depending on how one counts, up to 25% of the U.S. population in 1990 may be "minority." In 1990 African Americans represent over 12% of the nation's people; the "other races" category, largely Asian and Pacific Islander, constitutes 3.6%, and Hispanics total 8.4% (Waldrop & Exter, 1991). The fastest growing segments of the population are Asians and Hispanics. In fact, the Hispanic population in the 1980s grew at a rate four times that of the whole population (Waldrop & Exter,

1991). Between 1990 and 1995, while the entire U.S. population between the ages of 5 and 13 is expected to decrease by
about 3%, the African American population in this age cohort
is expected to grow by more than 12%, and the Hispanic population is likely to grow by almost 17% (Sternlieb & Hughes,
1987). By the same token, the total population from age 14 to
17 is projected to grow by 7%, but the African American high
school population will jump by more than 11%, and the
Hispanic population in this age group will increase by an estimated 11.5% (Sternlieb & Hughes, 1987). Immigration, often
spurred by unpredictable world political and economic
events, may accelerate these trends. On average, minority
populations are younger than the U.S. white population and
tend to have more children. Sternlieb and Hughes (1987) predict that these trends will result in the movement to promi-
nence on the public policy agenda in the 1990s of issues of
race and ethnicity, possibly even bringing on a return of the
urban crises as we saw in the 1960s.

The Maturation of America

The so-called baby boom generation, comprising those born
between 1946 and 1964, has had a profound impact on U.S.
society (Jones, 1980). This large population cohort led to the
rapid expansion of the U.S. public school system in the 1950s
and 1960s, with their maturing resulting in student enrollment declines in the 1970s. The "echo effect" of the children
of the baby boom generation attaining school-attending age
caused enrollments to modestly increase in many regions of
the nation in the mid-1980s. In 1991 the baby boomers are between 27 and 45 years of age; in 1995 they will be between 31
and 49. The oldest are seeing many of their children leave
public elementary and secondary schools, while many of the
youngest are settling in to raising families. As Sternlieb and
Hughes (1987) point out, between 1990 and 1995 the number
of Americans 34 years of age and younger is expected to decline
by 1.7%, while the number from 35 to 54 is likely to increase

by 16.0%, and the number 55 years of age and older will increase
by 3.9%. The "mature generation" will predominate. Those in
this age band tend to be more security minded, are interested in
recreation and cultural activities, will tend to become more
health minded with age, and will have less of a direct interest in
public schools as time passes. They are also very politically active and vote in larger proportions than younger groups. Their
primary interest may not be in public education, and their political support for education may be waning.

The maturation of the U.S. population also means a more experienced and productive work force (Sternlieb & Hughes,
1987). Career advancement may not be as rapid as in previous
decades because the age cohort approaching retirement—those
born during the late 1920s and 1930s—is much smaller than that
of the workers who are just behind them. The labor force will
become increasingly security minded, and intrinsic job rewards
will be important to many workers, partially because extrinsic
rewards like promotion and salary bonuses may not be available
to a large share of workers. Younger workers and new job en-
trants will become increasingly minority and more culturally diverse, possibly leading to cultural clashes in the workplace.
Immigration may become the source for many of the jobs that
fall into Reich's (1991) categories of "routine production services" and "in-person services"; however, it is worthy of note
that many persons who immigrate to the United States do fall
into Reich's "symbolic analyst" category. Broad, sweeping gen-
eralizations become difficult to make in these areas.

Fewer Traditional Families

The average household size in the United States fell from
2.76 in 1980 to 2.63 in 1990, and the average family size fell
from 3.29 to 3.17 during the same period (Waldrop & Exter,
1991). Fewer people per household or per family means fewer
traditional homes with two parents and children. In fact, the
percentage of "traditional family" households as a percentage
of all households fell from 31% in 1980 to an estimated 26% in

1990 (Waldrop & Exter, 1991). Therefore it is likely that over one half of all children in schools come from what would be considered "nontraditional" households. Caution needs to be exercised in the interpretation of these data because it is not fair to assume that, just because a household is not traditional, there is some degree of social instability. However, these data are one indicator that many assumptions school staff make about children and their families may not be true. In addition, the increasing number of dual-career families creates issues of before- and after-school care and support and assistance with schoolwork that must be considered.

Shifting Income Distributions

The income share of the top 20% of all households increased from 44% in 1980 to 47% in 1989 (Waldrop & Exter, 1991). Reich (1991) estimates that this figure has reached 50% by 1991. This supports the contention that the affluent are getting richer and the rest of society is becoming poorer, which has been well publicized recently (see Phillips, 1990; Reich, 1991). Waldrop and Exter (1991) attribute this to more working women, hence two-income households, and a stronger relationship between education and earnings potential, while Phillips (1990) holds that overt government policies have contributed to much of this income imbalance. Reich (1991) sees global economic trends as well as government policies at play here.

Reich (1991) makes the point that the increasing information base for our economy increases the economic power of "symbolic analysis"—the ability to manipulate words, numbers, and visual images—and that high-quality education is the key to high ability in symbolic analysis (see Reich, 1991, chaps. 14-19). This is supported by the analysis of Waldrop and Exter (1991), who show that between 1980 and 1990 the income, in constant dollars, of men aged 25 and older who are employed full-time year-round dropped over 21% for those who dropped out of high school, dropped 16.5% for those who are high school graduates with no college, and increased

4.5% for college graduates. For women aged 25 and older who
are employed full-time year-round, incomes increased 2.3%
for high school dropouts, 17.1% for high school graduates
with no college, and 30.5% for college graduates between
1980 and 1990, again in constant dollars. Both men and
women with more education have increased their economic
position compared with others during the last decade. This
attests to the power of education to increase incomes as well
as pointing out the difficult job of ensuring equal educational
opportunities among communities with greatly differing abilities to support public services.

The Nation Is Becoming More Suburban
and More Southern and Western

Between 1980 and 1990 the percentage of the total U.S. population living in the suburbs grew from 44% to 47.2%, while nonmetropolitan areas in the Midwest, South, and West all lost
population, and cities in most parts of the nation stagnated
(Waldrop & Exter, 1991). One of the best kept secrets during the
last few decades may be the steady and relentless suburbanization of the United States (Jackson, 1985). While nonmetropolitan
areas enjoyed a resurgence in the 1970s, the trend reversed in
the 1980s, and both nonmetropolitan and urban areas declined
or grew slowly compared with the suburban areas.

Earlier population trends toward the southern and western
United States continued in the 1980s and are likely to continue
through the 1990s. In 1990, 55.3% of Americans lived in a southern or western state, and the West passed the Northeast to become the third largest U.S. census region (Waldrop & Exter,
1991). Of the 25 U.S. counties with the highest projected job
growth between 1989 and 2000, five are in California, four each
are in Texas and Florida, and two are in Georgia; and 19 of the
25, or 76%, are in southern or western states (Exter, 1991). Significant growth in both Asian and Hispanic populations is occurring in California, and a major share of the population increase
in Texas and Florida is Hispanic. Immigration and the higher

birthrate of Hispanics is the engine driving a great deal of the population increase in metropolitan areas of the South and West.

Youth at Risk

In addition to the demographic trends discussed above, there are some disturbing statistics that indicate there are social trends toward the deterioration of the well-being of U.S. youth, placing many at risk for academic failure. While the percentage of 25- to 29-year-olds who have completed four years of college or more has increased from 11.0% in 1960 to 22.2% in 1985, the percentage who had not completed four years of high school is at an alarming 13.9% for the entire population in 1986. In the same year 16.7% of African Americans aged 25 to 29 had not completed four years of high school and 41.0% of Hispanics had not completed high school. Rapid advances were made in high school completion rates through 1975, but the rate of advance leveled off after the mid-1970s (U.S. Department of Education, 1988).

The percentage of children under age 18 living in poverty decreased from 26.5% in 1960 to 14.9% in 1970 but increased to 20.1% in 1985 (U.S. Department of Education, 1988). The poverty rate for children under 18 in 1985 was 43.1% for African Americans and 39.6% for Hispanics while 15.6% for whites (U.S. Department of Education, 1988). Slight advances were made in the late 1980s as the poverty rate for those under 18 decreased to 19.2% for the total population, 14.1% for whites, and 37.6% for Hispanics, but the poverty rate increased to 43.5% for African American children (U.S. Department of Education, 1991).

Challenges for the 1990s

These population changes in the United States suggest some major challenges in the 1990s and beyond for U.S. society and for public schools. While demographic trends may not be direct determinants of social, economic, and political changes, they do provide the basis for predicting certain trends.

First, the clientele served by public schools is already changing, and those changes will continue and accelerate in the future. Differential birthrates among different sectors of U.S. society and immigration would indicate that public school enrollments will continue to see an increase in children from poor families, children who lack desired proficiency in English, children whose home culture is significantly different from the culture reflected in the school, children who lack adult supervision before and after school, children who live in environments with drug and alcohol abuse, and children who live in violent environments. While we often associate these factors with urban areas, there are rural areas in the country where such situations are major problems, and the suburbs are not immune. None of these situations is necessarily a problem in and of itself, but they are all factors that correlate with some school difficulties. Wilson (1987), for example, has highlighted the plight of the urban underclass and suggests that major public policy initiatives are required to remedy this significant social problem. He argues that,

> despite a high rate of poverty in ghetto neighborhoods throughout the first half of the twentieth century, rates of inner-city joblessness, teenage pregnancy, out-of-wedlock births, female-headed families, welfare dependency, and serious crime were significantly lower than in later years and did not reach catastrophic proportions until the mid-1970s. (p. 3)

All indications are that this situation is not improving and will continue to be a major issue in the 1990s and early twenty-first century.

Second, evidence suggests that education is becoming even more important in financial and career success in adulthood. More unequal income distribution is documented in recent work in income distribution and public policy in the United States (Phillips, 1990; Reich, 1991). Thurow (1984) shows both the conceptual and the empirical complexity of demonstrating the relationship between levels of education and income, but Reich (1991) offers a possible solution to this human capital dilemma. He says,

> My argument thus far is that the economic well-being of Americans . . . no longer depends on the profitability of the corporations they own, or on the prowess of their industries, but on the value they add to the global economy through their skills and insights. Increasingly, it is the jobs that Americans do, rather than the success of abstract entities like corporations, industries, or national economy, that determine their standard of living. (p. 196)

After documenting the growing unequal distribution of income in the United States, he states, "the widening income gap is closely related to the level of education" (Reich, 1991, p. 205). He notes that those in the upper income strata are, for the most part, those who earn their living from the analysis of words, numbers, and visual symbols, and he also notes that their educational preparation follows a similar pattern. Symbolic analysts attend elite private schools or high-quality suburban public high schools, study at selective universities and the best graduate schools, have high parental interest and involvement in education, work with teachers and professors who attend to their academic needs, enjoy well-equipped schools with computers and good libraries, have small classes and intellectually stimulating classmates, have access to a tremendous array of cultural experiences and books, and receive very high-quality medical care (Reich, 1991, pp. 227-228). Most U.S. children simply do not have access to this quality of education and life. The education of symbolic analysts emphasizes four basic skills of abstraction, system thinking, experimentation, and collaboration, skills not often taught in the standardized education provided for most U.S. children (Reich, 1991). This rescues the case for reform of U.S. state school finance systems from sterile arguments about fiscal equity and places it squarely in the center of the quest for high-quality educational services for all children as a necessary requisite for continued life success.

Third, there is a growing gap between those who benefit from public services and those who make decisions about funding public services. Political power seems to be concentrating more in the hands of those who are white, middle aged, and middle class and live in the suburbs of major U.S. cities. These individuals have a high demand for certain public services, such as health care, recreational facilities, environmental protections, and police protection and corrections. They may be Republicans or Democrats, but they are generally fiscally conservative and protective of their own affluence. Nationally, they will be particularly evident in large numbers in southern and western states such as California, Texas, and Florida. They will be physically and culturally separated from what Sternlieb and Hughes (1987) see as increasing concentrations of African Americans, Hispanics, and the poor in central cities and "spillover suburbs." A dramatic demographic change in the first ring of suburbs next to large cities has already become evident in such places as Nassau County, New York, and Cook County, Illinois. We know that minorities and the poor are not as politically active, nor are their voting participation rates as high as those who are white, more affluent, or better educated. Major political battles will continue and increase over whether those in the affluent suburbs will be willing to tax themselves at a higher rate to finance public services—such as health care, public assistance, social services, and education—for minorities and the poor in the cities, poor suburbs, and rural areas. Legislative responses in 1990 and 1991 to school finance reform decisions in favor of plaintiffs in Texas and New Jersey may be indicative of this shift in political power and the battle over the public purse. If the plaintiffs prevail in a pending Illinois school finance lawsuit, the political response is likely to mirror the turmoil in Texas and New Jersey.

Implications for Public School Policy

These trends raise some important questions and issues for public policy in the United States relating to schools. While schools do not provide the answers for all the social ills of the nation—a role the public sometimes likes to foist on public schools—they are an important instrument of social policy.

Demographic trends in U.S. society raise critical questions relating to the organization and governance of U.S. public schools. The strong elements of local control present in so many state systems of public education seem increasingly to be outmoded in the face of the grave problems facing schools. Basing education policy decisions on local norms and community values often results in discriminatory and repressive school practices in culturally diverse communities. There is evidence to indicate that some communities use the excuse of responsiveness to local differences as a way of circumventing equal opportunities for schooling (Ward & Rink, 1991). Education in the United States is constitutionally a state function and state responsibility. The challenge of a changing public school clientele coupled with increasing cultural, social, and economic separation of those who pay for public services and those who benefit from public services require a reexamination of intergovernmental relations and the provision of educational services. States need to become much more active in ensuring that their organization and control of public schools protects the rights of all children and that high-quality schooling is available to all children in the state. This must be done with care, however.

As March and Olsen (1989, p. 118) remind us, public policies based on aggregative political processes, characterized by contractual relations, rationality, majority rule, and efficiency considerations, may not be as effective and as democratic as integrative public policies involving shared purposes and trust, a communal approach to politics, a sense of reasons and trusteeship, development of shared meaning through public debate, and an emphasis on integrity and competence. If we are to overcome what Reich (1991, p. 282) calls "the politics of secession," where the successful "undo the political and legal ties that bind them to their undesired compatriots," then we must look at new political institutions (i.e., rules, routines, and procedures) to integrate our educational system so that all are served well.

Current organizational and governance institutions in education allow the successful in U.S. society to functionally secede from the rest of society and, through governmentally sanctioned enclaves, provide high-quality educational services for their children while relegating the children of much of the rest of society to a substandard education. Current choice proposals and other attempts at privatizing education represent a further move in the direction of segregating society and protecting the affluent through exclusive enclaves of privilege. A solution may be to organize the provision of education around larger organizational units with smaller service delivery units. Great uniformity of opportunity may exist in larger organizational units, where the ability to secede from others is lessened, and larger units may actually be open to broader public scrutiny in a democratic society. Greater community involvement in the governance of these larger units will be necessary to build the shared vision and sense of common purpose that are needed. Larger organizational units, however, do not mean larger school buildings. In fact, larger school districts could protect smaller elementary schools, which seem to work quite well, and allow more flexibility in the delivery of secondary school students. The kind of standardized education that Reich laments seems more common in high schools in small and medium-sized districts, where adequate opportunities cannot be provided. Larger organizational units broaden the tax and revenue base and help to eliminate extremes in a district's financial ability to provide services.

School curricula, programs, and structure also need to be revisited. A centralized-decentralized structure may be the most appropriate for the changes taking place in U.S. education. All the factors discussed in this chapter indicate the need for a social consensus on what the results of schooling should be and the need for some mechanism to ensure that all schools provide the opportunity for all children to have access to the curriculum, program, and experiences that will let them achieve the level of education called for in this social consensus. It seems to me that states have an obligation to make clear and explicit what they want schools to achieve to meet the state's responsibility to provide an adequate education. This will take the form of a state curriculum for all learners. It then seems that school districts and schools have an obligation to exercise broad discretion to develop programs of instruction to achieve those ends. These desired ends should be uniform across the state, not with one curriculum for the affluent and another curriculum for the rest of society. School structures should be flexible enough to allow experimentation and different approaches to learning. Risk-taking behavior must be encouraged to foster greater creativity.

Another issue that merits greater attention is the coordination of social services for children among numerous agencies. The current system of providing social services for children in many states is fragmented with responsibility shared among so many agencies that no one agency can perform its function adequately. Schools often complain that they cannot provide education and be broad-based social service agencies at the same time. This is true to the extent that schools cannot perform this function alone. Schools may need to be at the center of a coordinated set of social services for children, however, and take the lead in bringing other agencies together in a coordinated system. Otherwise, for many children the school may not be able to perform even its education function well. In many states this requires a reevaluation of units of local government and governmental jurisdictions and boundaries that are not coterminous. It is not uncommon for a school district, a municipality, the county, and the state all to provide social services for children. They all have different boundaries, and coordination among so many agencies with different jurisdictions becomes an administrative and service delivery nightmare. One solution might be the establishment of units of government with broader geographic scope to coordinate all public services for children. Some states with county school districts come close to this model.

A final issue relates to new ways of thinking about the financing of education. Thro (1990) has noted that state school finance reform litigation in the United States in the late 1980s seemed to have moved from an emphasis on equal protection to greater dependence on making the argument for reform on the basis of the state constitution's education article or clause. This shift may be partially a matter of legal strategy and partially, as Ward (1990) has noted, a recognition that the early state school finance lawsuits failed to achieve their desired purposes. Whatever the reasons, this change signals a move in emphasis away from equity issues toward issues of adequacy and quality. The complexity of measuring the special needs of children and of equating one kind of need with another quantitatively to fit into a state distribution formula may outstrip our ability to deal with these issues conceptually and technically. This makes the application of the concept of equity to school finance a practical nightmare. As a result, most measures of student equity in school finance only include expenditures for "regular" children and exclude spending for special needs. Increasingly this approach only measures a somewhat narrow band of school expenditures. A shift toward providing high-quality educational services for all children, without comparing one with another, avoids some of this conceptual and technical quagmire. In this manner, equal educational opportunity is freed from the restriction of equal expenditures and is allowed to take on the greater meaning of serving all children well with a high-quality education. A logical extension of this line of thinking, however, is to move toward some form of full state funding of public education. Morrison (1930, p. 231) stated it as simply and as eloquently as anyone when he wrote, "from the purely fiscal standpoint, it would seem to be clearly sound public policy for the states to relieve overburdened communities, not by the distribution of state largess, but by the assumption of functions which in principle belong to the state." Of course he considered this issue from a much broader view than just the fiscal viewpoint but arrived at the same conclusion.

The broad sweep of demographic changes may indicate that current systems of public education are not adequate to meet current needs and those of the future. This analysis suggests that educators and policymakers in the United States should consider at least the following reforms to better serve the children of this nation:

(1) a thorough reexamination of our organization of schooling, with a view toward democratizing education;

(2) the establishment of state curricula and performance standards with maximum local discretion in designing educational programs to meet those standards;

(3) the coordination of social services for children among various levels and units of government, with some reorganization of governments to better accommodate the needs of children; and

(4) an emphasis on funding high-quality educational services for all children through full state assumption of the financing of education.

Population changes have the power to render old institutions and arrangements less functional in meeting social needs. This chapter has examined some recent population trends in the United States, explored changes that are anticipated during the next few decades, and suggested some education reforms that may allow U.S. public schools to achieve even greater success in the coming years.

References

Exter, T. (1991). Booming counties. *American Demographics, 13*(1), 55.

Heifetz, R. A., & Sinder, R. M. (1988). Political leadership: Managing the public's problem solving. In R. B. Reich (Ed.), *The power of public ideas* (pp. 179-203). Cambridge, MA: Harvard University Press.

Jackson, K. T. (1985). *Crabgrass frontier: The suburbanization of the United States.* New York: Oxford University Press.

Jones, L. Y. (1980). *Great expectations: America and the baby boom generation.* New York: Ballantine.

Majone, G. (1988). Policy analysis and public deliberation. In R. B. Reich (Ed.), *The power of public ideas* (pp. 157-178). Cambridge, MA: Harvard University Press.

March, J. G., & Olsen, J. P. (1989). *Rediscovering institutions: The organizational basis of politics.* New York: Free Press.

Morrison, H. C. (1930). *School revenue.* Chicago: University of Chicago Press.

Ornstein, A. C. (1984). Urban demographics for the 1980s: Educational implications. *Education and Urban Society, 16,* 477-496.

Phillips, K. (1990). *The politics of rich and poor: Wealth and the American electorate in the Reagan aftermath.* New York: Random House.

Reich, R. B. (1991). *The work of nations: Preparing ourselves for 21st century capitalism.* New York: Knopf.

Sternlieb, G., & Hughes, J. W. (1987). The demographic long wave: Population trends and economic growth. *Economic Development Quarterly, 1,* 307-322.

Thro, W. E. (1990). The third wave: The impact of the Montana, Kentucky, and Texas decisions on the future of public school finance reform litigation. *Journal of Law and Education, 19,* 218-250.

Thurow, L. C. (1984). *Dangerous currents: The state of economics.* New York: Vintage.

Usdan, M. D. (1984). New trends in urban demography. *Education and Urban Society, 16,* 399-414.

U.S. Department of Education, Office of Educational Research and Improvement. (1988). *Youth indicators 1988* (National Center for Educational Statistics). Washington, DC: Government Printing Office.

U.S. Department of Education, Office of Educational Research and Improvement. (1991). *Digest of educational statistics 1990* (National Center for Educational Statistics). Washington, DC: Government Printing Office.

Waldrop, J., & Exter, T. (1991). The legacy of the 1980s. *American Demographics, 13*(3), 33-38.

Ward, J. G. (1990). Implementation and monitoring of judicial mandates: An interpretive analysis. In J. K. Underwood & D. A. Verstegen (Eds.), *The impacts of litigation and legislation on public school finance: Adequacy, equity, and excellence* (pp. 225-248). New York: Harper & Row.

Ward, J. G., & Rink, F. J. (1991, April). *Analysis of local stakeholder opposition to school district consolidation: An application of interpretive theory to public policy making.* Paper presented at the meeting of the American Educational Research Association, Chicago.

Wheeler, J. O., & Mitchelson, R. L. (1991). The information empire. *American Demographics, 13*(3), 40-42.

Wilson, W. J. (1987). *The truly disadvantaged: The inner city, the underclass, and public policy.* Chicago: University of Chicago Press.

Wrigley, E. A. (1969). *Population and history.* New York: McGraw-Hill.

Zill, N., & Rogers, C. C. (1988). Recent trends in the well-being of children in the United States and their implications for public policy. In A. J. Cherlin (Ed.), *The changing American family and public policy* (pp. 31-115). Washington, DC: Urban Institute Press.

T W O

Diversity in Urban Schools

JAMES G. CIBULKA

Diversity has been a fact of life in the urban schools of America since the emergence of a common public school system in the mid-nineteenth century. As waves of immigrants came to America and as migrations occurred from farms to cities, the immigrants were absorbed by our city schools. Moreover, as these same schools sought to accommodate this diversity, they were chronically underfunded (Cibulka & Olson, in press; Katznelson & Weir, 1987).

In broad outline then, the topic of this chapter, demographic diversity in urban schools, deals with old educational and political problems. Yet in key respects the character of the problem has changed over time, both educationally and politically. This educational and political context is critical to any discussion of financing arrangements that address demographic diversity in urban schools. Accordingly, the chapter begins by trying to characterize the evolving character of the "problem" we are addressing.

Diversity as an Education Problem

At a rhetorical level, Americans prize diversity. As a nation of immigrants, our public culture emphasizes the strength that comes from this diversity. Our efforts to embrace cultural pluralism and multiculturalism bespeak this commitment.

Yet our public schools, particularly our urban schools, have been built on a unitary model that favored white, middle-class Protestants (Tyack, 1974). The function of the schools was to create an "urban discipline" that contained the diverse values and cultural traditions that immigrants brought to America. Thus U.S. urban schools were not really designed to accommodate cultural diversity (Gordon, 1978; Weiss, 1981).

Racial Change and Segregation in City Schools

As many have pointed out, the case of blacks illustrates the gap between rhetorical support for cultural pluralism and actual institutional practice. Whereas European immigrants were allowed to assimilate into the dominant society, blacks were subject to a caste system that at once prevented assimilation while also suppressing black culture to the extent possible within a system of segregated institutions (Ogbu, 1981). In particular, the racial segregation in U.S. public schools was a means to limit life chances for blacks, both through provision of inferior programs and facilities and through limiting the teaching of black culture. That legacy is by no means behind us and must be central to any analysis of student diversity in urban schools.

To be sure, racial segregation in U.S. public schools has a complicated history. That historical legacy varies in U.S. cities. Accordingly, the degree of segregation found in city school systems varies as well as the progress in creating desegregated environments.

Before examining segregation per se, it is useful to document the changes in racial composition in large-city school systems. In 1967, 11 of the nation's 60 largest school districts

Table 2.1 Trends in Black Enrollments in the Nation's Largest
School Districts, 1967-1986

	1967	*1976*	*1980*	*1986*
Number of districts 50% or more black	11	12	12	15
Number of districts 50% or more nonwhite	20	28	29	32
Number of districts 50% or more white	23	15	14	11

SOURCE: Adapted from Orfield and Monfort (1988, table 2).
NOTE: While the sample was the 60 largest school districts in the nation, 17 districts were eliminated due to missing data for one or more years. Thus computations are based on 43 districts. Columns do not total consistently due to the impact of other nonwhite enrollments.

had black enrollments of 50% or greater (see Table 2.1). By 1986 the number of districts had risen to 15. Thus black enrollments were still below 50% in a majority of these districts in 1986. On the other hand, white enrollments accounted for a majority in less than half of the districts, indicating that other minority group enrollments were rising. While this increase in black enrollments is not as dramatic as one might expect, as a percentage of total enrollments, black enrollments increased during this period in 49 of the 57 districts for which data were available. Similarly, white enrollments, as a percentage of total enrollments, fell in all districts (Orfield & Monfort, 1988). In short, the nation's central city school systems are becoming increasingly nonwhite.

Orfield and Monfort (1988) used several measures of segregation of black students in the nation's 31 largest urban districts. Only one sixth of these districts had as many as half their black students in majority-white schools, and these were districts where a significant white population can still be found in the city school system. By contrast, among the 13 metropolitan school districts with desegregation plans, more than 75% of these districts had most black students in majority-white schools. Also there are differences among cities in the progress made toward desegregation between 1968 and

1987. More than two thirds of the districts showed some progress in exposure of blacks to whites in this 19-year period.
Districts intensely segregated 19 years earlier rarely made any
progress. Several districts lost ground, due to some combination of demography and/or desegregation policy.

Because the data on segregation trends are drawn from a
smaller subset of districts than the above data on racial enrollment trends, we must exercise some caution in generalizing
about overall trends in U.S. cities. Nonetheless, it appears that
we can say the following with some degree of certainty: Most
urban school systems continue to have programs to desegre-
gate students and staffs. Of the 45 members of the Council of
Great City Schools (CGCS), 30 had active programs in 1990-
1991.[1] Half of these plans (15) have been implemented in the
1980s. Thus many urban school systems continue to confront
current desegregation demands and costs.

Poverty in Urban School Systems

The most serious educational problem facing central city
school systems is the prevalence of large numbers of children
in poverty. Nearly 21% of our nation's children are poor (U.S.
Bureau of the Census, 1988). They tend to be concentrated disproportionately in central cities and rural and southern areas.
In 1983, 31% of all children living in central cities of metropolitan areas were poor compared with 13% of the children living in noncentral (principally suburban) parts of these
metropolitan areas (U.S. House of Representatives, 1985).

Poverty, it bears pointing out, is not principally a minority
phenomenon. Almost two thirds of the poor are white. Blacks
and Hispanics are less than 35% of these poor. We would expect this because whites vastly outnumber minorities in our
population.

Yet minority children are much more likely to be poor than
white children; while they constitute a quarter of the child
population, nearly half of the poor children belong to minority groups. Among white children, 14% were in poverty in

1989, while 43% of black children and 36% of Hispanic children were poor.[2]

Poverty in our cities therefore has taken on a racial character: 58% of blacks make their homes in central cities, as do 50% of Hispanics, compared with only 27% of the white population (U.S. Bureau of the Census, 1982). Further, minorities remain disproportionately poor; 33.1% of black adults and children and 28.2% of Hispanics were poor in 1987. Consequently, 39% of all poor children live in central cities (U.S. House of Representatives, 1985, p. 266).

The relatively higher percentage of female-headed households in cities also increases poverty among urban children, because more than half of all children in single-parent families headed by a female are poor. While most of the poor in our country continue to live in households headed by two adults, the number of female-headed households has been growing. The number of such families with children doubled from 1959 to 1983, when 20% of all children were to be found living in such households. Black and Hispanic households with these characteristics are especially prone to poverty; in 1987, 68.3% of black children in female-headed families and 70.1% of Hispanic children were poor (U.S. Bureau of the Census, 1980). About two thirds of the nation's black and Hispanic female-head families live in central cities.

Children of never-married mothers are a growing segment of these one-parent households. In 1980 almost one fifth of all births were to unwed mothers, with 48% of black births and 11% of white births. Unmarried mothers tend to be young and to have limited education. They are part of a trend toward short-cycle families, a new form of poverty family that creates a new "generation" every 14 years (Hodgkinson, 1989). Not only are these children likely to be raised in persistent poverty, they are especially at risk of dropping out of school.

The emergence of a growing number of persons who are persistently poor is a particularly important, disturbing development. About a third of all children experience poverty at some time in their childhood, while only 1 in 20 experiences persistent poverty. Most poor white children experience poverty

Table 2.2   Free and Reduced-Price Lunch Eligible Children in 45
               Urban School Districts, 1989-1990

Percentage of Enrollments	Percentage of Districts
Under 20%	2 (1)
Between 20% and 40%	16 (7)
Between 40% and 60%	53 (24)
Between 60% and 80%	27 (12)
Over 80%	2 (1)

SOURCE: Based on unpublished data from the Council of the Great City Schools (1990);
these data are preliminary.
NOTE: Income eligibility ceilings for free lunches stand at 130% of the federal poverty
income guidelines and between 130% and 185% for reduced-price lunches. Because this is
an income-tested program, some otherwise eligible children do not identify themselves.

from 1-4 years of their 15-year period of "childhood." Much
white poverty is associated with changes in family structure
events, such as divorce, remarriage, or change in earnings.
Blacks, by contrast, are likely to be persistently poor for five
or more years (Duncan & Rogers, 1984). Not only does their
poverty last longer, it is less affected by the above family
changes. The persistently poor also are overrepresented
among children in female-headed households.

Most central city school systems now serve a majority of pupils who are poor (see Table 2.2). Among the 45 school districts
that were members of the Council of Great City Schools, the
average percentage of students who were eligible for free and
reduced-price lunches was 57.4%. The modal group of districts
falls between 40%-60%, and only one district had fewer than
20% of its pupils meeting these poverty criteria.

Other Indicators of Pupil Need

It is generally acknowledged that urban school systems
have above-average concentrations of pupils who are handicapped. The heavy concentration of handicapped pupils in

Table 2.3 Handicapped Children in 45 Urban School Districts, 1989-1990

Percentage of Enrollment	Districts (%)
5-9	18 (8)
9-10	22 (10)
10-11	13 (6)
11 and above	47 (21)

SOURCE: Based on unpublished preliminary data from the Council of Great City Schools (1990); U.S. Department of Education, *Digest of Education Statistics* (1989, table 45).
NOTE: The national average in 1987-1988 was 11.1%.

some disability categories reflects multiple causes—poor prenatal and postnatal health care, inadequate early intervention education programs, political demands from organized advocacy groups as well as migration to cities by parents of special education children who are aware of available programs for their youngsters. In 1989-1990 the average percentage of handicapped students among districts in the Council of Great City Schools was 10.9% compared with a national average of 11.1%. Considerable variation exists among these school systems in the incidence of identified special education children, however. Table 2.3 indicates that 8 districts had fewer than 9% of their students enrolled in special education programs, while 21 had more than 11% of their student bodies in such programs. These differences reflect at least in part the different practices employed by school districts in identifying such children and determining their eligibility for services. Some critics marshal evidence that too many minority youngsters are classified as special education pupils (Ogbu, 1981). On the other side, some urban school systems may underserve special education pupils because revenues are in short supply to fund the additional costs that these programs entail.

The costs of serving children whose mothers were drug dependent and HIV positive are only beginning to become clear. Many will require special education services, and such children are likely to be disproportionately located in central cities.

Table 2.4   Current per Pupil Expenditures in CGCS Districts,
1980-1988

Expenditure Trend	Districts (%)	Mean Change (%)	Coefficient of Variation
Decrease	3 (1)	10	NA
Increase	97 (33)	32	.65
Rustbelt	45 (15)	28	.39
Sunbelt	55 (18)	36	.74

SOURCE: Based on unpublished preliminary data from the Council of the Great City Schools (1990).
NOTE: 1988 dollars for each city or regional cost of living index (all items); data were available for 34 CGCS districts.

Urban school systems typically have disproportionate percentages of limited-English-proficient pupils. Council of the Great City Schools (CGCS, 1990) data indicate that 16 districts, over a third of the districts, had greater than 10% of the student body so identified in 1989-1990. Milwaukee, for instance, must cope with 33 language groups as it attempts to bring pupils to English proficiency (Wisconsin Department of Public Instruction, 1990). In Los Angeles, Chicago, and other large cities, there are more than 100 language groups.

Student Diversity and Financial Resources of Urban School Systems

Given this extraordinary burden of pupil needs in urban school systems, which appears to be worsening, is the financial base available to these school systems improving or at least holding its own?

Table 2.4 shows trends in current expenditures between 1980 and 1988 among 34 school districts that are members of the Council of Great City Schools. Only one, San Francisco, had falling expenditures. Among the districts experiencing increases, there was considerable dispersion, with just as many districts recording under 10% as those experiencing between

Table 2.5 Revenue Trends in CGCS Districts, 1980-1988

| | Revenue Source | | | | | | | | |
| | Local | | | State | | | Federal | | |
Revenue Trend	*Number Districts*	*Mean (%)*	*COV*[a]	*Number Districts*	*Mean (%)*	*COV*	*Number Districts*	*Mean (%)*	*COV*
Decrease	6	19	.19	8	20	.19	24	54	.1
No change	1	—	—	—	—	—	1	—	—
Increase	32	38	.11	29	42	.12	12	146	.1
Total	39	+28	.15	37	28	.17	37	+10	.1

SOURCE: Based on unpublished preliminary data from the Council of the Great City Schools (1990).
a. Coefficient of variation; 1988 dollars for each city or regional cost of living index (all items). Incomplete data account for variations in district totals.

40% and 50%. The modal group, however, experienced per pupil expenditure increases of 30%-40%. It should be kept in mind that these are real expenditure increases after adjusting for inflation.

Examination of revenue trends in these districts during the same period helps explain what bolstered these expenditures (Table 2.5). The bleakest spot was federal revenues, as the Reagan administration's education cuts beginning in 1981 took their toll. Twice as many districts (24) experienced losses as experienced gains (not shown in the table).

It is perhaps surprising to note that local revenues in many of these systems have grown (Table 2.5): 32 experienced local revenue increases, 1 stood constant, and only 6 coped with declines. One explanation is that city tax bases continued to grow in the 1980s, despite other manifestations of urban decline in rustbelt cities, fueled mainly by the office building boom in many downtown areas. Further, between 1980 and 1985 (the period for which data could be obtained), effective property tax rates (for schools as well as other locally financed services) increased in more than half the CGCS cities (Table 2.6). These increases were in some rustbelt cities such as Cleveland, Milwaukee, Detroit, and Philadelphia, which were experiencing various degrees of fiscal distress in the

Table 2.6   Property Tax Rates in CGCS Cities, 1980-1985

Tax Rate in 1985 Compared with 1980	Number of cities
Lower	7
Higher	10

SOURCE: Based on annual comparisons published by the government of the District of Columbia (1980-1985), *Tax burdens in Washington, D.C., Compared with Those in the Largest City in Each State.*
NOTE: Tax rates are for educational as well as other locally funded public services. Only cities were included for which data were available for 1980 and 1985.

1970s. Increased tax effort no doubt was used to offset slow growth or decline in fiscal capacity. Of course some cities in sunbelt areas with rapidly growing economies could finance public services with reduced tax effort. But most cities with reduced local tax effort in the early 1980s were older cities such as New York and St. Louis, which had to turn to their states to help them offset local financial problems.

Indeed, states did provide more revenues for city schools in the 1980s, along with the general trend toward increased state support for schools. Of the 37 CGCS districts for which data were available, 29 had state-aid increases in this period (Table 2.5). Among the six cities reported in this table as experiencing local revenue losses (Baltimore, Buffalo, Fresno, Long Beach, Los Angeles, and Milwaukee), all but Long Beach had more than compensated for the magnitude of local revenue loss with state-aid increases.

Despite this indication that during the 1980s most urban school systems were able to maintain a reasonably sound financial position, as the 1990s began, some city school systems such as New York were in dire financial straits. At the same time, New York was considering further political decentralization (Temporary State Commission on New York City School Governance, 1991). Boston's city officials were contemplating a new governance structure to reverse what critics characterize as gross financial mismanagement of the school system by its School Committee. In Wisconsin, Governor Tommy Thompson proposed dividing the Milwaukee school district into four separate entities. Chicago's restructuring with local school boards and local financial management was already under way, despite a state supreme court ruling that invalidated the original plan. In 1991 an unprecedented number of urban superintendencies were vacant, prompting considerable national discussion on what is wrong with urban school governance. Such developments signal that the 1990s could be a politically and financially turbulent decade for urban school systems.

Competing Perspectives on the Plight of Urban School Systems

Thus urban school systems find themselves in an ambiguous situation. As their pupil needs have risen, so in most cases have expenditures and overall revenues. Yet it is not clear that the future will be so kind. Moreover, whether their funding is equitable or adequate is an important issue. There are a number of alternative, competing ways of characterizing the relationship between pupil needs and funding of urban school systems. Depending on one's perspective, the growing student diversity in these systems may or may not be accompanied by effective management. Three alternative perspectives are discussed below.

An Equity Perspective

One point of view is that urban school systems will be unable to effectively cope with increasing student diversity until they have a resource base that is more equitable. Consider the data in Table 2.7, which compares expenditures and staffing levels in large school systems with the national average. By 1986 they were spending less than the national average and predictably had poorer pupil-teacher ratios. A study by the Advisory Commission on Intergovernmental Relations (1984) using 1981 data demonstrated that city schools consistently

Table 2.7 Expenditures and Staffing in Large School Systems
Compared With the National Average, 1979 and 1986

| | Current Expenditures per Pupil | | Pupil-Teacher Ratio | |
| | 1979 | 1986 | 1979 | 1986 |
	(dollars)			
Large Districts	2,691	3,501	20.7	20.3
Nation	2,095	3,977	19.1	17.8

SOURCE: Based on data from the U.S. Department of Education, *Digest of Education Statistics* (1989, tables 35, 56, 83) and *Digest of Education Statistics* (1982, table 32).
NOTE: 1979 data are for the 20 largest cities while 1986 data are for all school districts with greater than 20,000 enrollment (N = 235).

spend less than their suburban counterparts. A comparable analysis has not been done recently. Data for Milwaukee, however, indicate the persistence of this city-suburban disparity in that city (Table 2.8). Milwaukee has the highest pupil poverty rate of any school district in its metropolitan area, yet its expenditures are the third lowest in the metropolitan area.

Despite this apparent inequity, urban school systems have had difficulty in mounting legal challenges to financing systems. New York, Baltimore, and Milwaukee all challenged their state financing systems based on the theory that cities experience educational overburdens, cost overburdens, and municipal overburdens, but each case failed on appeal to the state's highest court.[3] While the factual circumstances in these cases vary, the relatively higher expenditures in many city school systems, and in some cases relatively high property valuations, complicate the inequality claim. In New Jersey, on the other hand, a recent court decision did favor cities.[4] Given the time and money absorbed in mounting such legal challenges, the courts are unlikely to afford any quicker remedy in the future than in the past.

Those operating from an equity perspective might be quick to point out that, while expenditures have been rising over time, this masks a general decline in educational services available to children. During the period of enrollment decline

Table 2.8 A Comparison of Milwaukee and Its Suburbs on Spending, Staffing, and Educational Needs, 1989-1990

Districts	Spending (dollars)	Pupil-Teacher Ratio	Poverty Pupils (percentage)
Milwaukee	4,308	16.5	62
Suburbs (19)	5,062	14.6	8.4
Number below Milwaukee	2	18	0
Number above Milwaukee	17	1	19

SOURCE: Based on data from fall budget reports for Milwaukee; poverty data from Wisconsin Department of Public Instruction, November/December, 1989 counts (unpublished); staffing data from the Public Expenditure Research Foundation (1990, table 1). NOTE: Elementary and high school districts are combined for comparison purposes. Spending is state and local shared costs. Free and reduced-lunch data are calculated as a percentage of enrollment.

that occurred in urban school systems beginning in 1972, but whose impact was felt principally in the late 1970s and early 1980s due to recessions and other economic problems, urban school systems suffered many cutbacks from which they never recovered. For example, both Chicago and New York laid off legions of art and music teachers. During its financial problems in the mid-1970s, New York laid off 14,000 teachers, and among this group very few art and music teachers were replaced.

While it is possible to cite a long-term trend toward reduced pupil-teacher (and staff-teacher) ratios in city school systems, this masks the fact that educational costs are higher in cities (and metropolitan areas), which means they buy less for a comparable expenditure. Thus a school system may be spending above the state average yet offering substandard services given its poverty overburden.[5] Accordingly, it is possible to estimate whether city school system expenditures are higher or lower than ought to be expected, given the poverty "overburden" in the city compared with the state as a whole (Table 2.9).[6] In 1980, 59% (17 of the 29 systems) were spending less than would be expected, while 38% (11 systems) were spending more. In 1986-1987 there was little change in this distribution; 62% were spending suboptimally in relation to

Table 2.9   Cities Whose Expenditures Are Greater or Less Than
Expected Given Their Poverty Incidences Relative to
Their States, 1980-1986

Cities Whose Expenditures Are:	1980 (%)	1986 (%)
Greater than expected	38 (11)	34 (10)
Less than expected	59 (17)	62 (18)
The same as expected	3 (1)	4 (1)

SOURCE: Based on data from Sherman (1983) and the U.S. Bureau of the Census (1990, table 16).
NOTE: Calculated by multiplying excess poverty incidence by 15.4% and comparing the degree to which urban expenditures exceed state expenditures. Cities with less than the state average on poverty are compared in reverse. This method is adapted from the School Finance Project (Sherman, 1983), Table XV, which assumed a required poverty weighting of 25% added instructional costs, prorated to 15.4% because instructional expenditures were estimated to be only 61% of current expenditures. Current dollars are used for both years. The poverty overburden uses 1980 census data for both years. School districts are those in Table XV: the largest school system in 35 states plus two or more additional large systems in 5 of the nation's most populous states.

what might be expected given the statewide poverty incidence, while 34% showed excessive expenditures. In the in-
terim, cities moved very little in their positions. Two cities
(Indianapolis and Milwaukee) became "underspenders"
while only St. Louis moved to an "overspending" profile.

Further, working within this equity perspective, it might be
pointed out that, for a majority of high-expenditure cities, expenditures have been regressing toward the state average, despite the escalating demands posed by the student bodies in
central city school systems. Between 1979-1980 and 1986-1987,
among 39 cities, more than two thirds (27) showed a slippage
in relation to state average expenditures (Tables 2.10 and
2.11). While expenditures remained above average in about
two thirds of the urban districts, by 1986-1987, 70% had pupil-
teacher ratios that were poorer than their states' average.

In sum, there are a plethora of data that can be used to support the argument that, given the rising pupil needs of urban
school systems, the systems are not spending enough to meet
the needs of these pupils.

Table 2.10 Expenditures and Staffing in CGCS School Districts
Compared With Their States, 1979-1986

Districts	Expenditures 1979 (%)	1986 (%)	Pupil-Teacher Ratios 1979 (%)	1986 (%)
Better than state average	87 (33)	66 (25)	32 (5)	30 (11)
At state average	0	5 (2)	0	0
Below state average	13 (5)	29 (11)	68 (11)	70 (26)

SOURCE: Based on data from the U.S. Department of Education, *Digest of Education Statistics* (1989, tables 58, 83, 146), *Digest of Education Statistics* (1981, table 45), *Digest of Education Statistics* (1982, table 32).
NOTE: Pupil-teacher ratios are based on a smaller set of the nation's 20 largest cities in 1979-1980. For 1986 a larger set of 37 CGCS districts (including all those reported in 1979) was used, owing to changes in data reporting over this period. District totals in various columns vary due to missing data for some districts. Because different districts are compared in different columns, these data should be viewed as suggestive only.

Productivity Perspective

Urban school systems by no means have been immune from the national alarm over the perceived "quality problem" in America's public schools. Although *A Nation at Risk* virtually ignored the special educational problems of cities, a succession of reports thereafter did begin to focus on underachievement among poor and minority children. While some reports have taken a human investment perspective, arguing for more resources (e.g., Carnegie Foundation for the Advancement of Teaching, 1988; Committee on Economic Development, 1987; CGCS, 1987; W. T. Grant Foundation, 1988), others draw attention to the alleged poor educational performance of urban schools in particular (e.g., Moore & Davenport, 1990).

This productivity perspective focuses on the bureaucratic dysfunctions of urban schools. The essential argument is that resources are diverted to matters that have little bearing on educational achievement or that actually impede it. The most trenchant critique using this institutional analysis is in Chubb and Moe (1990). They cite extensive research refuting any clear relationship between level of expenditure and student

Table 2.11   Expenditures and Staffing in CGCS School Districts
Compared With Their States

Districts	Expenditures (%)	Pupil-Teacher Ratios (%)
Improving in relation to state	31 (12)	18 (3)
Declining in relation to state	69 (27)	82 (14)
No change	0	0

SOURCE: Based on data from the U.S. Department of Education, *Digest of Education Statistics* (1989, tables 58, 83, 146), *Digest of Education Statistics* (1981, table 45), *Digest of Education Statistics* (1982, table 32).

achievement. Theirs is only the most recent in a legion of studies arguing that there is a weak or nonexistent measurable relationship between spending levels and educational outcomes (e.g., Coleman et al., 1966; Walberg & Fowler, 1987). Boyd and VanGeel (1988) review evidence that administrators, regardless of district location, do not give much attention to productivity issues. Thus some argue that it is the way resources are used that is the most critical to equity issues (Murphy & Hallinger, 1988). The current "generation" of equity issues focuses on equality of access to intellectual opportunities, which are affected not only by the level of fiscal resources but also by the way these resources are utilized through such means as course content, quality of instruction, homework, and related concerns. It is important to point out, however, that most school finance experts believe that there is some relationship between levels of spending and effective use of resources (e.g., Rossmiller, 1987).

Two specific studies in this productivity vein that have proven controversial are analyses of how much money is actually spent in classrooms. According to Cooper and Sarrel (1990) studying New York City and Fisher (1990) studying Milwaukee, the amount is 32% and 26%, respectively. While their analyses are controversial, for critics they demonstrate the misallocation of resources in urban school systems.

Hanushek (1981) among others has criticized reducing class size as a means of allocating new resources, because there is

Table 2.12   Teacher Salaries in CGCS Districts and the Nation, 1989

	Average Teacher Salary (dollars)	Percentage of National Average
Large City Districts	33,139	111
Rustbelt	34,780	121
Sunbelt	31,946	108
Nation	29,500[a]	NA

SOURCE: Based on data from the Educational Research Service, Inc. (1990).
a. Excludes District of Columbia; data with D.C. included are $31,304.

no evidence that this affects achievement until class sizes are extremely small. Yet pupil-teacher ratios in urban schools, like those in the nation as a whole, have been decreasing (see Table 2.7), principally due to teacher collective bargaining arrangements. Other critics, using a public choice perspective (e.g., Michaelsen, 1980), focus on resource allocations such as improved teachers salaries that ostensibly benefit teachers rather than pupils. In a longitudinal analysis of 10 cities based on developments until 1982, Cibulka (1988) did not find compelling the argument that teachers' salaries are excessive. On the other hand, if one simply compares salary levels in cities with the nation as a whole, the salaries in rustbelt cities exceed the national average by 21% compared with an 8% premium in sunbelt cities. While the latter are within a reasonable range considering the wage differentials in metropolitan labor markets, the 21% salary differential in rustbelt urban school districts seems hard to explain by cost factors alone (Table 2.12).

Data on the educational outcomes of central city youth do not clearly answer how accurate the productivity critics are. Longitudinal National Assessment of Educational Progress (NAEP) data show some improvement in scores of minority youth over time and a closing of the gap between white and minority youth. But these national trends, as Peterson (1991) points out, may mask poor performance by central city districts, an interpretation that would seem to be supported by anecdotal evidence of high minority dropout rates in central city schools. In an analysis of NAEP data, Jones (1987) reports on the educational progress of blacks between 1970 and 1984 in three types of communities—rural, disadvantaged urban, and advantaged urban.[7] (Blacks in each type of community constitute 8%, 30%, and 5%, respectively.) Jones's data indicate that at age 9 black children in central cities have made the same progress as blacks that age elsewhere. Yet at ages 13 and 17 they lag considerably behind other blacks in the progress demonstrated between 1970 and 1984. Similarly, the racial gap in scores narrowed in central cities for 9-year-olds but has shown no progress whatsoever for 13- and 17-year-olds, even though teenage counterparts in rural and advantaged urban areas did show considerable progress during this period. This disappointing finding could be interpreted to mean that central city school systems are not performing as well as they should.

Central city school performance, based on SAT scores and achievement data in CGCS school districts, provides a mixed picture (Table 2.13). About two thirds of the districts had below-average or mixed scores on secondary achievement tests, and less than half of the districts report that scores are improving. On the other hand, most districts with below-average scores report improvement. More than half of the CGCS districts score below average on national norms for the SAT. While these are crude measures of urban school performance, they are precise enough to set out an overall picture that leaves much room for increased productivity.

Increasingly urban school officials are asked to demonstrate that they are capable of spending money wisely before their case for additional resources to serve pupils will be taken seriously.

An Urban Ecology Perspective

There is still a third way to interpret the capacity of urban school systems to respond to the dramatic growth in pupil needs. This approach sees the problem, and concomitantly the

Table 2.13 Student Performance Data in CGCS Districts

Districts	Performance Indicator	
	Secondary Grade Achievement in Math and Reading (%)	SATs (%)
At or above national norms	36 (16)	44 (17)
Improving	44 (7)	
Decreasing or mixed	6 (1)	
Stable	50 (8)	
Below national norms	42 (19)	56 (22)
Improving	63 (12)	
Decreasing or mixed	32 (6)	
Stable	0	
Mixed[a]	22 (10)	0
Improving	10 (1)	
Decreasing	60 (6)	
Stable	30 (3)	

SOURCE: Based on unpublished preliminary data from the Council of the Great City Schools (1990).
a. Applied only to secondary achievement data where more than one grade level is tested. *Mixed* means that some grades are above the norm, some are below, or some grades or subjects show increases while others do not. All data are preliminary and based on most recent test data for which results are available. SAT scores are those for 1987-1988 and were not available for all CGCS districts; they should be interpreted cautiously because different segments of the student body may take this test in each school system.

solution, as more than a function of *either* spending levels or more productive deployment of resources.

Urban schools are part of a larger urban ecology that shows evidence of significant decline. Analysts can disagree on the causes of this decline yet still concur that it is under way. The urban neighborhoods in which many poor children must live have in many cases undergone steady deterioration in recent decades. Wilson's (1987) study of Chicago, Detroit, Los Angeles, New York, and Philadelphia documents the transformation of inner-city neighborhoods as middle- and working-class residents have left behind a large proportion of poor, heavily minority residents. An urban underclass born into poverty and

Table 2.14   Poor Persons Living in Areas of High Poverty
Concentration, 1980-1987

	1980 (%)	1987 (%)
All races	40	16
Whites	31	28
Blacks	67	83
Hispanics	NA	55

SOURCE: Based on data from the U.S. Bureau of the Census (1982, table 20, 1988, table 18).
NOTE: Poverty areas are those census tracts in metropolitan areas and minor civil
divisions in nonmetropolitan counties with a poverty rate of 20% or more in 1979 based
on the 1980 census.

isolated from middle-class values and life-styles has emerged,
owing to structural shifts in the economy and related deterioration in inner-city neighborhoods. Newspapers now run regular features on the rising tide of crime in central cities,
particularly escalating homicides.[8] The epidemic of drug use,
although it is a societal problem touching all classes and
races, has had a particularly devastating impact in central cities. Homelessness is a fact of life, often concentrated in central city neighborhoods and involving families and children.
The high prevalence of unemployment, deplorable housing
conditions, and inadequate health care and other services all
point to this deteriorating quality of life in our inner cities. It
is this negative community endowment that worsens the impact of childhood poverty and complicates the educational
tasks of inner-city schools.

The concentration of the poor in neighborhoods of high
poverty, characterized by a variety of social problems, has
gotten worse for blacks (Table 2.14). Between 1980 and 1987
the percentage of whites living in high-poverty neighborhoods dropped slightly (from 31% to 28%); the reverse occurred for blacks. In 1980 two thirds were living in such
neighborhoods; by 1987 it was 83%. In 1987, 55% of Hispanics
lived in areas of high poverty concentration. While not all
high-poverty areas are in cities, the latter tend to have higher

concentrations of poor persons than other poor areas. Accordingly, between 1975 and 1987 the proportion of poor children under 6 living in concentrated areas of poverty in central cities increased from 54% to 61% (National Center for Children in Poverty, 1990). Clearly, public schools educating children who are reared in such poverty areas face a major challenge. They must counteract a broader environment of poverty.

While some commentators point to overly generous welfare policies as the central problem (Murray, 1984), others cite the deterioration in government assistance that at one time compensated for failures of the private economy. Between 1980 and 1987 grant programs of special importance to cities were cut by 47%. Distressed cities (those with high concentrations of poverty, low income levels, and high unemployment) lost disproportionately compared with healthy areas (Cuciti, 1990).

An example of a major federal cutback is the decline in assistance levels within the Aid to Families with Dependent Children program between 1976 and 1988.[9] Further, the shortage of low-income housing affects the disposable income of the poor due to escalating rents (Hodgkinson, 1989), limits their access to jobs, and causes frequent moves that harm their children's achievement in school. Many of these cutbacks reflect the philosophy of the Reagan and Bush administrations. Unsatisfactory transportation, health care, and other services all affect the capacity of schools to work effectively with children. A pattern of major disinvestment in urban areas has contributed to the declining quality of educational services in these areas.

From this urban ecology perspective, it is impossible to mount an effective attack on educational underachievement in our central cities without integrated, comprehensive improvement in the living conditions that affect such children and their families. The lack of a coordinated set of policies for children constitutes one aspect of the problem (Herrington, 1990; Kirst, 1989). Indeed, many more resources are spent on the elderly than on children, accounting partly for the sharp reduction in rates of poverty among the elderly in recent decades.

More important, the larger opportunity structure of the society may have to be altered before school outcomes in our central cities can be expected to improve significantly. Thus the data showing that educational gains among blacks in central cities lag behind those in other areas can be read not as a productivity problem for the schools alone but more broadly as an indicator of "urban distress." Indeed, the work of Ogbu (1981), MacLeod (1987), and others explains how black youth lower their self-expectations in the face of such grim life chances.

To be sure, this third perspective does not answer the question of how public and private resources are to be deployed to resolve a growing urban crisis. It does call for improved coordination of current and new resources between schools and other institutions serving inner-city communities. Accordingly, an urban ecology perspective implies that a different set of structures and norms are needed for schools to be effective. For example, much more family involvement and community engagement may be necessary to close the hiatus now separating urban schools from their clients (Boyd, 1989).

Conclusion

The changing demographics of urban school systems indicate that they enroll a growing number of children who are difficult to educate. The policy implications of this trend, as this analysis has demonstrated, are open to dispute. After all, by superficial criteria such as per pupil expenditures and revenue trends, urban school systems have been able to garner additional resources to cope with their increasingly complex student bodies. Indeed, several alternative interpretations of these facts have been reviewed. An equity perspective shows that, for example, while expenditures and revenues indeed have risen over time, there still remain significant disparities between cities and suburbs in spending and needs. On the other hand, a productivity perspective argues that the problem will not be addressed with more money but with better use of it. Continuing high dropout rates and relatively poor performance on standardized tests bolster this perspective, despite some indications that improvements are occurring.

Finally, an urban ecology perspective looks to the social and cultural context within which central city schools are located. Their rising problems and resource requirements cannot be separated from the deteriorating quality of life in central cities. A renaissance for urban schools, it might be argued, will depend on significant societal investment in the regeneration of central city institutions and the public services that sustain them.

A traditional equity perspective, focusing on resource adequacy alone, is unlikely to remain compelling in the 1990s for reasons that have now become obvious—the reform movement's focus on productivity, concern about rising taxes, and continuing deficit problems at the federal level as well as in many states. Traditional equity arguments frequently assume a steady-state policy environment predicated on perceptions of incremental progress, but such assumptions increasingly lack credibility with policymakers and the general public. While some school urban systems can point to improved student achievement levels, this progress is not uniform or conclusive.

Yet a productivity perspective, while superficially appealing, can easily become a rationalization for inaction and continued neglect of a growing social problem in the nation's central cities. The perspective, like the equity one, is not so much wrong as it is incomplete, failing to account for the fact that excellence in schools cannot be disentangled from the broader conditions of urban life that motivate and sustain children and their families.

The urban ecology perspective thus offers a way of reconciling the seeming contradictions posed by the equity and productivity perspectives. It may be that more resources truly are needed for urban education, but urban school renewal is unlikely to come without a broad plan for reviving urban communities. Urban schools cannot be expected to achieve excellence amid a rising tide of social decay. At the same time, new resources for urban schools must be coordinated more effectively with other public and private resources for this renaissance to occur.

An urban ecology perspective offers a political vision that can sustain the future of urban school systems. The policy task of securing adequate funding and improved effectiveness for the nation's urban schools is less technical than political, one of reconciling competing values and interests.

In the years ahead the growing pupil needs in our urban schools will make it even more difficult to achieve educational excellence for all urban youth. Accordingly, the creativity of our institutional responses must be commensurate with the magnitude of this challenge.

Notes

1. The membership of the Council of Great City Schools includes most of the largest school districts of the nation as well as some medium-sized urban districts such as Oakland, California.

2. These data were reported in the *New York Times* ("Suffering in Cities Persists," 1991) based on recent Census Bureau data.

3. These cases in New York, Maryland, and Wisconsin are, respectively, *Bd. of Education, Levittown Union Free School District v. Nyquist* (1982); *Hornbeck v. Somerset County Bd. of Ed.* (1983); *Kukor v. Grover* (1989).

4. *Abbott v. Burke* (1990; *Abbott II*).

5. In Milwaukee, for example, an analysis by Wayne Wendling established a statewide cost differential of approximately 10% for professional salaries and wages, using a hedonic wage estimating approach. Milwaukee was at the top of the cost scale. For a more general discussion of cost-of-education methods and findings, see Chambers (1981).

6. These estimations are based on Sherman (1983), who also used other measures to determine local spending requirements such as local share of school expenditure, per capita income, per capita own-source revenue, aggregate revenue effort, and incidence of children under 5. Table 2.9, however, merely draws on poverty incidences to estimate spending requirements. It should be noted that these estimations are somewhat conservative because they make no adjustments for cost-of-education overburdens in cities. Neither do they make any assumptions about whether the entrenched nature of poverty in predominantly nonwhite central cities entails additional remediation costs compared with white poverty in suburbs, small towns, and rural areas.

7. Peterson (1991) reports these data as though they approximate rural, central city, and suburban areas.

8. A typical example was the three-part series in the *New York Times* beginning February 4, 1991, on life in a public housing project for the working poor in Harlem, the Martin Luther King Jr. Towers ("Project Tenants See Island of Safety Washing Away: A Young Man, a Short Life, a Needless Death.")

9. Figures are in constant 1988 dollars for a mother with two children and include families with no wages, those with wages at 50% of poverty level, and those at 75% of poverty level (U.S. Census Bureau and the U.S. House of

Representatives, Ways and Means Committee Reported, in "Suffering in Cities Persists," *The New York Times*, 1991).

References

Abbott v. Burke, 575 A.2d 359 (N.J., 1990).

Advisory Commission on Intergovernmental Relations. (1984). *Fiscal disparities in central cities and suburbs, 1981.* Washington, DC: Author.

Bd. of Education, Levittown Union Free School District v. Nyquist, 453 N.Y.S. 2d 643 (1982).

Boyd, W. L. (1989). *What makes ghetto schools work or not work?* Unpublished paper, University of Illinois, National Center for School Leadership, Urbana-Champaign.

Boyd, W. L., & VanGeel, T. (1988). The politics of educational productivity. In D. H. Monk & J. Underwood (Eds.), *Microlevel school finance: Issues and implications for policy* (pp. 271-310). Cambridge, MA: Ballinger.

Carnegie Foundation for the Advancement of Teaching. (1988). *An imperiled generation: Saving urban schools.* Princeton, NJ: Author.

Chambers, J. (1981). Cost and price level adjustments to state aid for education: A theoretical and empirical review. In K. F. Jordan & N. H. Cambron-McCabe (Eds.), *Perspectives in state school support programs* (pp. 39-85). Cambridge, MA: Ballinger.

Chubb, J. E., & Moe, T. E. (1990). *Politics, markets, and America's schools.* Washington, DC: Brookings Institution.

Cibulka, J. G. (1988). Theories of education budgeting: Lessons from the management of decline. *Educational Administration Quarterly, 23*(1), 7-40.

Cibulka, J. G., & Olson, F. (in press). The organization of the Milwaukee Public School System 1920-1986. In J. L. Rury (Ed.), *From consensus to crisis: The Milwaukee Public Schools, 1920-1990.* Madison: University of Wisconsin Press.

Coleman, J. S., Campbell, E. Q., Hobson, C., McPartland, J., Mood, A., Weinfeld, F., & York, R. (1966). *Equality of educational opportunity.* Washington, DC: Government Printing Office.

Committee on Economic Development. (1987). *Children in need: Investment strategies for the educationally disadvantaged.* Washington, DC: Author.

Cooper, B., & Sarrel, R. (1990, March). *The effects of choice on urban high school funding allocations and achievement of at-risk pupils.* Paper presented at the annual meeting of the American Educational Research Association, Washington, DC.

Council of the Great City Schools. (1987). *Assuring school success for students at risk.* Washington, DC: Author.

Council of the Great City Schools. (1990). *The condition of education in the Great City Schools.* Unpublished paper, Washington, DC.

Cuciti, P. L. (1990). A nonurban policy: Recent public policy shifts affecting cities. In M. Kaplan & F. James (Eds.), *The future of national urban policy* (pp. 235-252). Durham, NC: Duke University Press.

District of Columbia. (1980-1985). *Tax burdens in Washington, DC compared with those in the largest city in each state.* Washington, DC: Government of the District of Columbia.

Duncan, G. J., & Rogers, W. (1984). *A demographic analysis of childhood poverty.* Unpublished paper, University of Michigan, Survey Research Center, Ann Arbor.

Educational Research Service, Inc. (1990). *Salaries paid professional personnel in public schools, 1989-90.* Arlington, VA: Author.

Fisher, F. (1990). *Fiscal accountability in Milwaukee's public elementary schools: Where does the money go?* Milwaukee: Wisconsin Public Policy Research Institute.

Gordon, M. (1978). *Human nature, class, and ethnicity.* New York: Oxford University Press.

W. T. Grant Foundation Commission on Work, Family, and Citizenship. (1988). *The forgotten half: Non-college youth in America.* Washington, DC: Author.

Hanushek, E. A. (1981). Throwing money at schools. *Journal of Policy Analysis and Management, 1*(1), 19-42.

Herrington, C. (1990, October). *Children and intergovernmental relations: Finding a place for the kids.* Paper presented at the annual meeting of the Association for Public Policy Analysis and Management, San Francisco.

Hodgkinson, H. L. (1989). *The same client: The demographics of education and service delivery systems.* Washington, DC: Institute for Educational Leadership.

Hornbeck v. Somerset County Bd. of Ed., 458 A.2d 758 (1983).

Jones, L. V. (1987, May). *Achievement trends for black school children, 1970 to 1984.* Paper presented at the colloquium, "Black Families and Public Policy: Historical and Contemporary Perspectives," Yale Bush Center and Yale Child Study Center, New Haven, CT.

Katznelson, I., & Weir, M. (1987). *Schooling for all.* New York: Basic Books.

Kirst, M. W. (1989). *Conditions of children in California.* Berkeley: Policy Analysis for California Education.

Kukor v. Grover, 436 N.W. 2d 568 (1989).

MacLeod, J. (1987). *Ain't no makin it: Leveled aspirations in a low-income neighborhood.* Boulder, CO: Westview.

Michaelsen, J. (1980). The political economy of school district administration. *Educational Administration Quarterly, 17*(3), 98-113.

Moore, D., & Davenport, S. (1990). School choice: The new improved sorting machine. In W. L. Boyd & H. Walberg (Eds.), *Choice in education: Potential and problems* (pp. 187-224). Berkeley, CA: McCutchan.

Murphy, J., & Hallinger, P. (1989). Equity as access to learning: Curricular and instructional treatment differentials. *Journal of Curriculum Studies, 21*(2), 129-149.

Murray, C. (1984). *Losing ground: American social policy 1950-1980.* New York: Simon & Schuster.

National Center for Children in Poverty, Columbia University. (1990). *Five million children: A statistical profile of our poorest young citizens.* New York: Author.

Ogbu, J. U. (1981). *Minority education and caste: The American system in cross-cultural perspective.* New York: Academic Press.

Orfield, G., & Monfort, F. (1988). *Racial change and desegregation in large school districts: Trends through the 1986-1987 school year.* Unpublished report,

University of Chicago, Council of Urban Boards of Education and the National School Desegregation Project.

Peterson, P. E. (in press). Are big city schools holding their own? In J. L. Rury (Ed.), *From consensus to crisis: The Milwaukee Public Schools, 1920-1990*. Madison: University of Wisconsin Press.

Public Expenditure Research Foundation. (1990). *Wisconsin school district facts*. Madison, WI: Author.

Rossmiller, R. A. (1987). Achieving equity and effectiveness in schooling. *Journal of Education Finance, 12*, 561-577.

Sherman, J. (1983). *The financing of urban public schools: A report on selected school systems* (Unpublished supplement to the final report, Vol. 1 of the Congressionally mandated study of school finance). Washington, DC: Department of Education.

Suffering in cities persists as U.S. fights other wars. (1991, January 27). *New York Times*, p. 15.

Temporary State Commission on New York City School Governance. (1991). [Draft recommendations for public comment]. Unpublished document, New York.

Tyack, D. (1974). *The one best system: A history of American urban education*. Cambridge, MA: Harvard University Press.

U.S. Bureau of the Census. (1982). *Characteristics of the population below the poverty level* (Series P-60, No. 133). Washington, DC: Government Printing Office.

U.S. Bureau of the Census. (1988). *Money, income, and poverty status in the United States; 1987* (Series P-60, No. 161). Washington, DC: Government Printing Office.

U.S. Bureau of the Census. (1990). *1987 Census of governments: Vol. 4, No. 1. Government finances: Finances of public school systems*. Washington, DC: Government Printing Office.

U.S. Department of Education, Office of Educational Research and Improvement. (1981). *Digest of education statistics* (National Center for Education Statistics). Washington, DC: Government Printing Office.

U.S. Department of Education, Office of Educational Research and Improvement. (1982). *Digest of education statistics* (National Center for Education Statistics). Washington, DC: Government Printing Office.

U.S. Department of Education, Office of Educational Research and Improvement. (1989). *Digest of education statistics* (National Center for Education Statistics). Washington, DC: Government Printing Office.

U.S. House of Representatives, Committee on Ways and Means. (1985). *Children in poverty*. Washington, DC: Government Printing Office.

Walberg H. J., & Fowler, W. J. (1987). Expenditures and size efficiencies of public school districts. *Educational Researcher, 16*(7), 5-13.

Weiss, B. J. (1981). *American education and the European immigrant: 1849-1949*. Urbana: University of Illinois Press.

Wilson, W. J. (1987). *The truly disadvantaged: The inner city, the underclass, and public policy*. Chicago: University of Chicago Press.

Wisconsin Department of Public Instruction. (1990). *Census of limited-English-speaking students by school district within language*. Unpublished paper, Madison.

THREE

Youth Migration From Rural Areas

EMIL J. HALLER

DAVID H. MONK

There has been long-standing interest in the migration of young people from rural areas. This interest exists partly because the migration has been so large and persistent and partly because it has important implications for public policy. To the degree that rural areas are net losers of young adults, questions arise about their future viability. These questions in turn prompt questions about the public's interest in and responsibility for fostering the health of rural communities.

The net loss of the young adult population within rural areas has potentially contradictory implications for education policy. On the one hand, if rural communities are losing their young people, and if as a consequence they are becoming less "viable," it could follow that heroic efforts to preserve, not to mention strengthen, local schools within such regions are ill-advised. What is the point of maintaining or enhancing the school in a dying community if the community's condition is unalterably terminal? Alternative policies, typically involving the reorganization and consolidation of rural schools, become attractive in this context.

On the other hand, it is possible that the maintenance of a healthy local school is one means by which rural areas can retain or even regain their viability (Hobbs, 1987). And it could follow that state or federal governments are well advised to preserve and strengthen local rural schools as part of a more global commitment to the social and economic welfare of rural America.

These contradictory policy positions can be reflected at the local level in a rural school's curriculum. For example, a school board, believing that a net loss of its youth to urban areas is inevitable, might reasonably feel an obligation to prepare students for urban jobs and for making the transition to metropolitan living. And, in fact, there are curricula designed specifically to prepare rural youth to successfully adapt to life in the city (e.g., Swift, 1988). Another board might view such actions as a form of community suicide and feel an obligation to attempt to slow the tide of migration by orienting programs to rural living and the local job market (even though that market may be in decline and graduates risk unemployment). Indeed, Mulkey (1988) argues that one reason for the inadequate curricula of rural schools is the reluctance of rural people to invest in students who will simply carry away their (expensive) skills to the benefit of urban places.

These ambiguities surrounding education policy implications associated with a net out-migration of rural youth make it important to better understand the role schools and schooling play in the decisions young people make about where to settle. A second reason for inquiry along these lines arises out of the migration literature itself, where relatively little attention has been paid to the attributes of schools and their effects on resettlement. Much of the existing research relies heavily on status attainment models that have been criticized for their exclusive focus on individual attributes such as SES and intelligence.

We shall be concerned in this chapter with linkages between schooling and the migratory behavior of young people, and we shall place special emphasis on the migratory behavior of young people in rural areas. The chapter begins with a brief overview of previous migration research in addition to a rationale for the school and community attributes we selected for study. Next comes a review of our methodology, which is followed by a presentation of findings. The chapter ends with a discussion of conclusions and implications for policy.

Background

It is clear that young people in rural areas are more likely to leave their communities than otherwise similar people in suburban or urban communities (Brown, 1987; O'Hare, 1988; Swanson & Butler, 1987). Moreover, these studies demonstrate that, when people leave their rural homes, they are more likely to settle within either suburban or urban communities than they are to situate in other rural communities (Lyson, 1986).

It is also clear that this migration is selective in its nature. As Lyson (1986) notes, previous studies show that rural-to-urban migrants have a greater tendency to score higher on intelligence tests (Price & Sikes, 1974) and come from upper-status, nonfarm backgrounds (Price & Sikes, 1974; Willits, Crider, & Bealer, 1980) than their nonmigrant peers. These findings have potentially alarming implications for the future strength of rural communities. Moreover, the disproportionate loss of intelligent and high-status young people suggests that economic and social inequalities across communities are likely to increase over time.

Perhaps the most common interpretation of this selective migration has been in terms of the relative lack of economic opportunity in rural regions. The evidence is not entirely supportive of this interpretation, however. For example, Seyfrit's (1986) study suggests that rapid rural economic development has no effect on the out-migration of young people (see also Rhoda, 1983).

In all of this research, scant attention has been paid to the possibility that certain aspects of local schools might affect migration. And yet there are good reasons for supposing that schooling has important influences on the migratory decisions of youth. After all, schools can offer young people insights into opportunities that exist in regions far removed from their immediate locales. Students can also develop aspirations and skills that significantly broaden the range of available economic opportunities. Conversely, by narrowly focusing on a restricted range of outcomes, such as "the basics," and with an intellectual horizon that stretches not much beyond the local region, students' recognition of opportunities and the development of their aspirations could be severely blunted.

This thinking suggests that curricular offerings are likely to be among the strongest means by which schools influence the migration decisions of youth. For this reason, we chose to focus our analysis on relationships between schools' curricular offerings and the subsequent migration of students.

It would be inadequate to look simply at relationships between measures of curricular offerings and migratory behavior, however, for several reasons. First, previous research has shown that curricular offerings themselves are the result of complex decisions made within educational systems (Barker, 1985; Haller, Monk, Spotted Bear, Griffith, & Moss, 1990; McKenzie, 1989; Monk, 1987; Monk & Haller, 1991). Given an interest in considering the policy implications of our findings, we need to understand the determinants of curricular offerings themselves if we are to fully grasp their impact on migration.

Second, it is possible that these predictors of course offerings have their own direct effects on migration. If we hope to explain migration, we need to be open to influences that arise independently of a curriculum effect. We know, for example, that measures of ability and SES at the individual level have substantial effects on migration. It seems likely that such factors may play a role when the school is the unit of analysis.

Third, existing measures of curricular offerings are seriously limited. For example, simple counts of course titles offered by high schools are readily available. While such data are useful for the task here, it is also clear that more information about qualitative differences in the courses offered as well as information about actual course content would be highly relevant. Unfortunately, such data are not readily available, and our strategy has been to identify school structural characteristics that we believe are related to these more qualitative aspects of curricular offerings. As a consequence, some of the explanatory power we find for the structural characteristics may stem from the unmeasured qualitative differences in curricular offerings.

With all this in mind, we identified the following five school-level attributes for further investigation: (a) average socioeconomic status, (b) average student academic ability, (c) location in a rural area, (d) number of students served, and (e) location in an isolated area. Each of these can affect both curricular offerings and migration patterns.

Socioeconomic status and test score attributes capture differences in demand for different kinds of courses from both parents and students. Ruralness can make a difference, aside from its impact on curricular offerings, to the degree that rural youth face different economic opportunities relative to others. The two most traditional lines of work in rural communities (production agriculture and extractive industries) have been in decline for years, and rural youth have had to factor this reality into their decisions about where and how to live. Moreover, rural youth have been found to have lower educational and occupational aspirations than others (Monk & Haller, 1986), and these lower aspirations could affect the contents of offered courses.

School size is relevant because we know it has important implications for curricular offerings (Barker, 1985; Haller et al., 1990; Monk, 1987; Monk & Haller, 1991), and curricular offerings can provide insight into lives outside of local communities. Size can also have bearing on the content of courses in addition to the range of different courses offered. To the degree that economies of scale exist and are exploited, a higher-quality set of courses will be possible for a given per pupil expenditure level in larger compared with smaller schools. Size offers the further advantage of being a relatively mutable school characteristic. It has long been at the center of the policy debate pertaining to rural schools.

Finally, isolation can affect the ability of schools to offer courses, particularly for specialized and otherwise advanced courses where access to competent teaching resources may be seriously restricted. Isolation can also affect student aspirations, and this in turn can affect the contents of those courses that are offered.

We can take this analysis one step further by recognizing that the impact of curricular offerings on migratory behavior may vary depending on the degree to which the community being served is rural. In particular, there is some reason to believe that curricular offerings in rural schools will have a more important effect on the migration behavior of students than will be the case elsewhere.

The rationale for this belief arises out of critics' claims that recent curriculum reforms have had negative effects on those who seek to remain in rural areas (Hobbs, 1987; Sher, 1986). The critics' argument is that today's curriculum is driven by the more specialized urban-oriented economic needs of society. As a consequence, curriculum reform has the effect of equipping rural youth more for life in the city than for life in rural areas. Upon graduation, rural youth have little choice but to move to more urban environments.

According to these arguments, the more successful the school becomes at reforming its curriculum, the more likely students will be to leave and the more questionable such communities' future becomes. Educational "improvement" in this light is the means by which rural communities destroy themselves. If curriculum improvements are viewed from this perspective, it is not surprising to observe rural communities opposing state-led efforts to "improve schools" either through consolidation or through the strengthening (read "citification") of the curriculum.

These critics argue for more regionally oriented curricula that provide youngsters the option of remaining within rural communities. It is noteworthy that this regional orientation tends to involve a deemphasis of traditional academic fare and a greater emphasis on developing fundamental entrepreneurial skills. If schools were "strengthened" in this fashion, the expectation is that better schooling would contribute to the future social as well as economic viability of rural communities.

In light of these arguments, we decided to look separately at the effects of curricular offerings on migration behaviors in urban, suburban, and rural communities. Our expectation is that indications of efforts to "improve" the curriculum will have more powerful effects in rural areas than elsewhere. More specifically, we hypothesize that manifestations of curriculum "improvement" in rural schools will be more closely related to migration than elsewhere.

Data and Methods

Our data come from various files constituting the High School and Beyond data set (hereafter *HS&B*). Three files were of particular relevance to this study: a school file, a student file, and a course file.

Briefly, the HS&B study consisted of a nationally representative sample of 1,015 U.S. high schools, both public and private. Information regarding each of these schools was collected in 1980 and again in 1982 and concerned such matters as facilities, enrollment, and student and faculty characteristics. The school file comprises these institutional data.

Schools were selected using a complex stratified sampling scheme in which some strata were very substantially oversampled. Weights are provided in the data to compensate for this oversampling, and we have used these school weights in all of the analyses we report below. We did, however, rescale the weights so that our tests of significance do not yield inflated values.

From within each school, up to 36 sophomores and 36 seniors were randomly sampled in 1980 (there were approximately 30,000 students in each cohort). These students responded to questionnaires concerning their school experiences and their plans for the future. In 1982, 1984, and 1986 students were recontacted and responded to questionnaires regarding their post-high school activities. The student file contains these data. For our purposes, we focused on the senior cohort's responses during the base year and in the three follow-ups.

Finally, as part of the 1982 resurvey, data were collected on each of the courses offered in every school. This data file provides a classification of every course into 52 curricular areas (e.g., agriculture, mathematics) and, within each of these, a further classification that is descriptive of the course's nature. This course file provided us with information about the curricular emphasis in each of the sampled schools.

We selected from the school file all public, four-year high schools that reported themselves as general, comprehensive schools. We eliminated all specialized schools that dealt with handicapped and vocational programs. We further restricted the sample to those schools that participated in both the 1980 and the 1982 follow-up surveys. Finally, we excluded schools with fewer than five seniors participating in the 1986 cohort follow-up.

For our measures of family SES and academic ability, we relied upon the composite SES measure provided in the data set and the battery of ability tests administered as part of the HS&B survey. These data were collected at the individual student level. Given our interest in school-level phenomena, we aggregated these responses and used school means for each variable (AVSES and AVTEST).

We assessed ruralness on the basis of the self-designation of the school's administrator. In the survey, administrators were asked to classify their school as being in an urban, suburban, or rural area. We created a dummy variable (RURAL) from their responses in which schools designated as rural were coded 1. Thus for our purposes rural schools are schools whose administrator considers them to be rural.[1]

School size (SIZE) was measured by the number of students enrolled. We used a square root transformation of the size variable to reduce the degree of skewness in its distribution.

Isolation (ISOLATE) was measured using the mean of the school's distance (in miles) from three other educational institutions: the nearest two-year college, business, or trade school,

and four-year college or university. A square root transformation was also applied to this variable to reduce its skew.

We selected two measures of curricular offerings that we
constructed using the HS&B course file: the number of different advanced academic courses (ADVCRS) and the number of
different vocational courses (VOCED) found within each high
school. We selected these attributes as key indicators of how
the curriculum is structured within a school.

We interpret the number of advanced academic course offerings as a measure of how congruent the school is with the national emphasis on strengthening the academic curriculum. It is
our measure of local efforts to "improve" the curriculum and to
bring it into line with the prevailing sense of national priorities.

Advanced courses were identified as courses described
with one or more of the following terms: *accelerated, advanced
placement, college placement,* and *honors.* The only exception involved calculus. All courses with the term *calculus* in the title
were included in the count of advanced courses.

We chose a vocational course count to gauge emphasis
within the school on more immediate and more regionally
oriented economic opportunities. Our choice was based on a
presumption that curricular offerings are sensitive to parent
and student demands coupled with the proposition that local
demand for vocational offerings is more sensitive to local economic and regional characteristics than is the analogous demand for academic offerings.

Students and parents seeking vocational courses will be relatively knowledgeable about local labor market conditions;
such knowledge is likely to influence the kind of vocational
courses that are sought. Thus we expect to find more agriculture courses in regions where agriculture is important and
more distributive education courses in regions where retail
sales is an important local economic activity.

We are not claiming that an emphasis on vocational offerings reflects a sole interest in local economic matters. Certainly some vocational offerings have broad applicability and
are not place bound. Keyboarding skills are a good example
of such globally relevant skills. Moreover, the contents of the

vocational curriculum are only partly influenced by local parent and student demands. State- and regional-level advisory boards can also play important roles in developing the vocational curriculum. What we are claiming is that schools that have unusually rich vocational offerings are revealing a greater sensitivity to and orientation toward local rather than global economic concerns. We relied upon a square root transformation of both ADVCRS and VOCED to reduce skewness.

We measured three related aspects of migration. The first two variables constitute two of the most common routes out of one's home community: attending a four-year college and joining the military. We constructed a measure of each of these from the 1982, 1984, and 1986 senior follow-up surveys. Our variables are aggregated to the school level and measure the percentage of a school's seniors who reported that they were in a four-year college or university at any time during the six years of the follow-up period (PCTCOLL). We constructed a similar measure of the percentage reporting that they spent time in the service (PCTMIL).

Finally, we constructed a school-level measure of migration (PCTLEFT). This variable is the percentage of a school's seniors who reported living more than 50 miles from their high school community in 1986, six years after the base year survey.

Our analysis begins with an examination of the bivariate relationship between the rural identity of a high school and the incidence of out-migration. The fact that this relationship is substantial and statistically significant sets the stage for our subsequent analyses of the roles played by school and community characteristics. This inquiry into the nature of the migration process begins with an assessment of relationships between the five structural characteristics and the kinds of courses found in the high school curricula. Specifically, we regressed our two measures of curricular offerings on the five structural characteristics: (a) average parental socioeconomic status, (b) average student academic ability, (c) location in a rural area, (d) school size, and (e) location in an isolated area.

We next considered the roles played by the structural characteristics as well as curricular offerings on both the decision

Table 3.1   Mean Percentage Migrating by School Location (N = 570)

	Urban	Suburban	Rural
Mean PCT LEFT	23.9	32.0	41.3
SD	16.6	18.3	19.8
Weighted N	40	177	353

NOTE: df = 2, 567; p < .001.

to go to college and the decision to enter the military. Regression analyses permit an assessment of the effects of curricular offerings, holding constant the five structural characteristics.

Finally, our attention turns to the measure of migration. We regress this variable successively on the five structural characteristics, the curriculum variables, and finally the variables measuring participation in either college or the military.

The analysis concludes with a reestimation of the college going, military going, and migration models, looking separately at the urban, suburban, and rural strata of the sample.

Findings

Table 3.1 demonstrates the very substantial and statistically significant variation between rural, suburban, and urban schools in the percentage of their seniors who migrate within six years of their schooling experience. According to Table 3.1, in the average urban high school, 23.9% of the seniors had migrated to a community more than 50 miles distant within six years; the comparable figure for rural high schools was 41.3%. The figure for suburban schools was 32.0%.

Table 3.2 provides the zero-order correlation matrix as well as the means and standard deviations for all of the selected variables, with listwise delation of missing data in effect. There are several points of interest. First, the number of advanced academic courses found within a school is substantially conditioned by the structural variables. Isolation and

Table 3.2   Correlation Matrix (N = 494)

	SIZE	AVTEST	RURAL	ISOLATE	AVSES	VOCED	ADVCRS	PCTMIL	PCTCOLL	PCTLEFT
SIZE	1.000									
AVTEST	.146	1.000								
RURAL	-.537	-.207	1.000							
ISOLATE	-.598	-.068	.564	1.000						
AVSES	.312	.782	-.331	-.219	1.000					
VOCED	.644	.183	-.373	-.425	.257	1.000				
ADVCRS	.713	.345	-.499	-.532	.464	.586	1.000			
PCTMIL	.070	-.069	.080	.011	-.099	.086	.066	1.000		
PCTCOLL	.079	.514	-.185	-.076	.474	.043	.204	-.212	1.000	
PCTLEFT	-.267	.332	.299	.435	.150	-.226	-.183	.077	.196	1.000
Mean	24.07	48.97	.63	5.14	-.196	5.93	1.38	7.20	33.04	37.60
SD	11.11	3.52	.49	2.16	.323	2.04	1.18	8.26	17.04	20.56

ruralness have strong negative effects, while the average ability level, SES, and especially size have strong positive effects. The structural variables have significant but smaller effects on a school's vocational offerings.

Second, the correlations among the background variables are of interest. As we would expect, school size, ruralness, and isolation are strongly related. The significance of this fact is that it will be difficult to ascertain which of these factors has the most powerful effect on any of our dependent variables in subsequent regression analyses. It is also worth noting that, on average, rural schools serve distinctly less advantaged clienteles than do their urban and suburban counterparts and that, perhaps partly as a consequence, the average ability test scores of their students is also lower.

Third, the percentage of a high school's seniors who serve in the military is virtually unaffected by any of the factors considered. This is not true for the percentage of seniors who attend college. Both a school's average ability and its average SES have the expected substantial positive influence, while being in a rural area has a small but significant negative effect

on college going. Of more interest to us here is the small but
significant effect of the curriculum on college going: The
number of advanced academic courses a school offers is correlated .204 with the percentage of seniors attending a four-
year college or university. Vocational offerings have no effect
on college going.

Fourth, the zero-order correlation matrix suggests that the
percentage of seniors migrating (PCTLEFT) is significantly related to all of the factors we are considering, though the relation with military service is tiny. (This may suggest that many
who serve in the military return to their home communities
after that service.) Note particularly that migration seems to
be decreased when schools offer a strong vocational education program (r = −.226). This fits with our earlier speculation
that such programs are attentive to local labor market conditions. The zero-order correlation of the number of advanced
courses a school offers with the percentage of its graduates
who migrate, however, is opposite to our expectations. The
correlation of −.183 suggests that, the more academic courses
a school offers, the less likely are its graduates to leave home.
We shall return to this point later.

Turning now to the question of influences on curricular offerings, Table 3.3 reports the results of regressing the number
of different advanced academic courses and vocational
courses a school offers on the five structural variables. All
variables except a school's ruralness contribute independently to the number of different advanced academic courses
it offers. In contrast, only school size and the average level of
its students' ability contribute to the extensiveness of vocational offerings. It is worth noting that the latter effect is positive; that is, the higher the average ability level of the student
body, the greater the number of vocational courses offered.
While this effect is not large, it is opposite to what some
might predict. It suggests that schools serving relatively low-
achieving students, who, presumably, are less likely to attend
college, are also less likely to offer their students an extensive
vocational curriculum designed to prepare them for work
after high school.

Table 3.3 The Effect of Schools' Features on Course Offerings
(Standardized Regression Coefficients; N = 494)

	Course Offerings	
	ADVCRS	*VOCED*
SIZE	.543***	.597***
AVTEST	.134***	.120***
RURAL	−.059	−.003
ISOLATE	−.139***	−.067
AVSES	−.142***	−.039
Adjusted R²	.592***	.420***

NOTE: *p < .10; **p < .05; ***p < .01.

A simple comparison of the standardized regression weights in Table 3.3 suggests that school size is the most important predictor of both advanced academic and vocational course offerings. This result has policy significance, because for years it has been common to assume that school size is a critical determinant of curriculum richness.

Our results also indicate, however, that other factors are related to course offerings, even among like-sized schools (also see Monk & Haller, 1991). Moreover, it is at least conceivable that the relatively large beta weights revealed in Table 3.3 for size are upwardly biased because of collinearity with the remaining structural factors. For example, the zero-order correlation between size and isolation is −.60, between size and advanced courses .71, and between isolation and advanced courses −.53.

To get a second estimate of the independent contribution of each of these variables, we partitioned the total variance explained (59.2%) for advanced academic offerings into those parts uniquely associated with each of the five structural factors. School size uniquely explains 16% of this total, isolation only 1%, and the remaining factors even less than 1%. This suggests two things: First, size has a substantial effect on course offerings independent of other structural features of schools, but, second, most of the variation is shared among

Table 3.4 The Effect of Schools' Structural Features and Course
Offerings on College Going and Military Service
(Standardized Regression Coefficients; N = 494)

	PCTCOLL		PCTMIL	
SIZE	-.087*	-.046	.193***	.086
AVTEST	.364***	.372***	.047	.022
RURAL	-.088*	-.086*	.132**	.139**
ISOLATE	-.014	-.016	.023	.046
AVSES	.184***	.175***	-.148*	-.164*
ADVCRS		.034		.130*
VOCED		-.099*		.064
Adjusted R^2	.277***	.280**	.026***	.033***
Adjusted R^2 Increase		.003**		.007*

NOTE: $^*p < .10$; $^{**}p < .05$; $^{***}p < .01$.

the various combinations of these features. In short, while
school size seems to be a critical determinant of the magnitude of a school's curricular offerings, its actual importance
cannot be definitively determined with these data. Similar
conclusions using different types of analyses were reached in
our earlier work (Haller et al., 1990; Monk, 1987; Monk &
Haller, 1991).

In Table 3.4 we turn our attention to the two important
means by which young people migrate from their home communities: entrance into college and entrance into the military.
When we regress the percentage of a high school's seniors
who spend some time in a four-year college or university on
the structural variables, we see that the average ability level
of a school and its average SES level have substantial and statistically significant effects, both positive. Slight relationships
are revealed for both school size and ruralness, suggesting
that there is some tendency for students from small rural
schools to be less likely to go to college, although the standard errors are too large to satisfy a 5% level of statistical significance. Isolation has no discernible effect on college going.
The modest strength of the relationships for school size and

ruralness are intriguing given the common beliefs that young people from rural small schools tend to have lower aspirations than others. Indeed, there is some evidence that this belief is correct (McIntyre & Marion, 1989; Monk & Haller, 1986). Our finding suggests that the aspiration-college going link may be largely explained by an association of average ability levels and SES with aspirations. As we have seen, rural schools tend to be slightly lower on our measures of both ability and SES.

We can also see from Table 3.4 that, when course offering variables are entered, the positive bivariate relationship observed earlier between the number of advanced courses and college going disappears. Numerous vocational course offerings appear to have a slight depressing influence on college going, but this relationship falls short of a 5% level of statistical significance. Together, the number of advanced courses and the number of vocational courses add less than 1% to the explained variance in college going.

The right-hand panel of Table 3.4 deals with the incidence of military service and shows that none of the variables we have been considering has much explanatory power. At best, we explain only 3.3 of the variance in the incidence of military service, although it appears that rural schools contribute slightly more students to the services and higher-SES schools slightly less.

Finally, we regressed the percentage of each school's senior class who had migrated on all the variables in our model, entered successively. Table 3.5 shows that ruralness, higher average student ability levels, and higher levels of isolation are all associated with a greater incidence of migration. These results continue to appear even as additional variables are added to the model.

Table 3.5 also shows that, controlling for all structural factors, students from schools with more extensive vocational offerings have a greater tendency to remain within 50 miles of where they went to high school. Recall our assertion that an emphasis on vocational offerings reflects a more local or regional orientation on the part of the school and the larger

Table 3.5   The Effect of Schools' Structural Features, Course
             Offerings, and Migration Routes on Migration
             (Standardized Regression Coefficient; N = 494)

	PCTLEFT		
	1	2	3
SIZE	−.015	.077	.072
AVTEST	.436***	.455***	.417***
RURAL	.166***	.163***	.156***
ISOLATE	.350***	.336***	.332***
AVSES	−.055	−.053	−.052
ADVCRS		−.043	−.061
VOCED		−.117**	−.114**
PCTCOLL			.114***
PCTMIL			.114***
Adjusted R^2	.336***	.342***	.356***
Adjusted R^2 Increase		.006**	.014**

NOTE: $^*p < .10$; $^{**}p < .05$; $^{***}p < .01$.

community. It is worth emphasizing that this curricular effect
on migration remains even with controls in place for the more
conventional influences on migrations (e.g., ability, SES, and
ruralness). The increase in R^2 when course offerings are added
to the equation (.006), however, can only be termed splendidly
trivial. Thus, while the effect of vocational offerings is statistically significant, it is not clear that it has any practical significance. Note also that the unexpected negative zero-order
correlation of ADVCRS with PCTLEFT (−.183) disappears when
structural factors are controlled, suggesting that the apparent
depressing effect of advanced academic courses on students'
tendency to migrate was largely spurious.

The expected positive relationships between the incidence
of students with college or military service and the incidence
of out-migration is also revealed by Table 3.5. The tiny negative direct effect of a vocational emphasis within the curriculum on the percentage leaving remains despite the inclusion
of the percentage going to college, which we learned in Table 3.4

Table 3.6 Effects of Schools' Curricular Offerings on Migratory Behavior by Strata[a] (Standardized Regression Coefficients)

	Urban	Suburban	Rural
Percentage entering college:			
ADVCRS	.062	−.081	.112
VOCED	−.053	.071	−.211[***]
Percentage entering the military:			
ADVCRS	.064	−.119	.278[***]
VOCED	−.093	.004	−.088
Percentage leaving after 6 years:			
ADVCRS	−.277	−.090	.027
VOCED	.008	−.150	−.119[*]
N	35	150	309

NOTE: [*]$p < .10$; [**]$p < .05$; [***]$p < .01$.
a. Controlling for four structural variables: school size, average test scores, school isolation, and average SES.

has a slight negative relationship to vocational offerings. Thus an emphasis on vocational courses has a small direct as well as a small indirect effect, via the incidence of students going to college, on out-migration.

Table 3.6 presents our final analyses in which we look separately at the curricular effects on college going, entrance into the military, and migration for the urban, suburban, and rural strata of our sample. Recall that we had reason to suppose that curricular effects would be more pronounced in rural schools. The results in Table 3.6 provide limited support for this proposition. According to Table 3.6, all of the relationships we found between curricular offerings and the incidence of college going, entrance into the military, and migration out of the hometown arise from within the rural stratum of the sample. There appears to be no relationship between curricular offerings, as they were measured here, and migration behaviors within the urban and suburban strata.

Moreover, the signs of the relationships revealed are consistent with what the rural critics of curricular reform would expect. An emphasis on vocational offerings within rural high schools has a negative effect on college going, while an emphasis on advanced academic courses within rural schools has a positive effect on exiting via the military. Lest we be too impressed with this confirmation of the critic's proposition, it is worth noting that in all cases the magnitudes of these relationships are quite small, and contrary to what the critics would predict, advanced academic offerings are not more positively related to college going within rural areas.

Discussion

Our results make it clear that curricular offerings, as we have measured them, have little to do with decisions young people make about leaving their home communities. Our results also make it clear that school size has neither a direct nor an indirect impact on migration. Once size has had its substantial effect on course offerings, it has only a minor impact on college going, on entrance into the military, and ultimately on migration itself.

It thus appears that the two most mutable schooling characteristics that we examined, curricular offerings and school size, have only a minor impact on the out-migration of youth. In contrast, relatively immutable structural aspects of schools and communities (e.g., isolation, intellectual levels, and to a lesser degree ruralness) coupled with the individual traits of students appear to be the primary determinants of youngsters' tendencies to leave home.

These findings are relevant to the policy issues we raised at the beginning of our chapter. At least insofar as "improving the curriculum" means expanding either the academic or the vocational range of courses offered, there seems to be little merit in the notion that the migration from rural communities can be stemmed by such curricular reform. This is not an argument for a policy of benign neglect or for school consolidation; it is merely one to recognize the limitations of schools as useful tools in this area of public policy.

Our results also speak to the critics' assertions about the need to develop programs specifically targeted to rural needs and to reverse the "citification" of the curriculum. Whatever else "citification" means, it surely means a curriculum oriented to advanced academics, subjects that are of special use in complex, professional, and technical occupations—that is, those found in urban centers. But our results suggest that providing opportunities to develop these skills to youth in rural areas seems not to promote their subsequent migration. We also found that providing more locally oriented programs (i.e., vocational education courses) has only negligible deterrent effects on migration. It is clear that rural youth will migrate regardless of the range of curricular offerings. Arguably then, not providing "urban skills" risks letting young people leave for the city unprepared to play productive roles.

This lack of effect is also important beyond what it says about the critics' calls for more rurally oriented curricula in rural schools. It suggests that small and rural schools can comply, to the extent that they are able, with national and state pressures to strengthen their academic curriculum without running the danger of exacerbating the drain of talented young people. Adding calculus and advanced placement physics courses is not a means of hastening the demise of rural communities.

Thus it appears that decision makers in rural areas have no rational basis for a concern over what curricular offerings can mean for migration. But we need to be mindful of the broader context in which these local decision makers operate. Rural communities are losing substantial portions of their young people, and it seems safe to assume that local officials such as school board members are fearful of these losses and are alarmed. While an "urban-oriented" curriculum may not be a strong predictor of migration, it is a logical one, and it may loom large in these local decision makers' thinking. Moreover, we did find evidence of a modest negative relationship between vocational offerings and migration. Thus, given a reasonable concern over the loss of youth and the absence of alternative means of intervening, it would not be surprising if some rural school boards looked to augmented vocational programs (and perhaps weakened academic ones) to help stem that loss.

Finally, we need to keep in mind the limits to our study. While our premise was that mutable schooling practices could have bearing on migration, the only readily changeable schooling phenomena we measured were school size and course title offerings. These are poor measures for what may be truly important: the contents of courses, the degree to which a school actually broadens the intellectual horizons of its students, and so forth.

Nevertheless, our results ought to be sobering to any reformer convinced that the simple manipulation of schooling attributes can have far-reaching implications for external social phenomena such as migration. While there may be many excellent and compelling reasons for reforming curricular offerings or changing average school size, our results make it clear that such reasons ought not to include expected changes in the migration behaviors of youth.

Note

1. These administrators' assessments correlated at high levels with alternative indicators of ruralness. For example, the point biserial correlation of the administrator's assessment with the 1980 county population in which the school was located was $-.72$.

References

Barker, B. (1985). Curricular offering in small and large high schools: How broad is the disparity? *Research in Rural Education, 3*(1), 35-38.

Brown, D. L. (1987). *Demographic trends relevant to education in nonmetro America*. Washington, DC: Rural Education Symposium. (Eric Document Reproduction Service ED 283 666)

Haller, E. J., Monk, D. H., Spotted Bear, A., Griffith, J., & Moss, P. (1990). School size and program comprehensiveness. *Educational Evaluation and Policy Analysis, 12*, 109-120.

Hand, C., & Prather, J. E. (1990). *Investigating high school effectiveness using college performance: An analysis of residuals*. Paper presented at the American

Educational Research Association Annual Meeting, Boston. (Eric Document Reproduction Service ED 318 761)

Hobbs, D. (1987, October 16-17). *Learning to find the "niches": Rural education and vitalizing rural communities.* Paper prepared for the National Rural Education Research Forum, Lake Placid, NY.

Lyson, T. A. (1986). Migration selectivity and early adult attainments. *Rural Sociology, 51,* 328-342.

McIntyre, W. G., & Marion, S. F. (1989). Academic achievement in America's small school: Data from high school and beyond. In *Education and the changing rural community: Anticipating the 21st century* (Proceedings of the 1989 ACRES/NRSSC Symposium). (Eric Document Reproduction Service ED 315 250)

McKenzie, P. A. (1989). *Secondary school size, curriculum structure, and resource use: A study in the economics of education.* Unpublished doctoral dissertation, Monash University, Faculty of Education.

Monk, D. H. (1987). Secondary school size and curriculum comprehensiveness. *Economics of Education Review, 6,* 137-150.

Monk, D. H., & Haller, E. J. (1986). *Organizational alternatives for small rural schools: Final report to the New York State Legislature.* Ithaca, NY: Cornell University, Department of Education. (Eric Document Reproduction Service ED 281 694)

Monk, D. H., & Haller, E. J. (1991). *Predictors of high school course offerings: The role of school size.* Unpublished manuscript. (Originally a paper presented at the annual meeting of the American Educational Research Association, Boston, April 1990)

Mulkey, D. (1988). *Education policy and rural development: A perspective from the southern region.* Birmingham, AL: Southern Regional Rural Development Workshop. (Eric Document Reproduction Service ED 302 359)

O'Hare, W. P. (1988). *The rise of poverty in rural America: Population trends and public policy.* Washington, DC: Population Reference Bureau. (Eric Document Reproduction Service ED 302 350)

Price, D. O., & Sikes, M. M. (1974). *Rural-urban migration research in the United States: Annotated bibliography and synthesis.* Washington, DC: Government Printing Office.

Rhoda, R. (1983). Rural development and urban migration: Can we keep them down on the farm? *International Migration Review, 17,* 34-64.

Seyfrit, C. L. (1986). Migration intentions of rural youth: Testing an assumed benefit of rapid growth. *Rural Sociology, 51,* 199-211.

Sher, J. (1986). Rural development worthy of the name. In J. Dale & R. Wimberly (Eds.), *New dimensions in rural policy: Building upon our heritage* (Joint Economic Committee of Congress). Washington, DC: Government Printing Office.

Swanson, L. L., & Butler, M. A. (1987). *Faces and futures of the nonmetro workforce.* Madison, WI: Rural Sociological Society. (Eric Document Reproduction Service ED 292 597)

Swift, D. (1988). *Preparing rural students for an urban environment.* Las Cruces: New Mexico State University. (ERIC Clearinghouse on Rural Education and Small Schools ED 296 818)

Vaughn, D. L., & Vaughn, P. R. (1985). *Handbook for rural students: Finding employment and adjusting to urban areas.* Las Cruces: New Mexico State

University. (ERIC Clearinghouse on Rural Education and Small Schools ED 276 536)

Willits, F. K., Crider, D. M., & Bealer, R. C. (1980). *Twenty-four years later: Migration and success for a panel of rural Pennsylvanians* (Bulletin 831). University Park: Pennsylvania State University Agricultural Experiment Station.

FOUR

Economic and Demographic Dimensions of National Education Policy

DEBORAH VERSTEGEN

Economic performance and demographic shifts have varied widely among continents and countries throughout the world during the decade of the 1980s, although certain trends are evident. After the sharp recession at the beginning of the decade, the industrial countries began an expansion of uninterrupted growth but at lower rates than in the 1950s and 1960s. In contrast, for many developing countries, economic stagnation and decline have been accompanied by falling incomes, increasing poverty, falling standards of living, and increasing levels of marginality. Economic disruptions around the globe have also led to major setbacks in basic education in many of the least developed countries; in other countries, economic growth has been available to finance education expansion but millions remain in poverty, unschooled, and illiterate. In some industrialized countries, cutbacks in government expenditure during the 1980s have led to the deterioration of education (World Conference

72   WHO PAYS FOR STUDENT DIVERSITY?

on Education for All [WCEFA], 1990, p. 1). In the United
States, national support for education and children has plummeted, even as the number of needy children has grown and
the onset of the information age has placed new and more
stringent demands on the schools.

This chapter will examine the mismatch in national policy for
children and children's needs into the decade of the 1990s. First,
it will provide a brief review of the major economic and demographic changes at home and abroad during the 1980s as children and youth are profoundly affected by the society in which
they live. It will then discuss national antipoverty policy in education and the implications of economic and demographic shifts
for education policy and finance in the 1990s and beyond. It is
argued that the face of economic instability and decline of the
1980s—a decade of growing disparity—is the face of the child,
whose life prospects today and hopes for tomorrow are severely
affected by the economics of now (see UNICEF, 1989, p. 2).

Economic and Demographic
Changes in the United States

The decade of the 1980s in the United States could well be
characterized as the best of times and the worst of times. The
Reagan administration's restructuring of federal policy during
this time dramatically affected the creation and distribution of
wealth and income, entrepreneurialism, investment, and speculation. Tax reforms in 1981 and 1986, budgetary policy changes,
relaxed regulation, and a preference for creditors over debtors
benefited many individuals, but at a grave price (Phillips, 1990).
At the close of the decade, many persons found themselves
worse off than at its beginning. Notably, children grew to constitute the largest share of individuals in poverty and became the
fastest growing homeless subpopulation. But national policy for
children and education—long directed at ensuring equal opportunity to all sectors of the educational landscape—sustained
substantial reductions in real aid during this time, even as the
economy then declined and poverty rates for children grew.

The federal budget deficit tripled to (an estimated) $3.1 trillion during the decade (Council of Economic Advisors, 1989, tables B-76, B-77). Although the national debt was one third (33.5%) of the gross national product (GNP) in 1980, by 1987 it had climbed to over one half (52.5%) of the GNP. The interest payments on the federal deficit alone amounted to $143 billion a year by 1987. This equals $20 million an hour, 24 hours a day (ACIR, 1989, table 8), or $10,000 for every man, woman, and child in the nation.

Adding to the budget deficit was the annual international trade deficit that hovered around $200 billion by the late 1980s. The sharp rise in the twin pillars of budget and trade debt was accompanied by long-standing anemic productivity, recession, a decline in the already low national savings rate, a drop in the U.S. standing from first to ninth in terms of global GNP per capita, increasing income inequalities, rising poverty, and falling standards of living—in what was once considered the "Affluent Society" (see Ebel & Marks, 1990; Thurow, 1985). The United States shifted from being the largest creditor to the largest debtor nation in the world in 1985; once the economic leader, America slipped to parity with other major industrial nations.

Fiscal and monetary policies collided in the early 1980s. Tight money caused inflation to subside, but the growth in tax receipts slowed as increased subsidies for medicare, medicaid, and social security for growing numbers of the elderly jumped upward and interest payments on the national debt grew rapidly (Heilbroner & Bernstein, 1989, chap. 2). By 1982 the country was in the throes of the worst economic recession since the 1929 depression. Personal income fell in real terms (ACIR, 1989, table 1); by 1988 the median family income was lower than in 1973 measured in constant dollars, and average weekly earning were lower than in 1962 (During, 1989, p. 23; Phillips, 1990, pp. 14-18). The absolute numbers of unemployed, though falling steadily since 1983, were higher in 1987 than in 1979 (Committee on Ways & Means, 1989, p. 1064, appendix J; Phillips, 1990). By mid-decade, after the onset of a modest economic expansion that began in 1983, disparities in earnings were the worst on record. The rich were growing richer and the poor, poorer. After-tax incomes of the top 1% of the population increased 74.2% between 1977 and 1987; but for the lowest 10% of the population, there was a real drop in income of 10.5% (Phillips, 1990, p. 14).

Growing economic polarization was apparent in the widening gap between the top and bottom fifth of the income distribution. Total income among the poorest 20% of families in the United States decreased 7.3% between 1973 and 1987, but the total income among the richest 20% of families increased 10.7%. In 1987 the richest 20% of households held over 43% of total income—the highest ratio since the Census Bureau began its official measurements in 1949 (Phillips, 1990, p. 12); but the lowest 20% held only 3.9% of total income. Among major industrial nations—including France, Britain, Canada, West Germany (the Federal Republic), Sweden, the Netherlands, and Japan—the United States held the ominous distinction of leading in the disparity between the upper fifth and the lowest fifth of the income distribution (Phillips, 1990, p. 11).

The disparity in the distribution of wealth grew even wider than the disparity in the distribution of income during the 1980s. The top 10% of households controlled 68% of family net worth in 1987—in essence, 68% of the nation's wealth. The top 420,000 households also accounted for 26.9% of national wealth. In 1988 approximately 1.3 million Americans were millionaires by assets, up from 574,000 in 1980, 180,000 in 1972, and 90,000 in 1964. Even when adjusted for inflation, the number of millionaires doubled between the late 1970s and the late 1980s (Phillips, 1990, p. 10). In contrast, almost 20% of all U.S. families had zero or negative net worth (Thurow, 1985, p. 111). Growing income polarization brought on by government policies, the decline in the real average earnings levels, and a low minimum wage that failed to keep pace with inflation catapulted many individuals, families, and especially children into poverty.

In 1973, 11.1% of the population was poor; this is approximately 23 million people. In 1987 the poverty rate rose to 13.5%; 32.5 million people were poor. This is an increase of over 41%. And the poor were growing poorer. The average poor family in 1986 was further below the poverty line than at any time since 1963, except for the recession of 1981-1982 (Committee on Labor and Human Resources, 1988, pp. 38-39). Between 1973 and 1988 the poverty gap—the difference between a poor family's disposable income and the poverty level, summed across all poor families—grew from $28.6 billion to $41.4 billion (in 1987 dollars), representing an increase of $12.8 billion.

African Americans and Hispanics, in addition to individuals in female-headed households and children, had poverty rates that greatly exceeded the average. The poverty rate for all Hispanics remained near 30% during the decade. The poverty rates for African Americans and individuals in female-headed households remained above 30% from 1959 to 1987. Two out of every three Americans in poverty, however, were non-Hispanic whites.

Poverty rates in the United States were higher in 1987 for rural areas than for urban metropolitan areas for every race classification. Central city sections of metropolitan areas, however, continued to register the highest poverty concentrations of all municipalities. The number of poor who lived in inner-city poverty neighborhoods increased by about 66% between 1970 and 1980, but most of this growth was concentrated in New York, Chicago, Philadelphia, and Detroit. Therefore the "vast majority of the poor, even the urban poor, lived dispersed in suburbs, small towns, and cities, or mixed-income neighborhoods of central cities" (Committee on Labor and Human Resources, 1988, p. 24).

Notably, child poverty rose at an alarming rate throughout the 1970s and 1980s; and children replaced the elderly as the largest subpopulation in poverty. While many children fare well in households with low income, studies have shown that these children are more likely to suffer disproportionately—early death, serious illness, teenage pregnancy—because of their poverty status, and they are less likely to continue education beyond high school (Kirst & McLaughlin, 1989).

The child poverty rate grew from 8.4% in 1973, representing 9.4 million children, to 20.4% in 1987, when 12.8 million children—1 out of every 5—were in poverty (Committee on Ways

& Means, 1989, p. 942, and tables 2, 3, pp. 944-945). It is shocking to note that in America, 27 children die every day as a direct result of poverty (Reed & Sautter, 1990, p. K-3). International comparisons reveal that, of 20 industrialized countries, the United States has the highest infant mortality rate (Schorr & Schorr, 1988, p. 117). The United States also leads Australia, Canada, West Germany, Norway, Sweden, Switzerland, and the United Kingdom in child poverty. In all of these countries, children in one-parent families are considerably more likely to be in poverty than children in two-parent families.

Family structure also changed dramatically in the 1980s. The number of single-parent families and families where both parents work rose. In 1955, 60% of U.S. households consisted of a working father, a housewife mother, and two or more school-aged children. In 1980 that family unit characterized only 11% of homes, and by 1985 it represented only 7% of all households (Hodgkinson, 1985, p. 3). One-parent families increased 142% between 1970 and 1987, growing from 3.8 to 9.2 million. During the same period, two-parent families decreased 3.1%, from 25.8 to 25.0 million. Although the total number of children under age 18 years declined from 69 to 63 million, the number of children living with one parent grew 84%, from 8.2 to 15.1 million. More than 23% of all children lived in one-parent families in 1987, compared with 12% in 1970. Based on current trends, it is estimated that 70% of white children and 94% of African-American children born in 1980 will spend part of their childhood in a single-parent home before reaching the age of 18 (Committee on Ways & Means, 1989, p. 832).

Although the feminization of poverty has accounted for about 38% of individuals in poverty from 1978 to 1986, it is significant that female-headed families contributed almost nothing to the sharp increase in poverty from 1979 to 1983. The poor performance of the economy and federal budget reductions explained a large portion of the rapid increase in poverty during this time, particularly for the working poor (Committee on Labor and Human Resources, 1988, pp. 39-40).

Unlike previous generations, a large number of America's poor today are working poor. For example, full-time work at the minimum wage by the head of a family of three leaves that family $2,500 below the poverty line (Reed & Sautter, 1990). Michael Harrington, author of *The Other America*, notes: "Most Americans do not know there are more poor families headed by a working person in the United States than there are poor families headed by a welfare mother. They do not know that" (Harrington, 1988, p. 5). In fact, in 1987, 60% of all poor families with children were families where someone worked during the year, and 25% of all poor families with children were families with one or more full-time worker equivalents (FTWEs).

The number of prime-working-age individuals, aged 22 to 64, who work but are still poor has increased by 50% between 1978 and 1988; the number of prime-working-age people who work full-time year-round but are still poor has increased by 57% since 1978. There are an estimated 6 million individuals—including 2 million children—in households where someone works full-time year-round but the household is still poor (Committee on Labor and Human Resources, 1988).

Growing poverty during the 1980s and the lack of affordable housing have left many people homeless. The number of homeless in America has increased to between (an estimated) 680,000 and 2.5 million people. There are disproportionate percentages of African Americans and Hispanics among the homeless in comparison with the overall population; a large percentage of the homeless have not graduated from high school. In the homeless population, 77% are single but 23% are members of homeless families—8% are adults and 15% are children. Children represent the fastest growing subpopulation of the homeless population (Committee on Ways & Means, 1989, pp. 1060-1063).

Despite a rising number of homeless individuals in the United States and the sharp rise in individuals in poverty— particularly children—during the decade, national budgetary policy has favored military expansion over social investment. Between 1980 and 1988, $1.9 trillion was spent on national defense, but programs aimed at protecting poor children and families were reduced $10 billion (Reed & Sautter, 1990, p. K-5).

Defense spending rose from 4.9% of the GNP in 1980 to 6.2% in 1987. In 1980 this represented 22.2% of total budget outlays, by 1987 defense spending consumed 26.3% of the U.S. national budget.

Conversely, between 1980 and 1987 funding for transportation dropped from .74% to .58% of the GNP, and Housing and Urban Development assistance declined as a percentage of the GNP from .48% to .35% (Executive Office of the President, 1988, tables 1.2, 4.1). During the same period, total federal aid for education decreased as a percentage of the GNP from 0.6% to 0.4%, while funding for the Department of Education declined as a percentage of total budget outlays from 2.5% to 1.7%. Higher (tertiary) education revenue accumulated increases of 11% during this time; primary and secondary education revenues fell a total of 28% (Verstegen, 1990), and the U.S. position on spending on education declined. Of 16 industrialized nations including Sweden, Austria, Switzerland, Norway, Belgium, Denmark, Japan, Canada, West Germany, France, the Netherlands, the United Kingdom, Italy, Austria, and Ireland, the United States ranks 14th both in public spending for all levels of schooling and in spending for K-12 education. Only Australia and Ireland spend less than the United States (Rasell & Mishel, 1990). Of the 15 industrialized countries belonging to the OECD (Organization for Economic Development and Cooperation), the United States ranks 10th in the percentage of GDP (gross domestic product) devoted to public education (Nelson, 1990).

Currently, 39% of children from poor families do not receive free and reduced-priced lunches; one fourth of these children have no health insurance; 38% do not receive food stamps; and public housing accommodates only 21% of all families in poverty (Kirst & McLaughlin, 1989, p. 8). AFDC benefits (Aid to Families with Dependent Children) for a family of four with no other income have dropped about 33% in real terms since 1970; since 1980 AFDC support has fallen $7 billion. The unemployment insurance program reached only 33% of the unemployed by 1987 (Committee on Labor and Human Resources, 1988, p. 41). Although government benefit programs lifted one of five families out of poverty that would have been poor without them in 1979, in 1988 they lifted one of every nine families out of poverty.

Military outlays have aggravated the budget deficit and opportunity costs have swelled as a result of financing armaments rather than education, infrastructure, and the environment. The Committee on Education and Labor in the U.S. House of Representatives (1985) points to the reduction in services and hardship that have resulted from federal aid reductions, stating that "the difficult problems the nation confronts require more resources, not fewer." It finds the decreases in funding have been borne by those least able to sustain them and that poverty in the United States has risen as a direct result of the Reagan administration's budget reductions. National budgets in the 1980s have not only favored military over social expenditures, but, like state budgets, they have often been maldistributed within the sectors ostensibly aimed at children and the poor—rural development, education, and health. Phillips (1990, p. 53) observes that during the 1980s "accelerating maldistribution seemed to be a global phenomenon."

International Changes

The global poverty rate rose during the 1980s, after steadily declining since midcentury and, after decades of steady economic advance, large areas of the world slid backward into poverty (UNICEF, 1990, p. 1). Global poverty was 21.7% in 1980, but by 1989 about 1 billion people across the world— 23.4% of the global population—lived in absolute poverty. Two thirds of the world's poor are children, that is, under the age of 15 (During, 1990, p. 140). In the United Kingdom and Eastern Europe, as in the United States, poverty has been on the rise during this time (During, 1989, pp. 22-23). Rising poverty during the decade in Latin America, Africa, and parts of Asia has offset reductions in the number of impoverished in the two most populous countries on earth—China and India (During, 1989, p. 227; 1990, p. 139). As in the United States, rural poverty is pronounced: Of the world's poor, four fifths live in rural areas.

In most countries of the world, the poorest fifth of households collect less than 10% of national income while the richest fifth commonly receive half (During, 1989, p. 10). The disparity of wealth is wider, as it is in the United States. The situation in India is illustrative of developing countries generally. The richest tenth of households receive income 25 times greater than the poorest tenth of households but own assets worth 250 times as much (see Lipton, 1988, p. 14).

That poverty is increasing substantially in developing countries is apparent in the fact that 43 developing nations finished the decade poorer than they started it (based on per capita estimates). For most of the countries of Africa, Latin America, the Caribbean, and parts of Asia—unlike China, India, Malaysia, Pakistan, the Republic of Korea, Sri Lanka, and Thailand (nations where absolute incomes continue to rise and average living standards slowly improve)—along with rising population growth and environmental decline, per capita GNP has fallen, productivity has been reduced, and debt repayments have risen. Throughout most of Africa and much of Latin America, average incomes have fallen by 10% to 25% in the 1980s. In some countries in Latin America, real per capita GNP was lower in the 1980s than it was a decade ago. Today, one third of Latin America's population— 130 million people—live in dire poverty. In some African countries, the GNP is less than it was two decades ago (World Bank, 1990, p. 6). What safety nets have existed for many of Africa's poor have been torn away. Malnutrition is rising in many countries including Burma, Burundi, the Gambia, Guinea-Bessau, Jamaica, Niger, Nigeria, El Salvador, and Peru (During, 1990, p. 137). Between 1979 and 1983 life expectancy fell in nine African countries; more than 100 million people lacked sufficient food to sustain themselves (During, 1990, p. 138).

Poverty's greatest toll is measured in the lives of children. In Zambia twice as many children died from malnutrition in 1983 and 1984 than in 1980. The infant mortality rate in Brazil rose in 1983 by 25% and again in 1984, as it did in much of the Third World. In 1989 the deaths of at least a half million children were attributed to the slowing down or reversal of progress in the developing world (During, 1989, p. 16).

"Must we starve our children to pay our debts?" Tanzanian President Julius Nyerere has asked. That question has now been answered in practice, and the answer is "yes." Hundreds of thousands of the developing world's children have given their lives to pay their countries debts, and many millions more are still paying the interest with their malnourished minds and bodies (UNICEF, 1989, p. 30).

The links between poverty, population growth, and environmental degradation are often direct. Africa's population is growing faster than that of any other region in the world in this century. As increased numbers of people in poverty press upon limited natural resources in rural areas, the stock of renewable resources begins to be depleted. In South Asia, Africa, the Middle East, and arid and semiarid areas of the world, desertification, deforestation, or water scarcity have, in part, reduced the land available for agriculture, wildlife inhabitants, and recreation (World Bank, 1990, p. 15).

According to the U.N.'s International Children's Education Fund (UNICEF, 1990, p. 2), this tragedy of development's reversal is happening not because of "any one visible cause, but because of an unfolding economic drama in which the industrialized nations play a leading role." For example, as deficits have mounted in the United States, the need to attract funds to finance budget deficits has meant that interest rates maintained high levels, adding to the debt-service burden in many of the indebted developing nations (UNICEF, 1990, p. 24).

The total debt of the developing world in 1989 was $1.2 trillion—nearly one half of its collective GNP. Between 1985 and 1986 total debt increased by almost 10% ($70 billion); the debts of sub-Saharan Africa increased by almost 20% ($25 billion). Interest and principal payments claimed more resources than loans from industrial countries supplied. By 1988 the balance of payments reversed as developing countries in the South were paying the North's industrial nations $50 billion a year (During, 1990, p. 144). On average, repayments claimed almost 25% of export revenues. At the same time, real prices for chief export commodities fell by about 30%.

In an attempt to stave off balance-of-payments crises while at the same time meeting debt obligations, maintaining essential imports, and struggling to return to economic growth, most of the affected nations have been forced to adopt economic adjustment policies that included deep cuts in government spending. The services that have been most radically pruned, with some notable exceptions, were health services, free primary education, and food and fuel subsidies (UNICEF, 1990, p. 16). Military expenditures, however, have increased..

In 1988 the world's nation-states devoted $1 trillion—$200 for each man, woman, and child—to the means of warfare, but they failed to provide the $5 per child it would have cost to eradicate the simple diseases that killed 14 million or to raise the funding necessary to alleviate illiteracy among the 880 million adults who could not read or write their own names (ACDA, 1989; UNICEF, 1989). In the 37 poorest nations of the world, per capita spending on education has fallen by nearly 50% and on health care by 25% during the last 10 years (UNICEF, 1989, p. 17). School enrollment rates have fallen and dropout rates have risen in approximately one third of the developing nations (p. 18). As the U.N. Committee for Development Planning finds:

> There seems to be a clear bias within the political system towards a reduction of public expenditure on human development in times of distress . . . many governments believed it was easier to more expedient to reduce expenditures on human development than on other items in the central government's budget. (UNICEF, 1990, p. 19)

The Face of Debt and Recession

As the social effects of the debt and recession of the 1980s become more obvious into the 1990s, it can be seen that the heaviest burden is falling on the shoulders of those who are least able to sustain it. It does not take much imagination to realize what lies behind these statistics—the face of today's economic problems is the face of the child and individuals in poverty. It is children and the poor who bore the heaviest burden of debt and recession in the 1980s and whose prospects for the 1990s and beyond are, currently, dismal. It is "the child whose individual development today and social contribution tomorrow are being shaped by the economics of now" (see UNICEF, 1989, p. 2).

At all levels, the world's poor are overwhelmingly illiterate and therefore lack access to information and ideas that could help them escape the downward spiral of poverty. Equal opportunities for education that would allow them to break the cycle that has trapped generations in its grip remain an illusive ideal. More than 100 million children today, including at least 60 million girls, have no access to primary schooling; more than 960 million adults, two thirds of whom are women, are illiterate; more than one third of the world's adults have no access to printed knowledge, new skills, and technologies; more than 100 million children fail to complete basic education programs; millions more satisfy attendance requirements but fail to acquire basic skills (WCEFA, 1990, p. 1).

Where most children have access to schooling, as in the United States, the growing inequality that has characterized the decade of the 1980s and the early 1990s has become most apparent in the nation's public schools. Despite "reforms" that have steadily punctuated the decades, rich schools and poor schools persist, and within affluent schools, insidious "tracking" systems condemn many children to less than the best education, curtailing their future opportunities. Wide cleavages in the ability to provide equal opportunities for a quality education are apparent not only among schools, however, but among school systems and among states (see Table 4.1)—and they are growing wider (see Verstegen & Salmon, 1989). For example, in Illinois, spending for elementary education varies from $1,162 per student in one elementary school to $7,040 in another. In New Jersey, one elementary district spends $2,081 per pupil and another spends $12,556. In more than half the states, the range of differences in spending among school systems is at least twofold; in one third of all states, spending varies over threefold (Committee on Education and Labor, 1990; Riddle, 1990). However, in addition to large variations for spending on education within states, there are also substantial differences in spending for education between states.

In Alaska, for example, a high spending state, average per pupil expenditures ($7,971) are almost three times that of Mississippi ($2,548). This difference is reflected in each state's ability to support education (as indicated by their gross state product (GSP) per child and by their relative tax capacity). Alaska's GSP is $176,351 but Mississippi's GSP—$54,597—is three times lower. Alaska's relative tax capacity—its potential for raising revenue through tax effort at the national average—is 177 compared with 65 for Mississippi. States with the lowest wealth and the lowest per pupil expenditures are often the states with the highest concentrations of children in poverty (Taylor & Piche, 1990). In Alaska, for example, 12.7% of children under 18 are in poverty but in Mississippi, almost three times as many, 34.3%, are in poverty.

Children in poverty make up a disproportionate share of the population most at risk of dropping out of school. In 1984, 22.4% of people aged 22 to 65 years who had dropped out of high school were poor, but half as many—9.8%—of those who had completed high school but not gone on to college were poor. The poverty rate of those who attended college was 5.4% (Lyke, 1988). This affects opportunities directly. The real mean earnings for male dropouts who were between 20 and 24 years fell 41.6% between 1973 and 1984. The decline for Hispanic young men for the same period was 38.6%. The decline for black males was 61.3%.

Dropping out of school generally has high costs for society as well as individuals. On average, dropouts pay less taxes; are more likely to be less productive workers, to need welfare assistance, to commit crimes and delinquent acts; and are less likely to participate in community affairs. Dropouts are three

Table 4.1   Current Expenditures, Gross State Product, Tax Capacity, and Children in Poverty

State	1988 Current Expenditures per Pupil/Rank (dollars)	1986 Gross State Product per Child/Rank (dollars)	1986 Relative Tax Capacity (U.S. = 100)/Rank	1985 Percentage of Children Under 18 in Poverty/Rank
Highest spending:				
Alaska	7,971 (1)	176,351 (1)	177 (1)	12.7 (3)
New York	7,151 (2)	115,337 (6)	107 (13)	23.6 (41)
New Jersey	6,564 (3)	116,190 (5)	121 (6)	15.5 (11)
Connecticut	6,230 (4)	128,668 (2)	135 (4)	11.8 (2)
Massachusetts	5,471 (5)	120,340 (3)	124 (5)	14.1 (6)
Wyoming	5,051 (9)	109,093 (8)	151 (2)	15.5 (11)
Lowest spending:				
South Dakota	3,249 (41)	71,029 (43)	82 (42)	21.3 (33)
Kentucky	3,011 (45)	71,322 (42)	76 (47)	23.6 (41)
Arkansas	2,989 (46)	67,019 (45)	78 (45)	29.0 (46)
Idaho	2,667 (48)	59,058 (48)	77 (46)	21.7 (36)
Mississippi	2,548 (49)	54,597 (50)	65 (50)	34.3 (50)
Utah	2,454 (50)	55,703 (49)	80 (43)	13.2 (5)

SOURCE: Committee on Education and Labor (1990).
NOTE: Data collected from U.S. Department of Education (1990), Children's Defense Fund (1990, p. 90), and Council of Chief State School Officers (1989).

and a half times as likely as high school graduates to be arrested, six times more likely to be unwed parents, seven and a half times more likely to be dependent on welfare; and two and a half times as likely to be unemployed and to live in poverty (Schorr & Schorr, 1988). Children of dropouts often share their disadvantages perpetuating social inequality. In 1982-1983, 39% of all children in two-parent families were in poverty if neither parent had completed high school. If one parent had graduated from high school, 20% were poor; if both had, 7% were poor (Lyke, 1988, p. 9).

Currently, more than 20% of young people fail to complete high school; this amounts to about 750,000 new dropouts per year. Although the dropout rate has declined steadily from the

turn of the century, since 1969 it has increased. In 1985, an estimated 73.3% of all students completed high school compared with 77.1% in 1969. On average, dropout rates are
higher in urban (18.9%) versus suburban (11.8%) localities;
among Native Americans/Alaskans (29.2%), Hispanics (18%),
and African Americans (17%) compared with Euro-Americans
(12.2%); and for males (14.7%) versus females (12.6%).

As the numbers of children at risk of not completing high
school continue to encompass a growing circle of America's
youth, the nation's most pressing threat mounts from within its
borders and portends the emergence of a dual society with a
large and uneducated underclass, political instability, reduced
economic competitiveness, and higher costs of public services
associated with poverty and crime (Brazelton, 1990; Levin,
1989). At the same time, America's rich mix of ethnic and racial
groups provides a unique opportunity given the incredible potential for creativity, innovation, and diversity available to provide a competitive edge into the twenty-first century. Today,
14% of all adults and 20% of children under age 17 are members
of minority groups. By the year 2000, one third of all school-
aged children will fall into this group. In 25 of the largest cities
and metropolitan areas, at least 50% of public school students
come from minority groups. By the year 2000, almost 33% of all
public school students will be minority children; 42% will be
children in poverty (American Council on Education, 1988, p. 2).
Therefore, in the future, increased diversity coupled with growing poverty will be accompanied by a distinct challenge, because, historically, children of color and children in poverty
have not been well served by the nation's schools—and schooling provides a viable passport out of poverty.

Thus, the plight of children today represents society's most
hideous failure, but children also represent one of its best
hopes in the future. Schools are the one social institution that
touches every child every day and as such have a major role
to play in addressing the effects of child poverty. Although
schooling cannot redress deeply rooted social and economic
maladies, recently renewed attention has been given to the

importance of education to individual economic and social success in the information age; to national economic growth and increased productivity; and to the reduction of income inequalities, poverty, social welfare programs, crime, and incarceration. To briefly summarize, although there are important caveats, Tilak (1989, p. 60) establishes that

- the contribution of education is significant in reducing poverty and improving the income distribution (see Ahluwalia, 1974; Fields, 1980a, 1980b);
- education contributes significantly to economic growth—returns to investment in education are comparable with, if not more than, investment in physical capital (cf., Psacharopoulos, 1985);
- there are positive and significant relationships between education and nonmonetary returns such as physical productivity (cf., Jamison & Lau, 1982);
- the contribution of education is higher in developing countries compared to developed countries (cf., Psacharopoulos, 1984, 1985);
- the contribution is higher from investment in education of socioeconomic weaker sectors compared to investment in socially and economically advanced groups of the population.

In a two-part strategy for rapid and politically sustainable progress on poverty, investment in basic education for children and youth is highlighted by the World Bank (1990). The first part of that strategy calls for policies that harness market incentives, social and political institutions, infrastructure, and technology to promote the productive use of the poor's most abundant asset—labor. Lowering unemployment rates, raising wages, raising benefit levels, extending benefit coverage, or otherwise increasing income through such means as increasing child support collections and expanding the earned income tax credit have been found to provide large impacts on poverty (Committee on Labor and Human Resources, 1988, p. 42). The second feature of the two-pronged strategy to reduce poverty is to provide basic social services to the poor, including health care, family planning, nutrition, and

importantly primary education. This strategy was at the heart
of the 1960s "War on Poverty" in the United States. Now,
nearly one third of a century later, the demographic and economic imperatives of the nation call for another assault on
want and deprivation, another War on Poverty. Lessons from
the last 20 years show that a War on Poverty can be won, but
only if the commitment is mounted to fight it.

The Federal Role in
Children's Antipoverty Policy

The idea of education as a weapon against poverty has
strong roots in the traditional U.S. conception of education as
the key to social integration and mobility that accompanied
attempts to assimilate successive waves of immigrants
through schooling in the nineteenth century. This idea was
strengthened after World War II by human capital theorists
who showed that investments in schooling yielded ample returns in the form of higher lifetime earning streams. As Levine and Bane (1975, pp. 3-4) observe, education

> had inherent attractions because of its very indirectness.
> Publicly supported education, it seemed, could give the
> poor the tools they needed to escape from poverty by
> dint of their own efforts. It would not oblige Americans
> to violate the work ethic by creating a dole.

Education was the Johnson administration's major weapon in
fighting the War on Poverty and the principal tool in building
the "Great Society." According to President Johnson, however,
there were "interlocking effects" of deprivation. Although traditionally measured in terms of income, poverty's true horror ex-
tends to all aspects of life: susceptibility to disease, lack of access
to most services and information, lack of control over resources,
subordination to higher social and economic classes, extreme
vulnerability to sudden misfortunes, and utter insecurity in the
face of changing circumstances (During, 1989, p. 7). According

to Robert McNamara (1981), poverty is a "condition of life so limited by malnutrition, illiteracy, disease, squalid surroundings, high infant mortality, and low life expectancy as to be beneath any reasonable definition of human decency." The Johnson program therefore provided a multifaceted attack on the many faces of poverty with a premium placed on job training and education that would provide a "hand up" rather than a "handout" for the poor (Graham, 1984, p. 53). Passage of the Economic Opportunity Act of 1964 established 10 programs to address these goals—among them Head Start, the Job Corps, and VISTA. Other major programs followed: medicare and medicaid, federal aid for elementary and secondary education, federal scholarships for college students, the Partnership for Health program, and an assortment of consumer protection laws ("Health, Education and Welfare," 1969, p. 663).

The explicit idea of education as a weapon against poverty was given form in 1965 through enactment of the cornerstone of the War on Poverty: the Elementary and Secondary Education Act (PL 89-10). The program's aim under Title I (now Chapter 1), from that time until the present, was to provide supplemental educational and related services to economically disadvantaged children who attended schools serving low-income areas (Riddle, 1981, p. 1). Passage of Title I broke the logjam of nearly a century in the enactment of large-scale federal aid to elementary and secondary education; it tripled expenditures for the schools and made economically disadvantaged children a legitimate concern of the federal government.

Although early evaluations of War on Poverty programs were mixed, recently a number of scholars, analysts, and others have found that, while funding never reached estimated levels of need, what was spent worked. Head Start worked—preschool programs have provided benefits sixfold compared with costs. Jobs programs worked—the numbers of unemployed went down every year in the 1960s. Changes in social security worked—they raised the level of benefits and indexed them against inflation. The attack on poverty worked—economic growth and prosperity cannot nearly account in full for the decline in the number of poor people from 40 million in 1961 to

24 million in 1969, a number that was 24 million in 1972 before dipping to 23 million in 1973 (see House Select Committee on Children, Youth and Families, 1990; Kennedy in Committee on Labor and Human Resources, 1988; Okun, 1975, p. 117; Schorr & Schorr, 1988; Schweinhart & Weikart, 1986).

Other successes have been documented in improving maternal and child health during the last two decades in four War on Poverty programs: Medicaid and Medicaid's Early and Periodic Screening, Diagnosis and Treatment (EPSDT) program, the Special Supplemental Food Program for Women, Infants and Children (WIC), and federal support of neighborhood health centers and maternal and child health clinics (Schorr & Schorr, 1988, p. 124). Moreover, federally supported compensatory education under Chapter 1 has been shown to have succeeded in narrowing the performance gap between economically disadvantaged and more fortunate children (see Hawley, 1985; Schorr & Schorr, 1988, p. 224; Smith & O'Day, 1991). The National Assessment of Educational Progress found that disadvantaged 9-year-olds showed significant improvement in reading ability between 1970 and 1980, with the greatest gains occurring among black children and children in the Southeast, where federal money, particularly under Title I, had been concentrated. The Sustaining Effects Study also found a narrowing of the achievement gap in basic skills between historically lower-achieving children and their more affluent counterparts. Title I programs were found to have produced significant gains among disadvantaged children in grades 1 to 3 in reading and in grades 1 to 6 in math (Schorr & Schorr, 1988, p. 225).

Nonetheless, others point out that the effectiveness of federal programs for children and the poor, though real, never reached their full potential. This resulted from a number of factors. First, although the War on Poverty was conceived of as an integrated attack along the many fronts of poverty (Johnson, 1969, p. 75), over time, services have become fragmented and segregated. Today, federal aid for children is scattered across multiple agencies and consists of more than 100 major authorizations (House & Stephan, 1987). What is currently missing is a national organizational and structural center to coordinate services on behalf of needy children and youth, as well as incentives for inter-agency collaboration for localities and states as well, so they may plan education programs across multiple domains of youth services. Increasingly research has shown that an integrated approach that coordinates multiple services on behalf of the needy is most effective (see Kirst & McLaughlin, 1989, p. 10; Schorr & Schorr, 1988). An integrated, coordinated approach for children's services can bring enhanced results in education—but only if programs are funded to provide full benefits for all eligible children.

Second, many have argued that War on Poverty programs have been so inadequately funded that they have not had a fair opportunity to prove their merit. Early cost projections indicated that the federal government should be spending more than $30 billion on education by 1976 (Johnson, 1969, p. 109)—a level still not reached a decade and a half later. This has resulted in underservice or nonservice for all eligible recipients. Except for the program's first year, Chapter 1 appropriations have been substantially below the maximum eligibility level, often serving less than half of eligible recipients (Riddle, 1981, p. 5). A current estimate of youth in need of other federal assistance programs compared with those actually being served by federal funds shows servicing levels well below levels of need. Federal programs serve only half of all eligible for the supplemental food program for women, infants, and children (WIC); 1 out of 5 low-income children in need of preschool education; 2 out of every 5 children in need of remediation; 1 out of every 4 children in need of bilingual education; and 1 out of every 20 youth in need of job training (Haas, 1991). Federal budgetary policy during the 1980s has exacerbated this situation. At a time when the number of needy children has increased substantially and the dual requirements of a global economy and knowledge society demand a highly educated work force, funding for children and education has declined (Verstegen, 1990). Reductions in aid have affected a generation of federal aid recipients and signal further erosion in recipient benefits, cutbacks in programs and services, or decreased numbers of children, young adults, and adults that are served by federal aid programs.

National divestment in children during the 1980s and a policy of decentralization for provision of education for economically disadvantaged children and youth—long the cornerstone of federal aid to education—have strained state budgets and made the quality of a child's education a growing function of the wealth of the state and locality in which that child resides. Vast disparities exist in education support—both between the states and within the states—creating disparate educational opportunities for children. This is in contrast to the widely held and long affirmed American ideal that all children should have an equal opportunity for a quality education regardless of the circumstances into which they have been born or their place of residence. Without federal intervention to provide incentives, mandates, or sanctions to equalize resources within states and to provide assistance to poorer states to guarantee equity and access, vast disparities in educational opportunities will prevail for children, not only diminishing their opportunities but diminishing the future of the nation as well (see Verstegen, 1990). A large and uneducated underclass raises the specter of a dual society, political instability, reduced economic competitiveness, and higher costs of public services associated with poverty, crime, illness, dependency, and homelessness (Levin, 1989).

The Rights of Children

The challenge for the future, if continued improvement for children and youth at home and abroad is to be realized and poverty abated, is to raise both the level and the distribution of resources for children and to give to the many what has been reserved for the fortunate few. This includes decent health care, housing, proper nutrition, and basic quality schooling. UNICEF's Convention on the Rights of the Child affirms this as a child's *right,* calling for a new ethic for children. The essence of the new ethic for children is the principle of "a first call for children"—a principle that the essential needs of children should be considered more than a priority in the allocation of resources and that protection for the lives and the development of the young should be an absolute.

The ethic of "a first call for children" demands not the kind of commitment that can be superseded by other priorities that suddenly seem more urgent but the kind of commitment "that will not waver in the winds of change which will always blow across the world of human affairs" (UNICEF, 1990, p. 27). There will always be something more immediate; there will never be anything more important. The mental growth, development, and opportunity of all children cannot be asked to wait until economies return to growth, until there are no wars, or until debt repayments have been rescheduled. According to UNICEF (1990, p. 27):

> In the past, it may often have been inevitable that the physical, mental and emotional development of children should be exposed to the slings and arrows of adult society. But in our time, for the first time, we have the chance to begin shielding the lives and the normal growth of children from the worst excesses, misfortunes, and mistakes of the world into which they are born. And the fact that our societies do not now do so will one day be regarded as being as strange and uncivilized as is the notion of slavery today.

Reversing the trend toward inequality and focusing on justice and fairness for all children as a basis for public policy is therefore important not just from an economic point of view. As Thurow (1985, p. 112) has contended, "For most Americans to allow such conditions is to demean themselves as well as to permit real deprivation among those who are unable to help themselves." Failure to end the scourge of child poverty will not only stain the history of our age, it will predestine the destruction of much of the progress achieved thus far. Although poverty and ignorance penalize the poor more consistently and severely than they do the rich, they will do more than condemn the weakest elements of our society to lives of desperation and want on the edges of society. The downward spiral of poverty eventually becomes a circle embracing all of humanity, rich and poor alike (see During, 1989, p. 67).

References

ACDA (U.S. Arms Control and Disarmament Agency). (1989). *World military expenditures and arms transfers 1988*. Washington, DC: Government Printing Office.

ACIR (Advisory Commission on Intergovernmental Relations). (1989, January). *Significant features of fiscal federalism* (Vol. 1, No. M-163). Washington, DC: Author.

American Council on Education. (1988). *One-third of a nation: A report on minority participation in education and American life*. Washington, DC: Author.

Brazelton, T. B. (1990, September 9). Why is America failing its children? *The New York Times Magazine*, pp. 1-2, 50, 90.

Children's Defense Fund. (1990). *Children 1990: A report card, briefing book, and action primer*. Washington, DC: Author.

Committee on Education and Labor, Together with Minority Views. (1985, March). *Budget for the United States government for the fiscal year 1986* (U.S. House of Representatives, 99th Congress, 1st Session). Washington, DC: Government Printing Office.

Committee on Education and Labor. (1990). *Fact sheet on the Fair Chance Act*. Washington, DC: House of Representatives. (mimeo)

Committee on Education and Labor. (1990, December). *A report on shortchanging children: The impact of fiscal inequity on the education of students at risk*. Washington, DC: Government Printing Office.

Committee on Labor and Human Resources, U.S. Senate. (1988). *Poverty in the 1980s: Examining poverty and policy issues in the 1980s and to explore innovative methods to improve the current poverty situation in the United States* (100th Congress, 1st Session, October 7, 1987; No. S. Hrg. 100-433). Washington, DC: Government Printing Office.

Committee on Ways & Means, U.S. House of Representatives. (1989, March 15). *Background material and data on programs within the jurisdiction of the Committee on Ways & Means* (WMCP: 101-4). Washington, DC: Government Printing Office.

Council of Chief State School Officers. (1989). *State education indicators*. Washington, DC: Author.

Council of Economic Advisors. (1989, January). *Economic report of the president.* Washington, DC: Government Printing Office.

During, A. B. (1989, November). *Poverty and the environment: Reversing the downward spiral*. Washington, DC: Worldwatch.

During, A. B. (1990). Ending poverty. In *State of the world* (pp. 135-153). New York: Norton.

Ebel, R. D., & Marks, L. (1990). American competitiveness in the world economy. *Intergovernmental Perspective, 16*(1), 9.

Executive Office of the President, Office of Management and Budget. (1988). *Historical tables: Budget of the United States government*. Washington, DC: Government Printing Office.

Graham, H. D. (1984). *The uncertain triumph*. Chapel Hill: University of North Carolina Press.

Haas, L. J. (1991). Stalled rescues. *National Journal, 23*, (3), 162-164.

Harrington, M. (1988). *Statement of Michael Harrington* (Hearing before the Committee on Labor and Human Resources). In U.S. Senate, *Poverty in the 1980s: Examining poverty and policy issues in the 1980s and to explore innovative methods to improve the current poverty situation in the United States* (100th Congress, 1st Session, October 7, 1987; No. S. Hrg. 100-433). Washington, DC: Government Printing Office.

Hawley, W. D. (1985). False premises, false promises: The mythical character of public discourse about education. *Phi Delta Kappan, 6*(7), 183-187.

Health, Education and Welfare. (1969). In *Congress and the nation: Vol. 2. 1965-1968.* Washington, DC: Congressional Quarterly Service.

Heilbroner, R., & Bernstein, P. (1989). *The debt and the deficit: False alarms/real possibilities.* New York: Norton.

Hodgkinson, H. (1985). *All one system: The demographics of education from kindergarten to graduate school.* Washington, DC: Institute for Educational Leadership

House Select Committee on Children, Youth and Families. (1990). *Opportunities for success.* Washington, DC: Government Printing Office.

House, S., & Stephan, S. (1987). *Federal programs affecting children.* Washington, DC: Congressional Research Service, Library of Congress.

Johnson, L. B. (1969). *The choices we face.* Johnson City, TX: Bantam Books and the Johnson Foundation.

Kirst, M. W., & McLaughlin, M., with Massell, D. (1989). *Rethinking children's policy: Implications for educational administration.* Stanford, CA: Stanford University, Center for Education Research.

Levin, H. M. (1989). Financing the education of at-risk students. *Education Evaluation and Policy Analysis, 3,* (1), 474-460.

Levine, D. M., & Bane, M. J. (1975). *The "inequality" controversy: Schooling and distributive justice.* New York: Basic Books.

Lipton, M. (1985). *Land assets and rule poverty.* Staff working paper, 744. Washington, DC: World Bank.

Lyke, R. F. (1988). *High school dropouts* (No. IB87167). Washington, DC: Congressional Research Service.

McNamara, R. S. (1981). *The McNamara years at the World Bank: Major policy addresses of Robert S. McNamara 1968-1981.* Baltimore, MD: Johns Hopkins University Press.

Nelson, F. H. (1990). *An international comparison of public spending on education* (draft). Washington, DC: American Federation of Teachers.

Okun, A. (1975). *Equity and efficiency: The great tradeoff.* Washington, DC: Brookings Institution.

Phillips, K. (1990). *The politics of rich and poor: Wealth and the American electorate in the Reagan administration.* New York: Random House.

Rasell, M. E., & Mishel, L. (1990, January). *Shortchanging education: How U.S. spending on grades K-12 lags behind other industrial nations.* Washington, DC: Economic Policy Institute.

Reed, S., & Sautter, C. R. (1990). Children of poverty. *Phi Delta Kappan, 71*(10), K1-K12.

Riddle, W. (1981). *Education for disadvantaged children: Federal aid* (No. IB81142). Washington, DC: Library of Congress.

Riddle, W. (1990, January 17). *School expenditure variations in the states.* Washington, DC: Congressional Research Service.

Schorr, L. B., & Schorr, D. (1988). *Within our reach: Breaking the cycle of disadvantage.* New York: Doubleday.

Schweinhart, L., & Weikart, D. (1986, November). Early childhood development programs: A public investment opportunity. *Educational Leadership, 44*(3), 4-12.

Smith, M. S., & O'Day, S. (1991). Educational equality: 1966 and now. In D. A. Verstegen & J. G. Ward (Eds.), *Spheres of justice in education* (pp. 53-100). New York: HarperCollins.

Taylor, W. L., & Piche, D. M. (1990, December). *Shortchanging children: The impact of fiscal inequity on the education of students at risk* (Committee on Education and Labor, U.S. House of Representatives, 101st Congress, 2nd Session; (Serial No. 101-U). Washington, DC: Government Printing Office.

Thurow, L. C. (1985). *The zero sum solution.* New York: Simon & Schuster.

Tilak, J. B. G. (1989). *Education and its relations to economic growth, poverty, and income distribution: Past evidence and further analysis* (No. 3). Washington, DC: World Bank.

UNICEF (U.N. International Children's Fund). (1989). *The state of the world's children, 1989.* Oxfordshire, UK: Oxford University Press.

UNICEF (U.N. International Children's Fund). (1990). *The state of the world's children, 1990.* Oxfordshire, UK: Oxford University Press.

U.S. Department of Education. (1990, May). State education performance chart (Supplement). In *A report on shortchanging children: The impact of fiscal inequity on the education of students at risk* (for the Committee on Education and Labor, U.S. House of Representatives, December 1990, Serial No. 101-U). Washington, DC: Government Printing Office.

Verstegen, D. A. (1990). Education fiscal policy in the Reagan administration. *Education Evaluation and Policy Analysis, 12,* 355-373.

Verstegen, D. A., & Salmon, R. G. (1989). The conceptualization and measurement of equity in school finance in Virginia. *Journal of Education Finance, 15*(3), 124-150.

World Bank. (1990). *World development report 1990: Poverty.* Oxford: Oxford University Press.

World Conference on Education for All. (1990, March 5-9). *World declaration on education for all and framework for action to meet basic learning needs* (Jomtien, Thailand). New York: Inter-Agency Commission (UNDP, UNESCO, UNICEF, World Bank).

F I V E

Special Needs Students
A GENERATION AT RISK

DAVID C. THOMPSON

There are large and growing numbers of young people in the United States who face severe economic and social consequences resulting from the failure to obtain an appropriate education. The consequences are striking, as in almost all instances there is a history of school failure and low achievement that can be linked to high rates of unemployment, underemployment, low wages, and unfulfilled potential. A line can be drawn that connects in-school problems, dropping out, and future unemployment and underemployment. With increasing frequency, the line cuts across a broad range of school clients, leading some critics to argue that the public schools of the future may contain mostly special needs students who will require concerted attention to prevent an entire generation from risk of failure.

These children often share unifying commonalities. Almost without exception, they are poor, are frequently minority, lack basic skills, and are consequently prone to dropping out of school. Beyond these barriers, they face formidable high-risk conditions. First, they are economically at risk in a society fueled by a postindustrial economy that no longer values unskilled labor. Second, they are socially at risk in a nation that increasingly exhibits signs of racial and class segregation brought about by economic stratification based on educational skills. Third, their risks are joined with those of the traditionally defined special populations, swelling their numbers and exponentially driving up costs and straining current resource levels. Fourth and finally, they are all at risk because they are dependent on federal, state, and local governments to intervene.

Such conditions argue for effective federal, state, and local education policies aimed at providing every child with a full slate of educational opportunities. Yet federal and state mandates have largely been concerned with traditionally defined special populations, and local policies have been shaped and restrained by both inadequate resources and an unwillingness to exceed minimum federal and state mandates. The problem has been compounded at all levels as these organizations have become increasingly ambivalent due to their need to respond to political constituencies. But without strong governmental intervention to ensure educational opportunity, the future of these children is predictable from the failure of those of similar origin who have already been failed by the system. Whether federal, state, and local units will be able or willing to meet the challenge becomes a critical question for the future.

This chapter argues five major points. First, it is suggested that, consonant with much current information, the nation is being fragmented into the schisms referenced previously. Second, the chapter maintains that federal interest in special needs populations has been narrow and inadequate while simultaneously reflecting an incomplete acceptance of the changes that are recasting the nation. Third, it is argued that states have been left to their own initiative—an initiative hindered by both federal and state indifference that stems from a failure to recognize that ignoring a seemingly endless onslaught of special needs children will not change the basic truth that national, state, and local economic fortunes will eventually depend on their skills. Fourth, it is argued that local units of government have had to lead the way in some instances because of the failure of federal and state governments to engage in total warfare against inequality. Fifth and finally, the chapter suggests that, in the changing demographic context, the way federal and state levels of government respond to the ideal of public education will play a large part in the continued viability of democracy.

A Generation at Risk

There can be little doubt that the nation is experiencing startling demographic changes. Nowhere are these changes as evident as in the effect on the public school population. As Hodgkinson (1985) notes, the combination of age, births, and family status *is* the future.

In the United States, this combination spells enormous changes because of wide differences in birthrates among races, increases in immigration, and changes in family demography. Birthrates, for example, clearly demonstrate the declining dominance of the white majority that has characterized the nation for more than 200 years. Given current population growth, which requires 2.1 children per female to stay even, white births (1.7) are slipping rapidly, while black births (2.4) are nearly 50% higher, and Hispanic births (2.9) are more than 70% higher. Although less publicized, other minority groups have also added to the changing complexion of the nation, leading some demographers to claim that America is rapidly becoming a majority of minorities (Hodgkinson, 1985).

Increasing minority representation is also being aided by significant changes in the current adolescent and adult population. The 1980 census, for example, showed that whites accounted for only 31% of the total population of the nation, while the largest minority groups constituted nearly 50%,

Table 5.1   Public School Enrollment, by Race and Ethnicity, 1976-1986

| | 1976 | 1986 | |
	(number in thousands)		Percentage
Total	43,714	41,156	−5.9
White	33,229	28,957	−12.9
Black	7,774	6,622	−2.2
Hispanic	2,807	4,064	44.7
Asian	535	1,158	116.4

SOURCE: U.S. Department of Education (1990a).

with the fastest growing groups being blacks (25%) and Hispanics (22%). These numbers are expected to increase over the next two decades as the nation's 26.5 million blacks are expected to nearly double to 44 million by the year 2020, and the nation's 14.6 million Hispanics are expected to more than triple to 47 million by the same year (Hodgkinson, 1985). When these changes are added to rapidly increasing immigration groups such as Asians, whose population increased by 116% from 1976-1986 and represents 44% of all immigrants into the United States each year (see Table 5.1), it is not surprising that by the year 2000 the majority of America will be nonwhite. As the total population is predicted to have changed very little during the same period of time, enormous shifts within the population of the United States are highly evident.

The demographic makeup of the family structure is having a further dramatic impact. More than any other institution, the family is undergoing changes that significantly affect the public schools. As Hodgkinson (1985) notes, unwed births have reached epidemic levels, with 50% of all illegitimate children born to teenage mothers. Every day, 40 teenage girls have their third child, many of whom are malnourished infants born to child mothers who are themselves undernourished. The grim statistics on life chances for children have become familiar but are no less shocking as the data declare that, of every 100 infants born in 1988, 20 will be illegitimate,

12 will have parents who divorce before the child is 18, 5 will have parents who separate, 6 will lose a parent in death, 40 will live in a female-headed household, 13 will be born to teen mothers, 15 will be born to homes where no parent is employed, 15 will be born to homes with wages below poverty, and 25 will be on welfare at some point in life (Children's Defense Fund, 1989).

These difficult dilemmas add even greater significance to the knowledge that poverty is growing, especially in single-parent households headed by black or Hispanic females. And 50% of all such households are in poverty compared with only 12% of households where a male is present. In a nation that declared war on poverty and unequal opportunity under the sweeping social reforms of the 1960s and in which the current level of society's affluence is unparalleled in history, almost half of all children remain poor in 1990, a 10% increase over 1983 when 14 million children (40%) were in poverty. A child under 6 years of age in 1990 has a 600% greater chance of being poor than a person over 65, in part because government spending for elderly programs has increased significantly while child spending has decreased (Hodgkinson, 1985). While poverty has declined in this century, the trend has steadily reversed since 1979 (see Table 5.2). These changes have been felt most strongly among minority groups, as both birthrates and poverty have increased faster for these groups, with 86% of all poor children also of minority status.

At the same time, almost all available evidence leads to the contention that two of the most influential factors affecting a child's adult life chances are socioeconomic status and level of education (Coleman et al., 1966; Illinois State Board of Education, 1986; Kennedy, Jung, & Orland, 1986). Poverty, with all the accompanying social and family disruptions, has strong effects on the level of care before a child is born, on health and nutrition, on the security of family and home, and on the quantity and quality of education. Where low-income students constitute 24% or more of a population, those children suffer particular risk, and children of families in poverty for more than eight years and with parents of low education

Table 5.2 Percentage of Children in Poverty

Year	Total	White	Black	Hispanic
1960	26.5	20.0	65.5	—
1965	20.7	14.4	47.4	—
1970	14.9	10.5	41.5	—
1975	16.8	12.5	41.4	34.5
1980	17.9	13.4	42.1	33.0
1981	19.5	14.7	44.2	35.4
1982	21.3	16.5	47.3	38.9
1983	21.8	17.0	46.2	37.7
1984	21.0	16.1	46.2	38.7
1985	20.1	15.6	43.1	39.6
1986	19.8	15.3	42.6	37.1
1987	20.0	15.0	45.1	39.3

SOURCE: U.S. Department of Education (1990b).

attainment are also at greater risk (Illinois State Board of Education, 1986; Kennedy et al., 1986). To be poor from a low-achievement home is to greatly increase economic, social, and educational risks.

To be at risk in a society that ties economic and social rewards to education implies a failure of the system to meet the needs of those children who most desperately need economic and social mobility. Under such conditions, the ultimate failure of the system is epitomized by the school dropout. That any child should drop out is evidence of system failure, but if those for whom the system most often represents failure are poor, of minority status, or come from the backgrounds of disadvantage that make up the change in demography of the nation, the system itself can be seen as contributing to the line that links undereducation, unemployment, and intergenerational poverty.

At the very least, the system fails approximately 25% of the nation's high school students each year. While various reports place the dropout rate at between one quarter and one third of all high school students, the results are no less emphatic. The

Table 5.3   Dropouts, 1968-1988

Year	Total	White	Black	Hispanic
1968	5.3	—	—	—
1970	5.5	—	—	—
1975	6.1	5.7	9.2	9.2
1980	6.2	5.7	9.2	11.1
1985	5.0	4.8	6.3	10.9
1987	4.8	4.6	6.7	9.5

SOURCE: U.S. Department of Education (1990a).

U.S. Department of Education, for example, estimates the dropout rate at 29.1% (in 1986), resulting in a loss to society and the economy of approximately 750,000 persons who fail to complete basic schooling each year. Males represent 2.26 million (52.4%) of all dropouts, while females represent 2.06 million (47.6%). When the data are examined for ethnic trends, dropout rates are much less evenly distributed. Barro and Kolstad (1987), for example, report much higher male dropout rates than are represented by figures typically accepted by the public. The National Center for Education Statistics (NCES) report *The Condition of Education* (U.S. Department of Education, 1990a) notes that, while dropout rates have declined during the period (1968-1988; see Table 5.3), there are distinct levels of imbalance. Although dropout rates for both black (−27%) and white (−10%) students have improved greatly, the dropout rate among blacks still remains more than 45% greater than for whites, and the Hispanic rate has actually worsened (+3.2%), more than double the white dropout rate and nearly 42% worse than for blacks (see Table 5.4). While some improvement can be seen in that children are staying in school longer rather than dropping out before grade 9, the data still cannot mask the reality that whites show the lowest dropout rates and the greatest improvement in years of schooling, that minorities still complete far fewer years and drop out in far greater proportions than whites,

Table 5.4   Dropouts by Race, Age, 1986—United States

		(data in thousands)					
		Noncompleters		Dropouts		Dropouts	
Race/Age	Total	N	%	Early	%	Late	%
White:							
18-19	6,051	2,152	34.1	213	9.4	1,949	90.6
20-24	17,712	2,701	15.7	697	25.8	2,004	74.2
25-29	17,829	2,347	13.2	703	30.0	1,644	70.0
30-34	16,846	1,888	11.2	696	36.9	1,192	63.1
Black:							
18-19	1,092	536	49.1	64	11.9	472	88.1
20-24	2,694	549	20.4	87	15.8	462	84.2
25-29	2,617	508	19.4	89	17.5	419	82.5
30-34	2,289	491	21.4	134	27.3	357	72.7
Hispanic:							
18-19	626	373	40.4	94	25.2	279	74.8
20-24	1,768	724	40.1	362	50.0	362	50.0
25-29	1,693	661	39.0	385	58.2	276	41.8
30-34	1,397	620	44.4	384	61.9	236	38.1

SOURCE: National Commission for Employment Policy (1988).
NOTE: *Early* means prior to grade 9; *late* means after grade 9.

and that the dropout condition still describes the social and economic failure of more than a quarter of the young people in the nation. When viewed as a total loss to the economy and social fabric of the nation, the system appears to be disenfranchised from the rapidly increasing populations that herald its economic and social future.

The cumulative data point to growing problems for a democratic society and threaten a tidal wave of special needs students. Secured by Hodgkinson's (1985) observation that age, births, and family status spell the future, and armed with the bleak reality that schools have not been able to prevent large losses of at-risk populations to the dropout condition, the new face of America must be seen to bring an influx of high-risk populations to the public schools. With increasing frequency, schools are being asked to deal with victims of minority status, family turmoil, poverty, limited English proficiency, migrancy and homelessness, and new special education conditions stemming from society's struggles with drug use. When these groups are added to existing special education populations whose costs already anger many constituents and whose children have fled to private schools, public schools are in danger of becoming a repository for high-risk children whose needs will require enormous resources and concerted attention to prevent entire future generations from risk of failure.

Minority and poverty problems are being exacerbated by large numbers of children with limited or no English proficiency. National school enrollment for 1988 indicates that, of the 40 million children in public schools, nearly 2 million have only limited English proficiency (LEP). The full impact has yet to be measured because there are indicators that the LEP problem is growing rapidly as districts that have previously had high LEP enrollments are experiencing sudden growth and with a wide variety of native languages. Additionally, the number of schools enrolling LEPs is increasing significantly, including districts that have not previously had to deal with LEP issues. As the problem has grown, school systems are suffering under the added weight. LEP enrollment in Los Angeles, for example, grew from 15% of total enrollment in 1980 to more than 31% in 1989 while the state's LEP enrollment increased 16% in 1989 over the prior year. Cities like New York and Chicago have also experienced large increases accompanied by rapidly increasing language diversity. For example, New York and Chicago each has more than 100 primary languages, with more than 30% speaking such languages as Apache, Tagalog, Urdu, Chinese, Cherokee, Greek, and Russian (OBEMLA in Macias, 1989). Smaller districts have also had to cope with increased LEP demands—for example, Long Beach experienced a 20% increase in LEP enrollment to 18,000 students in 1989 representing 44 languages, and Brownsville's LEP incidence is now one third of total enrollment and 51% of kindergarten through grade 6. Almost no one has escaped the problem of language diversity as LEPs have spread out in search of jobs, with towns like Fall River, Massachusetts, reporting an LEP increase of 67% from 1985 to 1990 and with one third of its total enrollment qualifying for LEP status.

Growth in language minority students creates enormous problems. Los Angeles, for example, lacks 2,900 bilingual teachers, and the California State Department of Education's (1990) latest report estimates the state's shortage of teachers and specialists at 20,000 with over half the staff under waivers. In Florida, Dade County could place 1,500 bilingual teachers but lacks authorized vacancies. The LEP problem includes staffing needs for psychologists, counselors, nurses, and therapists. Even if funding for increased enrollments could be resolved, qualified staff are hard to find and equally difficult to retain because of burnout, racial and gender tones, lack of support from monolingual colleagues, demanding schedules (e.g., home visits, late evening community activities), testing systems that ignore language dominance, strain of no-prior-schooling arrivals, and the lack of local support systems for teachers (OBEMLA in Macias, 1989). The national demand is estimated at 175,000 teachers (Macias, 1989), but, as many bilingual teachers migrate for higher pay and others seek transfers to nonbilingual positions, a severe shortage has left many districts in the nation in noncompliance with state regulations on minimum LEP services, with 50% of districts in some states currently not in compliance (OBEMLA in Macias, 1989). Yet the problems of these children must be met because, as Steinberg, Blinde, and Chan (1984, p. 117) note, "individuals from homes where no English is spoken and who do not speak English themselves drop out at a rate four times that of individuals from an English background."

For many at-risk children, the barriers to economic and social mobility are compounded because they often belong to other subgroups at risk. Migrant children are among the worst affected as they are not only transient but are often simultaneous members of language minority or poverty groups. Although precise data are not available, Picou (1982, in Macias, 1989, p. 43) places the number of school-age migrant children at about 300,000 and the dropout rate at 90%. While the number has no doubt grown since 1982 with awareness of the urban homeless problem, there is no indication that migrant risks are exaggerated. Migrant problems are also likely to continue to grow, as the Immigration and Naturalization Service estimates another 2 million migrants will eventually be identified by the Immigration Control and Reform Act of 1986 (Public Law 99-603), which will move previously illegal aliens into documented status. In a complex and overlapping scenario, significant barriers to quality socioeconomic opportunity and the difficulty of providing educational services to needy populations exist given the accumulated effects of low SES, language deficiency, minority status, and other handicaps.

The problems of at-risk children are also being increased by the sheer numbers of current and prospective special education students. In recent years, there has been tremendous growth in the numbers of traditional special populations, especially since the passage of the Education Handicapped Act (EHA) in 1975. Most of the growth has been in mild/moderate areas (LD, SED, EMR), with the greatest concentration in learning disabilities. The growth in special education promises to continue, as there is unmistakable evidence that a new wave of special needs children is nearing school age or already beginning to swell classroom enrollments. For example, it is estimated that less than half of all students who could qualify for SED or behavior disorder placements are being served, and a national coalition of education and human services organizations is proposing to Congress that a new definition (Emotional and Behavioral Disorders) be mandated. There is further strong sentiment to push for a new Attention Deficit Disorders classification that would be distinct from LD and Seriously Emotionally Disturbed (SED). Even more startling is the dramatically increasing incidence of crack/cocaine babies and children with fetal alcohol syndrome effects. Much like the spread of LEPs into nontraditional minority regions, these incidences spell enormous changes throughout the nation, even in small midwestern states, such as Kansas and Iowa, with each estimated to have 4,000-5,000 such births annually.

These children will have irreversible physical and neurological handicaps that severely affect school performance, and many will be multiply handicapped with learning or behavioral disorders and special medical needs.

That the problems of these children overlap is beyond doubt as many attend or will attend school as simultaneous victims of urban poverty, family turmoil, minority status, language barriers, and traditional or new handicapping conditions. All these events, however, lead to two clear certainties: escalating costs and increased likelihood of dropping out of school due to personal and system failure. The question becomes twofold: whether there are intervention steps that can reduce the risks faced by these children and whether federal, state, and local units of government have put necessary programs in place to deal effectively with needs or are capable and willing to do so. Because the plight of these children can be summed up as the risk of dropping out, with all its economic and social consequences to underprivileged populations, it is critical for government to enact programs that prevent or reduce the loss to society of children who drop out.

Taken collectively, the best available predictors of dropping out are startling and offer a stern admonition to policymakers.[1] When a child has experienced grade failure or low academic achievement, is overage for modal grade level, reads below grade, lives in a single-parent household, has a parent who dropped out, comes from a low-socioeconomic or poverty background, is pregnant, or holds disadvantaged group membership, the risks of social and economic failure through the act of dropping out are greatly enhanced. While no single category is conclusive, each category increases the likelihood of failure at least proportionally if not exponentially. Yet a series of interrelated studies (Lazar, Darlington, Murray, Royce, & Snipper, 1982) suggest that a combination of infant, preschool, and primary grade programs for at-risk children with active parent involvement can improve test scores and social behaviors of children from low-SES and minority families. For example, the Perry Preschool Project (Berrueta-Clement, Schweinhart, Barnett, Epstein, & Weikart, 1984) reported that at age 19 recipients of high-quality preschool/early childhood services made greater gains in education, employment, and selected social behaviors than nonrecipients, in that fewer were mentally retarded (15% versus 35%), more completed high school (67% versus 49%), more attended college/job training (38% versus 21%), more held jobs (50% versus 32%), more were self-supporting (45% versus 25%), more had lower birthrates (64/100 versus 117/100 women), fewer were arrested (31% versus 51%), fewer committed crimes of property or violence (24% versus 38%), and fewer were on welfare (18% versus 32%). Information about programs that work for at-risk children indicates that predicted admission test scores, college attendance and achievement, and success in vocations not requiring a college education can be improved through planned intentional intervention strategies (Berrueta-Clement et al., 1984; Bronfenbrenner, 1974; Lambie, Bond, & Weikart, 1974; Lazar et al., 1982; Seitz, Rosenbaum, & Apfel, 1985; Wang & Walberg, 1988).

The problems of an increasingly at-risk population spell the future of the nation and occur in a time when ideals and realities are in conflict. As the bottom line, a society's advancement can be measured by its ability to meet the needs of its most at-risk children. Yet at a time when dropouts are increasing, minority college applications are shrinking, and fewer than 14% of the 3 million children eligible for Head Start are currently being served due to inadequate resources, the response by many states in the 1980s was to strengthen graduation requirements, institute merit pay, provide no remediation money, and generally abandon the children who were already having trouble meeting school standards. Because dropouts are accurately profiled as low-income or poverty children, minorities, and often non-English-language dominant and see themselves as failures, the problem of school failure also becomes a question of whether federal, state, and local governments are addressing problems or are themselves adding to school push-outs. When these burgeoning numbers of children are joined with traditional special populations, they are at enormous risk because they are dependent on federal, state, and local governments to redress their needs at a time when resources and public sympathy are in short supply. The question of federal and state responsiveness to special needs students becomes critical to the nation's future.

An Inadequate Federal Response

Federal interest in special needs populations has been sporadic and limited. The first significant initiatives took place during the Depression and World War II in the form of support for women in the work force, but those programs ended with the war. No other sweeping federal legislation targeting disadvantaged elementary and secondary students occurred until the 1960s when the War on Poverty began.[2] The federal response to special needs is discussed in the previous chapter.

By some accounts, federal expenditures for education belie the notion of limited interest. The NCES (U.S. Department of Education, 1989) notes that, in fiscal year 1989, federal funds totaled $19.6 billion for elementary and secondary education, $11.9 billion for higher education, $11.8 billion for research, and $3.2 billion for other programs. In 1989, $7.2 billion went to school districts, $3.5 billion to higher education, $3.4 billion to college students, $2.5 billion to SEAs, and another $4.1 billion went to banks as subsidies for college loans. Yet, of the total $46.5 billion, only 42% went to elementary and secondary children, which represented a 3% decline in federal aid since 1980. From 1980 to 1988 federal funds fell by 12%, student aid rose 23%, and federal tax expenditure for education dropped 19%.

Within categories of disadvantaged children, traditional special needs populations appear to have received the bulk of resources. In the decade 1980-1989, grants for the general category of disadvantaged children increased from $3.2 billion in 1980 to almost $4.6 billion in 1989, an increase of approximately 44%. Grants for bilingual education rose from $169.5 million in 1980 to $197.4 million in 1989, increasing nearly 16%. Although disadvantaged and bilingual classifications appear to have taken sizable increases, total dollars were small compared with other federal aid for the handicapped, which in contrast rose from $1.5 billion in 1980 to $4.2 billion in 1989, an increase of nearly 200%, with the largest increases going to early childhood education and handicapped rehabilitation. Enrollments increasing most were learning disabilities (+43.4%), seriously emotionally disturbed (+8.4%), and preschool handicapped (+8.2%),[3] reflecting the broadening of the LD category, preschool mandates, and a surge of students with emotional needs. In a total scheme of federal spending that saw decline in expenditure for education, shifts and increases were consumed by traditional special populations rather than redirected toward a more global view of special needs children.

When viewed in the context of expanding special needs populations, federal interest can be seen as loose and limited benevolence because increased funding has not followed observable outcomes. A prime example lies in the impact of Head Start and Chapter 1 programs. Comparative data have shown a return of $8:1 on investment in Head Start (Berrueta-Clement et al., 1984), showing that participating children were more likely to be employed (60% versus 32%), more likely to graduate (54% versus 50%), more likely to enroll in college (40% versus 23%), more likely to be functionally competent (60% versus 50%), less likely to be arrested (30% versus 60%), and less likely to be on welfare (20% versus 40%). Yet Head Start has never had sufficient funding, serving only about 20% of eligible children. Legislation beyond Head Start has been introduced but not passed in Congress at least six different times since 1970 (Administration for Children, Youth, and Families, 1987). Similarly, despite the findings of the Subcommittee on Elementary, Secondary, and Vocational Education (U.S. Congress, 1986b) that Chapter 1 appears to be the legislation providing the broadest sweep and effect for economically and educationally disadvantaged students, the Education Consolidation and Improvement Act (ECIA; Public Law 97-35, 1981) returned responsibility and control to the states, reduced funding even though eligibility under poverty guidelines increased, authorized paperwork reduction whereby efficacy of the program can no longer be determined, reduced parent interaction, increased pupil-teacher ratios nearly 13%, and increased incidence of beginning teachers being assigned to Chapter 1 (Dougherty, 1985). There appears to be little sentiment to change as the Reagan 1989-1990 federal budget provided no increase for Title XX income support for the fourth straight year and deleted funds for independent living and juvenile justice. The Bush administration has proposed elimination of the Administration for Children, Youth, and Families administered by the U.S. Department of Health and Human Services and has reduced aid for the Office of Adolescent Pregnancy Programs. Additionally, the Act for Better Child Care (S. 1885/H.R. 3660), which would have provided $2.5 billion in child care for working families, died in the Senate.

In the face of such data, federal interest in a full definition of special populations cannot be seen as overwhelming. The historical stance of narrowly defined interests has been exacerbated in recent years by budget reductions and turning control back to the states and by failure to commit resources to programs with known positive effects. Unfortunately, there is no national plan for education; nor does there appear to be a strong desire to have one. Rather, the federal government sets policies and leaves the states to decide whether and how they will address the needs of growing numbers of children at risk.

State Responsiveness

States have thus largely been left to their own initiative—an initiative that has found them faced with federal mandates and the fury of two opposing political camps that simultaneously demand increased services and reduced taxes. Additionally, states have experienced very different individual fortunes, with some states facing an overwhelming increase in special needs populations and creating a strain on scarce financial resources. While many states have faced these issues,

Florida and California are among the worst outcomes of demographic change.

Hodgkinson's (1985) argument that the combination of births, age, and family status predict the future is typified by Florida's experience. In the first half of the 1980s, 6 of the 11 fastest growing areas in the nation were in Florida, and its population growth is projected to increase through the year 2000. Even more important is diversity of population, as Florida stands as the main port of entry to the United States from South and Central America and the Caribbean. Much of the state's growth is due to immigration as its Hispanic population doubled in the eight-year period 1980-1988, making it the fourth largest Hispanic state in the nation. Florida also has other large minority groups, ranking sixth in black citizens and with Asian representation increasing as well. By the year 2000, the state's white population is expected to decline from the current 35% to 31%, its black population to stabilize at 14%, and its Hispanic population to grow to more than 50% (Hodgkinson, 1988).

But growth has not necessarily brought prosperity. *The Sunrise Report* (1987) notes that 62% of Florida's children receive no preventive health care, 50% have no safe child care, 90% of teen mothers are not in school, and 30% of children are in poverty. Hodgkinson (1988) argues that half of all children new to the state are at risk—socially, educationally, and occupationally. Yet the state ranks 41st in general revenues per capita and 49th in federal grants to states and localities (Hodgkinson, 1988). A major task exists for this state, which faces the highest crime rate in the nation, where 3 million Floridians are under court surveillance, which ranks fourth in unwed births, and where only 26% of single mothers receive federal or state support (Hodgkinson, 1988).

The impact on schools has been phenomenal, and resources to meet increased needs are not evident. The report *Priority Policy Issues* (Florida State Department of Education, 1987) estimated that 841 new schools will be needed before the turn of the century to accommodate the growth of 60,000 new students each year. Construction costs for new schools alone exceed revenues by more than $4 billion, and the cost of growing populations promises to be high because so many students are among groups at risk. Expenditures per pupil in Florida ($4,699) for 1989-1990 were barely above the national average ($4,607), and the balance of federal (6%), state (53%), and local (43%) revenue showed a loss of federal aid (-.4%) and increases in state (+.4) and local (+.1%) shares. When combined state and local spending is compared with other categories of state expenditures, Florida spent only 31.7% for education compared with the national average of 34.4% (National Education Association, 1990). The average teacher salary in the state in 1987-1988 was $26,611, more than 8% below the national average of $28,896 (U.S. Department of Education, 1989). Yet Florida's educational track record is not good—between 1986-1987 and 1987-1988, the percentage of handicapped preschoolers increased 17.2% compared with the national average of 8.1%, only 62% graduated from high school, and the economy has worsened at the same time the state is experiencing rapid growth in children whose characteristics make them at risk. Because most of the state's wealth rests with people who make Florida's the oldest population in the nation, the two sides of the state's demographic picture do not promise a simple resolution. Under such uncertain conditions, the state must prepare to cope with the number of children eligible for preschool programs, increase graduation rates for growing numbers of poverty and minority youth, and tax persons whose children do not reflect the state's new demographics.

If Florida's problems are significant, California's dilemma is overwhelming. Kirlin (1989) argues that the state is in a five-sided box that is slowly squeezing it to death. One side is Proposition 13, the tax initiative of 1978 that reduced property taxes by $7 billion (-60%) resulting in reduced state support for county services such as health, welfare, and transfers to cities and required state takeover of education funding. The second side of the box is Proposition 4, adopted into the constitution in 1979 and, in contrast to the one-time loss by Proposition 13, tied spending to the state economy—an effect

Table 5.5   Demographics of California, 1970-2020

Year	White	Hispanic	Black	Asian
1970	72.8	15.6	8.4	3.3
1980	56.5	27.1	9.2	7.2
1990	45.5	34.9	8.8	10.9
2000	40.2	38.9	8.6	12.3
2010	34.7	44.0	8.5	12.8
2020	31.7	46.0	8.6	13.7

SOURCE: Adapted from Thiel (1989).

permanently reducing spending nearly 16% (California Tax-payers Association, 1988). The third side of the box came from indexing personal income tax rates in 1982, braking the rapid growth in income tax revenues. The fourth side of the box is taxpayer resistance, and a fifth side also exists in reduced federal transfers to state and local governments amounting to 10% between 1978 and 1986 (Kirlin, 1989).

At the same time, the state's demographics require more, rather than fewer, public resources. The state's rapid growth, which by the year 2000 will reach nearly 30 million, largely comprises special needs populations, ranking second in blacks, first in Hispanics, and first in the foreign born. The drama of these changes is seen in Table 5.5, showing that minorities were 27.3% in 1970, 54.6% in 1990, and projected to reach 68.3% by 2020. The largest group will continue to be Hispanic, increasing threefold from 15.6% under age 19 to 46% by 2020, while Asians will grow from 3.3% in 1970 to 13.7% in 2020. Only 15% of school children in Los Angeles are white, with Asians predicted to reach 10 million by the year 2000. When nearly 2 million illegal aliens are included, the state contains half of the nation's illegal residents (Hodgkinson, 1986).

California faces more than just an influx of nonwhite populations. The problems of children at risk are growing phenomenally, as one in four California children under age 6 lives in poverty. More than 42% of women with children under age 6 use child care, and 50% of single mothers with children under 6 are working. The state's child-care program administered by the Department of Education provided subsidized care to 110,000 children in 1985-1986, less than 25% of the demand by low-income parents, with unmet need between 155,000 and 405,000 (Thiel, 1989).[4] Latchkey children are estimated at 600,000 to 800,000. The state ranks second in teen pregnancy and first in juvenile incarceration. Since 1985 emergency responses to child abuse have increased over 100% and foster care caseloads over 50% (Thiel, 1989). Ethnic children's problems begin before birth and persist: Hispanic and black women are twice as likely to receive poor prenatal care, black infant mortality and low birth weight are double the state average, and black and Hispanic children are three times more likely to live in poverty. Two thirds of all teen pregnancies, half of all dropouts, and the majority of incarcerated juveniles are minorities (Thiel, 1989).

California's demographic problems are affecting schools. The quality of public education has been declining for a decade, a phenomenon that has paralleled a net drop in funding. Enrollments are soaring, with the NCES (U.S. Department of Education, 1989) reporting increases of more than a half million students from 1980 to 1988. With the largest class size in the nation, reducing classes to the national average would require 160,000 new teachers, costing $4 billion (Hodgkinson, 1986). Yet funds are not present under tax limitations, despite the fact that state support (69.5%) for schools is much higher than the national average (49.8%). Revenue from local taxpayers in 1988-1989 was 23.5%, increasing to 25.1% in 1989-1990, while state revenue dropped from 69.3% in 1988-1989 to 66.8% in 1989-1990. At the same time, expenditure per pupil for 1989-1990 was only $4,303, compared with the national average of $4,607, and combined state and local spending as a percentage of all functions was only 30.5% compared with the national average of 34.4% (U.S. Department of Education, 1989). Yet the shift back to local taxpayers, low expenditures, and tax limitations has been accompanied by increasing populations characterized by lack of English skills, poverty, or handicap.

Hodgkinson's (1986) conclusions about California are grim: The state is in the bottom 20% on retention to graduation with only 68% graduating in 1981 while 76% graduated in 1976; dropping out by blacks and Hispanics is 50% higher than by whites; test scores are falling; education reform has increased requirements without remediation; and new monies will go simply to meet enrollment costs.

While California and Florida represent the extremes of demographic changes affecting school finance in the nation, they predict the enormous problems that are building around economic and social mobility, and they are not dissimilar to problems of other major population centers in the nation. In addition, problems of poverty, non-English-speaking background, and social disadvantage are having notable effects on previously unaffected areas of the country. With evidence of decreasing federal participation, it is in large part up to individual states and local units of government to respond to populations in need.

A search of state legislation affecting special populations yields a mixed picture that prevents encouraging conclusions about success and concerted effort on the part of states to redress these needs. While almost all states provide meaningful assistance to traditional special education populations, legislation providing compensatory or similar education reveals a more noncommittal posture on the part of states. Compensatory education statutes are lacking in 21 states,[5] and bilingual education provisions are absent in 28 states.[6] While there is no argument that each state faces unique population characteristics, there are few states that can legitimately claim that there are no bilingual children in need of services and even fewer states where no compensatory conditions such as poverty and low income exist. All states are subject to evidence that points to the fact that children do not all enter school at the same level, and the "cumulative deficit effect," whereby an uncorrected basic skills problem in the early grades will increase exponentially by grade 6 (Kluender & Egbert, 1989) fits every state without exception. Because all states contain significant numbers of disadvantaged students on some plane and because nearly half of all economically disadvantaged students score in the bottom quartile on achievement tests and their dropout rate is three times higher, it is unfortunate that states have not exerted intense effort to avert the chronic economic and social loss that follows educational failure.

The most far-reaching programs appear to have occurred as a combination of state and local initiatives. Particularly encouraging is that at least 15 states have enacted some form of early childhood education in recent years (Kluender & Egbert, 1989). Many appear to have been enacted in response to a recent spate of reports recommending the importance of early intervention (e.g., Council of Chief State School Officers, 1988; National Association of State Boards of Education, 1988; National Governors' Association, 1986). The report by the National Governors' Association (1986), for example, called for assistance to low-income parents of high-risk children, cooperation with community and religious organizations, kindergarten for all 5-year-olds, early childhood programs for 4-year-olds, parenting information, improved day-care centers and preschools, and state and local structures for agency collaboration. Without exception, the reports stressed family responsibility, society's need to aid parents, valuing those who work with children, and formulation, implementation, and funding of state policies that encourage local programs.

In a climate of strained resources, however, states often appear to have followed the lead of local districts rather than setting the tone themselves. For example, Orange County's Early Intervention for School Success program has demonstrated significant improvement in 4- to 7-year-old performance on standardized tests as well as reductions in kindergarten repeaters. The program has served 4,100 students, and the state has proposed using the county as the contract agency to phase into 200 additional schools by the end of 1991 (Thiel, 1989). Such programs offer hope as well as the opportunity to reduce costs. Case management appears to be among the more effective ways of dealing with staff shortages and high costs. Barnett, Escobar, and Ravsten (1989), for example, found that teaching parents to help language-handicapped preschoolers at home produced more gains than a five day per week school program—at a one semester cost of $700 compared with $6,000 for school-based services. Cost-benefit analysis in the Perry Preschool program serving handicapped disadvantaged children showed an annual cost of $6,200 said to obviate over $20,000 in the elementary years (Barnett, 1988). Finally, Shoor (1988) argues that early intervention is highly cost-effective, as in California's Adolescent Family Life program, which for $1,200 funds case managers to reduce teen pregnancy, repeat pregnancies, dropping out, and long-term public assistance.

The benefit of addressing the problems of special needs populations cannot be mistaken. Yet the high costs and relatively noncommittal posture of both the federal government and the individual states leave an enormous hole in the fabric of equal opportunity. Whether a disadvantaged child receives additional assistance depends greatly on the happenstance of residence and time, so much so that opportunity varies according to the current administration in Washington and the state of residence. The additional variable is whether the local unit of government has taken the initiative to go the extra step, either in response to current pressure or in anticipation of emerging needs. The fortune of children hangs in a delicate balance of power, without the benefit of concerted effort in most of the nation and well beyond the fiscal and physical capacities of local school districts.

Conclusion

The person with good life chances is one with a relatively high probability of being happy, productive, participating socially, employed, and self-sufficient. Conversely, the opposite is economic, social, and personal tragedy. Whatever society does to improve opportunities for children increases their chances of becoming adults with positive personal, social, and economic dimensions. The data increasingly demonstrate that the hallmark of many young Americans is the lack of economic and social mobility because the public schools are not prepared to meet their needs. If this is what the children of tomorrow can expect, a generation is truly at risk. The data speak to critical needs that must be addressed at all levels of governments. The federal government must redefine its role in education to encompass an understanding that the economic fortune of the nation and the preservation of democracy are at stake in children of disadvantage because they are the future. The federal government must provide structures and resources to develop and disseminate information about disadvantage while reaffirming commitment to programs that work. States must take a vital interest in bringing disadvantaged children to the national forefront because, absent such action, states will continue to deal with the problems in isolation. Above all, the decline in state support for education must be reversed, and states must take the lead in convincing the private sector of its stake in developing economic skills. States must also help local districts with career ladders to build quality professional staffs and provide the necessary impetus to prevent the agenda of disadvantaged children from becoming an adjunct program. Colleges and universities must be urged to provide in-service, training, and the research knowledge base that is needed to erase the line that connects in-school problems, dropping out, and the waste of human lives.

There is no doubt that America is changing. Whether it will change for the better depends on the effectiveness of public schools in equipping a disadvantaged population with skills leading to economic and social mobility. In the foreseeable changing demographic context, the way government responds to the ideal of public education will play a critical role in the continued viability of our democracy.

Notes

1. Many factors have been shown to contribute to dropping out. Family background and socioeconomic status yield the most consistent correlates

(Barro & Kolstad, 1987; Wehlage & Rutter, 1987). The most common predictors are low SES level, parents' educational attainment, large family, broken home, and parental punitiveness. Closely attuned to family and SES are findings that many children who drop out of school actually do so because of adult and family roles, including the need to generate income, sibling care, pregnancy, need to care for infants, and marriage. Numerous reports emphasize that a regular job outside school is critical to dropping out based on number of work hours, where 20 or more hours generally increased dropout risk. School-related factors include grade failure, grade performance, program of study, standardized and intelligence tests, interest and attitude (Eckstrom, 1987), discipline problems, delinquency, and truancy (Wehlage & Rutter, 1987). Such data lead to widespread consensus that the dropout rate for youth from low-income/low-skill/low-education backgrounds is about three times the rate of those from the highest end.

2. Federal interest in education actually dates back to the 1700s beginning with the Northwest Ordinance (in 1787). Similarly, the federal government has also engaged in other activities such as the civil rights movement, which attempted to bring racial equality to the nation. In this discussion, however, the focus is on actual government programs that feed funds to disadvantaged populations. Under such conditions, federal interest may been seen as focused on other projects such as support for higher education or defense as in the National Defense Education Act (in 1958), which spurred the development of science and technology.

3. The increase is for the single fiscal year 1986-1987 to 1987-1988. Increases in preschool handicapped services are not directly comparable for the time period because service requirements are the result of new federal mandates. The Education of the Handicapped Act was amended in October 1986 to extend the right to a free and appropriate education to handicapped children aged 3-5 years, with states required to meet the mandate by 1990-1991.

4. Thiel also notes that at the same time the state's schools have become social agencies with great overlap and fragmentation of services. The state education department administers programs for substance abuse, child care, and nutrition with services ranging from prenatal care to infants to preschool/school-age children to special populations to behavior problems. In addition, Thiel cites at least 47 programs for children administered by 13 agencies spending $5.9 billion annually, exclusive of K-12 education. For child-care alone, 13 agencies administer 49 programs for $747 million and 6 state agencies administer 27 programs for pregnant or parenting adolescents. As Thiel notes, there is even confusion regarding how to count and classify services because of a lack of standardized reporting and duplication in client counts.

5. No separate provisions for compensatory education are evident in the states of Alabama, Alaska, Arizona, Arkansas, Idaho, Indiana, Iowa, Kansas, Kentucky, Maine, Mississippi, Montana, Nevada, New Hampshire, New Mexico, North Dakota, South Dakota, Tennessee, West Virginia, Wisconsin, and Wyoming (Education Commission of the States, 1988).

6. No bilingual legislation is apparent in the states of Alabama, Arkansas, Delaware, Florida, Idaho, Indiana, Iowa, Kentucky, Maine, Maryland, Mississippi, Missouri, Montana, Nebraska, Nevada, New Hampshire, North

Carolina, North Dakota, Ohio, Oregon, Pennsylvania, South Carolina, South Dakota, Tennessee, Vermont, Virginia, West Virginia, and Wyoming.

References

Administration for Children, Youth, and Families. (1987, January). *Head Start fact sheet.* Washington, DC: Author.

Barnett, W. S. (1988). The economics of preschool special education under Public Law 99-457. *Topics in Early Childhood Special Education, 8*(1), 116-131.

Barnett, W., Escobar, C., & Ravsten, M. (1989). Parent and clinic early intervention for children with language handicaps: A cost-effectiveness analysis. *Journal of the Division of Early Childhood, 12*(1), 81-97.

Barro, S. M., & Kolstad, A. (1987). *Who drops out of high school? Findings from high school and beyond* (National Center for Education Statistics). Washington, DC: Department of Education, Office of Educational Research and Improvement.

Berrueta-Clement, J. R., Schweinhart, L. J., Barnett, W. S., Epstein, A. S., & Weikart, D. P. (1984). *Changed lives: The effects of the Perry Preschool program through age 19* (Monograph No. 8). Ypsilanti, MI: High Scope Educational Research Foundation.

Bronfenbrenner, U. (1974). Is early education effective? *Teachers College Record, 76*(2), 274-303.

California State Department of Education. (1990). *Superintendent's task force on LEP student issues.* Sacramento: Author.

California Taxpayers Association. (1988). *Growth within limits: Reshaping Article XIIIB.* Sacramento: Author.

Children's Defense Fund. (1989). *A vision for America's future: An agenda for the 1990's: A children's defense budget.* Washington, DC: Author.

Coleman, J., Campbell, E., Hobson, C., McPartland, J., Mood, A., Weinfeld, F., & York, R. (1966). *Equality of educational opportunity.* Washington, DC: Government Printing Office.

Council of Chief State School Officers. (1988). *Early childhood and family education: Foundations for success.* Washington, DC: Author.

Dougherty, J. (1985). A matter of interpretation: Changes under Chapter 1 of the Education Consolidation and Improvement Act. In *Report on changes under Chapter 1 of the Education and Improvement Act* (Serial No. 99-B; GPO Pub. No. 1985 50-5240). Washington, DC: Congress, House of Representatives, Committee on Education and Labor.

Eckstrom, R. B. (1987). Who drops out of high school and why? Findings from a national study. *Teachers College Record, 87*(1), 17-33.

Education Commission of the States. (1988). *School finance at a glance.* Denver: Author.

Florida State Department of Education. (1987). *Priority policy issues.* Tallahassee: Author.

Hodgkinson, H. (1985). *All one system: Demographics of education, kindergarten through graduate school.* Washington, DC: Institute for Educational Leadership.

Hodgkinson, H. (1986). *California: The state and its educational system.* Washington, DC: Institute for Educational Leadership.

Hodgkinson, H. (1988). *Florida: The state and its educational system.* Washington, DC: Institute for Educational Leadership.

Illinois State Board of Education. (1986). *Performance profiles: Illinois schools report to the public.* Springfield: Author.

Kennedy, M. M., Jung, R. K., & Orland, M. E. (1986). *Poverty, achievement, and the distribution of compensatory education services.* Washington, DC: Department of Education, Office of Educational Research and Improvement.

Kirlin, J. (1989). Fiscal policy choices. In J. Kirlin & D. Winkler (Eds.), *California policy choices* (Vol. 5). Sacramento: University of Southern California, Sacramento Center, School of Public Administration.

Kluender, M., & Egbert, R. (1989). Improving life chances for children in Nebraska. In M. Bryant, P. O'Connell, & C. Reed (Eds.), *Nebraska policy choices.* Omaha: University of Nebraska, Center for Public Affairs Research.

Lambie, D. Z., Bond, J. T., & Weikart, D. P. (1974). *Home teaching with mothers and infants, the Ypsilanti-Carnegie infant education project: An experiment* (Monograph No. 2). Ypsilanti, MI: High Scope Educational Research Foundation.

Lazar, M., Darlington, I., Murray, R. H., Royce, J., & Snipper, A. (1982). Lasting effect of early education. *Monographs of the Society for Research in Child Development, 47*(1-2, Serial No. 194).

Macias, R. (1989). Bilingual teachers supply and demand in the United States. In National Forum on Personnel Needs for Districts with Changing Demographics, *Staffing the multilingually impacted schools of the 1990s.* Washington, DC: Department of Education, Office of Bilingual Education and Minority Languages Affairs.

National Association of State Boards of Education. (1988). *Right from the start.* Washington, DC: Author.

National Commission for Employment Policy. (1988). *An investigation of education options for youth-at-risk, ages 9-15: Demographics, legislation, and model programs.* Washington, DC: Author.

National Education Association. (1990). *Rankings of the states, 1990.* Washington, DC: Author.

National Forum on Personnel Needs for Districts with Changing Demographics. (1989). *Staffing the multilingually impacted schools of the 1990s.* Washington, DC: Department of Education, Office of Bilingual Education and Minority Languages Affairs.

National Governors' Association. (1986). *Time for results: The governors' 1990 report on education.* Washington, DC: Author.

Seitz, V., Rosenbaum, L., & Apfel, N. (1985). Effects of family support intervention: Ten-year follow-up. *Child Development, 56,* 376-391.

Shoor, L. (1988). *Within our reach.* New York: Anchor.

Steinberg, L., Blinde, P., & Chan, K. S. (1984). Dropping out among language minority youth. *Review of Educational Research, 54,* 113-132.

The Sunrise Report. (1987). (Prepared by the Speaker's Advisory Committee on the Future, Tallahassee, FL).

Thiel, K. S. (1989). Providing services to children in need. In J. Kirlin & D. Winkler (Eds.), *California policy choices* (Vol. 5). Sacramento: University of Southern California, Sacramento Center, School of Public Administration.

U.S. Congress, House of Representatives, Subcommittee on Elementary, Secondary, and Vocational Education of the Committee on Education and Labor. (1986a). *Hearings-H.R. 3042, the dropout prevention and reentry act* (GPO Pub. No. 63-276 O). Washington, DC: Government Printing Office.

U.S. Congress, House of Representatives, Committee on Labor, Subcommittee on Elementary, Secondary, and Vocational Education. (1986b). *Targeting students for Chapter 1 services: Are the students in greatest need being served?* Washington, DC: Government Printing Office.

U.S. Department of Education, Office of Educational Research and Improvement. (1989). *Digest of education statistics* (National Center for Education Statistics). Washington, DC: Government Printing Office.

U.S. Department of Education, Office of Educational Research and Improvement. (1990a). *The condition of education* (National Center for Education Statistics). Washington, DC: Government Printing Office.

U.S. Department of Education, Office of Educational Research and Improvement. (1990b). Children in poverty 1960-87. In National Center for Education Statistics, *The condition of education*. Washington, DC: Government Printing Office.

Wang, M., & Walberg, H. (1988). *The national follow through program: Lessons from two decades of research and practice in school improvement.* Philadelphia: Temple University, Center for Research in Human Development and Education.

Wehlage, G. C., & Rutter, R. A. (1987). Dropping out: How much do schools contribute to the problem? *Teachers College Record, 87*(1), 69-77.

SIX

Rising Hispanic Enrollments
A NEW CHALLENGE
FOR PUBLIC SCHOOLS

CONCETTA RAIMONDI HYLAND

As we stand on the threshold of the twenty-first century, a sweeping shift in the U.S. population is taking place. Prominent demographers have clearly described the nature of the changes that will occur during the next generation. For educators, these changes and the impact they will have upon U.S. public schools must be examined carefully, for the public schools of the next generation, both student and staff, will be made up of individuals whose demographic characteristics are rather clearly visible today.

The current population shifts in the United States are ones that are transforming the nation with respect to both age (in 1983 there were more people over 65 than there were teenagers) and ethnicity. These demographic changes indicate a school-age population that is becoming more ethnically diverse than ever before. Hodgkinson (1985) predicts that by the year 2000 one in three Americans will be nonwhite. Considering also the trend toward increased childhood poverty and the increases in handicapping conditions, one can rather accurately envision the profile of U.S. public school children through the first decade of the next century.

The demographic study of school-age children in the United States is a helpful tool in planning for more productive schools, schools that can effectively meet the needs of all students. We *know* the essential characteristics of the graduating senior class of the year 2003, for these children have already entered school. Differential fertility rates of population subgroups enable experts to make additional projections. With this knowledge, policymakers can begin now to plan educational programs that will most effectively meet the needs of this changing population and improve the educational gains of all children.

More specific to the central focus here is the status of the U.S. Hispanic population—a subgroup who has experienced the most dramatic growth in the last 20 years. According to 1980 census figures, there were 14.6 million Hispanics in the United States. This represented a 61% increase over the 1960 figure. By comparison, the general U.S. population during that same time period grew only by 11% (Diaz, 1984). Although the 61% figure has been criticized as possibly inflated because of changing census methods, the 1980 population figure is dramatic nonetheless. This dramatic surge in the Hispanic population growth has not diminished. It appears instead that it is continuing to increase, providing some demographers with the data to suggest that by the year 2000 the Hispanic population will equal and surpass the black population in the United States.

The rapidly expanding population figures are a powerful and interesting phenomenon. But of serious concern to educational, corporate, and civic leaders is the contention that Hispanics are the most undereducated population group in America. Currently, Hispanics have the highest dropout rate of all major population subgroups at approximately 36%, more than doubling the dropout rate of the white population. In addition, Hispanic children tend to be excessively represented

in remedial tracks, to be underrepresented in gifted programs, and to exhibit low academic achievement levels overall. This group also has the distinction of being the most
highly segregated of all school children, both within and
among public schools (Diaz, 1984; Orfield & Associates, 1984;
Orum, 1986).

The future course of public school education should be defined with respect to the population moving through the system. Because the Hispanic population is expanding rapidly
and the current status of Hispanic school-age children is one
of low attainment, educational policymakers must give special consideration to the implementation of measures that will
foster success for this group.

Experts predict that by the year 2020 the population in the
United States will be made up of 265 million people. Of that
population, Hispanics, experiencing a tremendous period of
growth, will constitute 47 million, and 44 million will be
black. In addition, the number for the Hispanic population
may be even higher if Hispanic immigration rates increase
(Hodgkinson, 1985).

America has always been a nation of immigrants, and we
continue to be the recipient of massive migrations. In 1984,
544,000 people migrated legally into the United States. If one
adds the 300,000 to 500,000 illegal aliens presumed to have
entered the country, 1984 becomes the year of greatest immigration in our history (Hodgkinson & Mirga, 1986).

Immigration trends are just one factor used in analyzing the
growing Hispanic population. Two other demographic indicators also have special significance as we anticipate the growth in
the number of Hispanic citizens: birthrate and age. Differential
fertility rates suggest that significant shifts have occurred in the
birthrates of the racial and ethnic groups within America. Demographers agree that a birthrate of 2.1 children per female is
required to maintain the presence of a group at a constant number. It follows therefore that groups with birthrates below 2.1
will be less represented numerically in the next generation. Conversely, groups with a birthrate exceeding 2.1 will have higher
numbers of citizens in the future.

It is of significance then that Mexican Americans, with a birthrate of 2.9, will be a much larger part of our future, while white Americans, with a birthrate of 1.7, will be less represented in the next generation. Blacks, with a rate of 2.4, will be greater in number than today.

With respect to age, the 1980 census indicated that the average white American was 31 years old, the average black 25 years old, and the average Hispanic only 22 years old. These figures disclose that the typical Hispanic female is just moving into peak childbearing age while the average white female is moving out of childbearing age (Hodgkinson, 1985).

These demographic trends indicate that the Hispanic population in America is undergoing enormous growth. Hispanic children will have significant influences upon the U.S. public school system because they bring to that experience different needs and problems than the students who have preceded them (Hyland, 1989). Chief among these issues are three main concerns: isolation, performance in school, and intracultural diversity.

Isolation

Contrary to the stereotypical image of the farm laborer, America's Hispanic population is highly concentrated in urban areas. According to Orfield (1984), 88% of Hispanics lived in metropolitan areas in 1984. Within these cities, the Hispanic population typically lives in racially isolated neighborhoods.

In addition, most Hispanic students attend schools where the student population is predominantly minority. A report by Orum and Vincent (1984) noted that 61% of Hispanic children attended schools with a minority enrollment of 50% or more. Orum stated: "Hispanics now have the dubious distinction of being not only the most undereducated group of American children, but also the most highly segregated" (Orum & Vincent, 1984, p. 7). In addition, she found that more than one fourth of Hispanic children attended schools with minority enrollments of 90%-100% (Orum, 1986). Orfield (1983) contended that Hispanics were more likely to attend segregated schools than blacks.

A study of the segregation of Hispanic students also revealed regional implications. For example, California, New York, Texas, New Jersey, and Illinois are among the states with the largest Hispanic public school enrollment. These states also exhibit the highest incidence of school segregation for Hispanics.

In addition to frequently isolated housing and predominantly segregated schooling, Hispanic American students are also isolated with respect to their linguistic skills. These students tend to be placed in classrooms or schools where children of limited English proficiency predominate. This isolation in programs such as English as a Second Language and bilingual education has a tendency to reduce the possibilities for contact with the native English discourse of peers. Sometimes school practices heighten the problem of isolation by grouping students according to language ability for purposes of instruction. In these instances, there may be no English-speaking peers (Arias, 1986).

Programs for limited-English-proficient students are not the only ones that tend to isolate Hispanic students. Even within "integrated" schools, Hispanic children are represented disproportionately in a number of school programs. For example, Hispanic children are less likely to be placed in programs for the gifted. In 1986 Hispanic students accounted for 6.8% of the total school population, yet they constituted only 5% of all children enrolled in gifted programs. At the high school level, it was found that Hispanics were underrepresented in the honors, academic, or college-bound tracks and disproportionately represented in general or vocational programs (Arias, 1986; Orum, 1986). According to a report issued by then Secretary of Education William Bennett, Hispanic students were about twice as likely to be in remedial classes as whites (Bennett, 1988). Additional evidence suggests that assignment of special education programs also increased the segregation of Hispanic students within the school (Orum, 1986).

School Performance

Hispanic American students also differ significantly from their peers in other ways. Educational attainment, measured by years of schooling completed, scores on standardized tests, grades assigned by teachers, or type of academic preparation (including the nature of courses taken), finds Hispanic students significantly behind the general population.

In 1985 the average number of school years completed by Hispanics 25 years old or older was 11.5, while the general population had completed 12.6. In 1980, 74% of all the 17-year-olds in the United States had high school diplomas, while only 40% of Hispanics had graduated from high school (Arias, 1986). One study found that only 13% of Mexican immigrants received a diploma (National Coalition of Advocates for Students, 1988).

As measured by performance on standardized tests, Hispanic students have been found to score poorly compared with other groups. By the third grade, 80% of Hispanic students are attending schools that average below the 50th percentile on standardized achievement tests. This pattern of low student achievement continues through high school. In addition, the data reveal that early losses in achievement are never recovered (Espinosa & Ochoa, 1986). On both the Scholastic Aptitude Test (SAT; Bennett, 1988) and the American College Test (ACT; "Gap in Admissions," 1988), Hispanic students scored significantly below white students. A study of the National Assessment of Educational Progress (NAEP) for 1981-1982 indicated that Hispanic students performed below white students in reading, science, and mathematics (Arias, 1986).

When measuring achievement in terms of teachers' grades, the pattern continues. A study of grades attained by 1980 high school seniors showed that Hispanic students were less likely to receive As and more likely to receive Ds or Fs than their white counterparts in every subject area, including foreign language. Hispanic students were in fact twice as likely to have earned a grade of D or F. Data also indicated that one third of all Hispanic high school graduates had a D or F average in one or more academic subject areas (Orum, 1986).

Regarding the course selections within their school programs, Hispanic students took fewer classes in the college preparatory curricula than other students in 1980. On the other hand, they participated more in general and vocational curricula than did their white or black counterparts (Arias, 1986). A longitudinal study by the National Center for Education Statistics indicated that 52% of Hispanic students were in vocational courses compared with 34% of whites ("Hispanic Academic Achievement," 1988).

A review of Carnegie units completed by 1980 high school seniors indicated that Hispanic students had fewer credits in mathematics, natural science, and business than did others. In fact, the only subject in which they exceeded both white and black students in credits earned was "trade and industry" (Orum, 1986). The results of the Fourth Mathematics Assessment of Educational Progress disclosed that Hispanic students reported taking almost a full year less of advanced mathematics than did white students (NAEP, 1988). Finally, a 1987 study observed that Hispanics had earned fewer credits in the "new basics"—English, mathematics, science, social studies, and computer science—than whites and blacks (O'Malley, 1987).

Intracultural Diversity

Any discussion of Hispanic students must address the fact that there are really several different subgroups of Hispanics in America with similar yet sometimes distinct characteristics as students. Because of this fact, any attempt to analyze the nature of the problem must account for these distinctions.

Broadly speaking, researchers of Hispanic students have commonly referred to the following subgroups: Mexican American, Puerto Rican, Cuban, and Central/South Americans (Matute-Bianchi, 1986; Melville, 1988; Orum, 1986). Some researchers have further distinguished within a subgroup. Matute-Bianchi (1986) observed that Mexican Americans were a composite of Mexican immigrants, Mexican oriented, Mexican

American, Chicano, and Cholo. Each of the major subgroups has distinctive characteristics and, more to the point, experiences different degrees of success in U.S. public schools.

In March 1985 the Census Bureau reported 16.9 million Hispanic residents in the United States (U.S. Department of Commerce, 1985). This figure did not include the 2 to 5 million undocumented Hispanic workers believed to be in the country.

Three subgroups account for more than 80% of the Hispanic population. Mexican Americans, the largest group, accounted for 60.6% of the total. Puerto Ricans made up 15.1%, while Cubans accounted for 6.1%. Other groups, including Spanish immigrants, Central/South Americans, and Hispanic persons identifying themselves as Latino or Hispano, accounted for 18.2% (Arias, 1986).

Regional residency is another point of differentiation among Hispanic Americans. Mexican Americans reside primarily in California and Texas. Puerto Ricans are concentrated for the most part in New York and New Jersey, while Cubans live primarily in Florida (Arias, 1986; Orum, 1986).

Regarding family income, earnings for employed Hispanics averaged about 30% less than for whites. Within the Hispanic group, however, significant differences with respect to poverty were discernible. While only 11% of the non-Hispanic population was below the poverty level in 1984, 24% of the Mexican Americans fell below the poverty level, and 42% of the Puerto Ricans were in poverty. On the other hand, only 13% of the Cuban families were identified as below the poverty level (Orum, 1986).

Distinct variations occurred within the Hispanic population with respect to school success and participation. One study found that only 26% of the Mexican American students were enrolled in academic programs while 53% of the Cuban students were so enrolled (O'Malley, 1987). Further differentiation within the Mexican American subgroup, comprising recent Mexican immigrants (Spanish speaking), Mexican oriented (bilingually fluent), Mexican American (born in the United States), Chicano (of Mexican descent, resisting U.S.

culture), and Cholo (gang oriented, rejecting U.S. culture), noted that the Mexican American, probably as a function of the highest degree of assimilation to the American language and culture, was the most academically successful. The Chicano and Cholo, the least successful groups, "appear to resist certain features of the school culture" to maintain their ethnic identity (Matute-Bianchi, 1986).

Additional analysis of subgroups within the Mexican American population has led other researchers similarly to conclude that the most salient point of differentiation among Mexican Americans was English language proficiency. They observed that the most pronounced differences between the subgroups of Mexican Americans appeared along lines of language rather than nativity. They reported that English speakers achieved a high educational attainment, level of income, and rate of naturalization (Hurtado & Arce, 1986).

Regarding school completion and dropout concerns, continued differentiation occurred within the major subgroups of Hispanic Americans. A study of dropouts of the senior class of 1982 noted that 18.7% of the Hispanics who were sophomores in 1980 were not seniors in 1982. Puerto Ricans had the highest dropout rate (22.9%), followed by Mexican Americans (21.5%), Cubans (19.4%), and other Hispanics (11.5%). This report did not include the students who dropped out before the tenth grade. According to the commission, about 40% of all Hispanic dropouts leave school before the spring of their sophomore year (National Commission on Secondary Schooling for Hispanics, 1984).

School Responses to Changes in Hispanic Population

Because of these imminent demographic shifts and because of the knowledge that Hispanic students have been less successful in America's public schools than other substantial population groups, a study was undertaken that focused upon this problem (Hyland, 1990). More specifically, 25 educators from

across the country in academia, public schools, and state and
national organizations were used to discern what changes in
the U.S. public school system would be necessary to successfully adapt to the growing number of Hispanic students in
America's cities.

In terms of the conclusions from the study, there appear to be
several points about which there was substantive agreement.
Items discussed below are indicative of those changes that the
study participants felt would be most effective in adapting public schools to meet the needs of the Hispanic student.

*Tracking is a very important issue in the education of Hispanic
children.* The practice of tracking students according to ability
level and the use of standardized tests for the purpose of
tracking was rejected by experts who participated in the
study as an effective measure for educating Hispanic students. These practices, along with segregated facilities, were
targeted for reexamination or elimination.

Based upon the collective recommendations of the group of
experts, schools must aggressively examine the practice of
grouping or tracking as it might hinder the opportunities for all
students to gain access to successful educational experiences
and to district resources. The literature on tracking (Oakes,
1986a, 1986b; Slavin, 1988) is virtually unequivocal regarding
the impact of grouping on achievement and collateral issues
such as the opportunity to learn, access to knowledge, and affec-
tive influences that in turn affect student achievement.

Unquestionably, the powerful political influence and expectations of the gifted and talented movement in America will
have to be met in any solution that removes ability grouping
from its current widespread use in U.S. public schools. Parents of the more able will have to be convinced that any dis-
solution of current practices will, at the very least, not have a
deleterious impact upon their students' ability to achieve or
their ability to be secure in the classroom setting.

In a similar vein, the use of standardized tests, so common in
our public schools, particularly as they might be used as entrance
requirements into programs, must be carefully reconsidered.

Certainly the potential for initial language barriers and the potential for cultural bias exist in sufficient degree to cause thoughtful school leaders to tread carefully in this area and to depend upon additional factors when selecting students for special programs.

Significant changes in bilingual education programs were indicated. An emphasis on bilingual education emerged as a change the experts in the study warranted as necessary to better meet the needs of Hispanic students. Panelists strongly voiced the need for bilingual education in a variety of settings to increase the success of the Hispanic student in U.S. schools; however, total immersion as a form of bilingual instruction was rejected by the majority of individuals participating in the study. Clear emphasis was given to the systemic rather than the remedial approach that this instruction should take. In addition, the panelists indicated that bilingual instruction must begin at an early age.

Early intervention programs were recommended in the study. Another conclusion drawn from the results of the study was a need for a more widespread early intervention program for educating Hispanic youth. *Early success, early childhood,* and *preschool* were terms that were common to these recommendations. It was clear that the experts put great stock in the effects of early intervention on the successful educational outcomes of Hispanic students.

Early intervention and the extension of bilingual opportunities were strong recommendations by the panelists. In this regard, the funding mechanisms that generally do not enable school districts to extend prekindergarten opportunities to students who are not seen as "special education" or perhaps "at risk" must be reviewed and revised. The public schools of today are generally unable to provide funding that would be adequate to staff, equip, or house such necessary programs.

Study participants felt that there was not sufficient attention paid to cultural differences among students. A greater awareness of and sensitivity to the cultural differences of U.S. school-age children by educators and policymakers was an imperative change expressed as needed by the experts. They emphasized the need for greater sensitivity to the cultural pluralism that is America. The recommendation that educators adopt a more positive attitude was coupled with the recommendation that our delivery systems and curricula be changed to reflect this reality.

There was strong support for the curricular acceptance of the fact that Americans live in a culturally pluralistic society. Though textbooks may occasionally address the diversity of our heritage and current situation, the clear contention of the group was that schools are still based almost exclusively upon the values and traditions of the Anglo society. Certainly, if Hispanic students are to be afforded the opportunity for achieving their academic potential, this narrow view must be broadened.

Dropout prevention programs received emphasis. Another conclusion drawn from the study indicated the need to create or improve dropout prevention programs. Specifically, the panelists participating in the study urged the establishment of programs and practices that would have the effect of keeping a greater number of Hispanic students in school. Experts clearly supported the emphasis on dropout prevention as an effective strategy for better meeting the needs of Hispanic children.

With documented excessive dropout rates, the economic and political potential of the next generation of Hispanic American adults will be severely diminished. As a result, the panelists recommended aggressive action to prevent both dropouts and push-outs, those students who are counseled out or are simply harangued to the point where they see no value in returning to school. The experts did not, however, condone in any great numbers the use of punitive methods such as the withdrawal of a driver's license to meet this end.

It remains then for public school leaders and perhaps even legislators to face this continued drain on potential in America's future. In the final analysis, there remains something of the "chicken and the egg" in the problem of the Hispanic drop-out. If there exists little evidence that a high school diploma has any extrinsic value, there will be little impetus to stay in school.

The role of the teacher emerged as an important issue in the study. The teacher as a professional is a critical component in en-hancing the educational attainment of Hispanic students. The experts supported this notion by indicating the importance of staff selection and teacher attitude. Participants in the study recommended that staff be given strong consideration in shaping the solution. The quality of the staff that is recruited and retained was also emphasized as well as the need for Hispanic and Hispanic-sensitive teachers. Collectively, the study participants indicated that staff selection would be a key change for consideration. Many expressed that, without multiculturally aware teachers, the maintenance of an Anglo, white, middle-class system of values and attitudes would have the tendency to produce a sense of alienation on the part of the American Hispanic student.

Schools therefore need to institute staff development pro-grams that will assist in the education of those instructors al-ready in service. For those new teachers entering the profession, universities, as training institutions, bear a responsibility to as-sist in the multicultural sensitivity and awareness of their edu-cation graduates.

Systemic change will be necessary to properly service Hispanic chil-dren. There was an appeal for systemic rather than cosmetic changes that might better adapt the schools of America to meet the needs of the Hispanic student. It remains to be seen whether today's "restructuring movement," with its rhetoric of substantive change, will be the vehicle for this transforma-tion. To date, restructuring has more frequently meant teacher empowerment, site-based management, or parental choice. None of these movements has shown signs of dealing with the major issues that this study generated.

In evaluating the recommendations of the experts who participated in the study, one must consider the implications on public school finance and funding. Though the issue of adequate funding was the subject of several recommendations, none of those suggestions was among the most highly rated by the expert participants. In fact, the issue of adequate funding was also the subject of some disagreement between panelists, as evidenced by their individual responses. Many respondents underscored the essential nature of adequate funding by such comments as these: "Never enough funds for education," "Money talks," and "Money is the name of the game."

Yet other panelists challenged the notion that financial resources were of prime import. One respondent stated that "throwing money at problems seldom solves anything." Another expert also subscribed to a similar notion by stating, "Finance levels alone have little effect." One respondent stated, "[The] most important resource is not money."

It is important to note, however, that, although the experts in the field of Hispanic education did not emphasize the importance of adequate funding as a criterion for better meeting the educational needs of Hispanic students, many of the measures they emphasized as extremely important for student success would require fiscal support. Creating or expanding bilingual programs, instituting a more broad-based early intervention program (preschool), and designing and implementing effective dropout prevention or dropout recovery programs are all measures that would require additional public school funding. In addition, programs stressing a greater sensitivity to cultural differences would require additional funding to revamp the curricula, redesign the instructional delivery system, and retrain teachers through staff development. Finally, the research component for defining the most effective design and implementation of any of the above-mentioned programs would require substantial fiscal support.

In sum, there is a critical challenge facing U.S. public school educators. There is a steadily increasing Hispanic student population, one that demographers predict will eclipse the current black population of school children within the next generation. This is coupled with data suggesting that Hispanic students are the most "undereducated" of all major population groups in terms of educational attainment. Though experts in the field agree upon many measures that would enhance the educational prospects for this particular group, much of what they endorse would require additional funding. It is clear that the allocation of resources must be reviewed and revised at local, state, and federal levels if this current challenge facing educators is to be met.

References

Arias, M. B. (1986). The context of education for Hispanic students: An overview. *American Journal of Education, 95,* 26-57.
Bennett, W. (1988). *American education: Making it work.* Washington, DC: Department of Education.
Diaz, W. (1984). *Hispanics: Challenges and opportunities* (Report No. 435). New York: Ford Foundation.
Espinosa, R., & Ochoa, A. (1986). Concentration of California Hispanic students in schools with low achievement. *American Journal of Education, 95,* 77-95.
Gap in admissions: Test scores linked to income, coursework. (1988, March 9). *Education Week,* p. 3.
Hispanic academic achievement surveyed. (1988, January/February). *Education Network News,* p. 3.
Hodgkinson, H. (1985). *All one system.* Washington, DC: Institute for Educational Leadership.
Hodgkinson, H., & Mirga, T. (Eds.). (1986, May 14). Here they come, ready or not. *Education Week,* pp. 13-37.
Hurtado, A., & Arce, C. (1986). Mexicans, Chicanos, Mexican Americans, or Pochos . . . Que somos? The impact of language and nativity on ethnic labeling. *Aztlan, 17,* 103-130.
Hyland, C. R. (1989). What we know about the fastest growing minority population: Hispanic Americans. *Educational Horizons, 67,* 131-135.
Hyland, C. R. (1990). *Recommended responses to increasing Hispanic student enrollment upon urban American public school education through the year 2010: A Delphi study.* Unpublished doctoral dissertation, University of Illinois.
Matute-Bianchi, M. E. (1986). Ethnic identities and pattern of school success and failure among Mexican-descent and Japanese American students in a California high school: An ethnographic analysis. *American Journal of Education, 95,* 233-255.
Melville, M. (1988). Hispanics: Race, class or ethnicity? *Journal of Ethnic Studies, 16,* 67-83.

NAEP: Results of the fourth mathematics assessment. (1988, June 15). *Education Week*, pp. 28-29.

National Coalition of Advocates for Students. (1988). *New voices*. Boston: Author.

National Commission on Secondary Schooling for Hispanics. (1984). *Make something happen*. Washington, DC: Hispanic Development Project.

Oakes, J. (1986a). Keeping track, part 1: The policy and practice of curriculum inequality. *Phi Delta Kappan, 68*(1), 12-18.

Oakes, J. (1986b). Keeping track, part 2: Curriculum inequality and school reform. *Phi Delta Kappan, 68*(2), 148-154.

O'Malley, J. M. (1987). *Academic growth of high school age Hispanic students in America*. Washington, DC: National Center for Educational Statistics.

Orfield, G. (1983). *Public school desegregation in the United States, 1968-1980*. Washington, DC: Joint Center for Political Studies.

Orfield, G., & Associates. (1984). *The study of access and choice in higher education: A report to the Illinois State Committee on Higher Education*. Chicago: University of Chicago, Committee on Public Policy Studies Research Project.

Orum, L. (1986). *The education of Hispanics: Status and implications*. Washington, DC: National Council of La Raza.

Orum, L., & Vincent, A. (1984). *Selected statistics in the education of Hispanics*. Washington, DC: National Council of La Raza.

Slavin, R. E. (1988). Synthesis of research on grouping in elementary and secondary schools. *Educational Leadership, 46*(1), 67-77.

U.S. Department of Commerce, Bureau of the Census. (1985). *Current population reports: Population characteristics* (Series no. 404). Washington, DC: Government Printing Office.

SEVEN

Cultural Diversity and Political Turmoil
THE CASE OF SCHOOL FINANCE IN TEXAS

WILLIAM E. SPARKMAN

TRUDY A. CAMPBELL

Bob Dylan was right—"the times they are a'changing." To suggest that the people and economy of Texas are changing is to suggest the obvious. After all, most things do change over time, and the states certainly are not immune to the inevitability of change. The changes we document in this chapter are not of epic proportions that define a period of history; they instead reflect incremental shifts in the vital statistics of the State of Texas. The nature and magnitude of the changes, however, have major implications for the state and its political and educational systems. The collective response to these changes will define the state's character into the twenty-first century.

Overall, Texas is following certain trends in population, education, employment, and economic activity that mirror the nation as a whole. It has been predicted that by the year 2000 the following changes will characterize the United States and the southern states, including Texas (Southern Regional Education Board, 1989, p. 1):

- the overall population and the labor force will be older;
- minorities will constitute a larger percentage of the population;
- 80% of the new jobs will require a high school education, and an increasing number will require postsecondary education;
- the national and state economies will be increasingly interrelated with the global economy;
- too few students will be ready for the first grade, and too few will graduate from high school;
- minority students will continue to have lower levels of academic achievement, higher dropout rates, and lower levels of literacy than whites; and
- college enrollments will decline, and the disparity in attendance rates for whites and minorities will continue.

Many of the changes that have been documented or predicated for Texas will have consequences for the public education system. In this chapter, we will discuss certain demographic, economic, and social characteristics unique to Texas and explore their impact on the state's education system. We will give particular attention to the way the education system is responding to or coping with the changes in student diversity, with an emphasis on school finance policy issues. Of course any discussion of school finance in Texas must address the question of student equity, which has become a dominant issue in the state's legal and political system for more than two decades.

As we approach these several issues, we believe that it is not sufficient to look simply at broad trends in population growth, birthrates, economic patterns, and other socioeconomic or demographic indicators. It is important to disaggregate the data and look at the specific characteristics of the changes in the state's population or economy. For example, it is not enough to know that the population is growing. What is more important is to have an understanding of the composition of the population and how the different segments have changed over time when considering such variables as age, ethnicity, and race.

Some changes will have had a direct impact on the state education system. Increased public school enrollments beyond those predicted by state fiscal planners resulted in state school funds being prorated to the local districts in the 1990-1991 school year. Other changes will have more of an indirect and uncertain impact on the education system. For example, the aging of the population, with fewer families having children in the public schools, could jeopardize the legitimacy of the public system and make it increasingly difficult to garner political support for school funding increases.

This chapter begins with a profile of the State of Texas and reports selected demographic, economic, and social trends and indicators. These data are presented and discussed in context of selected national trends. Following the state profile, we highlight the impact of the reported changes on the state's education system. This provides the basis for the next section, which includes our analysis of the system's response to the demographic and socioeconomic changes. We have included in this section a discussion of student equity concerns by focusing on ongoing school finance litigation. The final section contains our assessment of the state's capacity and willingness to respond to the many issues raised in the chapter.

The Changing Profile of Texas

This section documents changes in several key indicators that are shaping the profile of the State of Texas in the closing years of the twentieth century. These indicators include population, educational attainment, enrollment, employment, and poverty. There obviously are many other factors that could be presented to provide a more comprehensive view of the state, but the ones presented appear to have the greatest impact on the state's education system. The information for Texas is presented in the context of broader national trends.

Population

The National Planning Association predicts the U.S. population will increase by 12.3% by the year 2000. Southern states will be growing much faster (14.8%), and the State of Texas is predicted to grow by 17.1% (Southern Regional Education Board, 1989, p. 4). According to the latest figures from the 1990 census, the population of Texas rose 19% just in the past decade ("Census Figures Show," 1991).

All minority groups in Texas grew faster than the white population during the past decade. In 1990 Anglos accounted for 75.2% of the population, down from 78.7% in 1980; Hispanics accounted for 25.5%, up from 21%; blacks accounted for 11.9% of the population, down from 12%; Asians or Pacific Islanders accounted for 1.9% of the population, up from 0.8%; Native Americans, Eskimos, and Aleuts accounted for 0.4%, up from 0.3%; and other races accounted for 10.6%, up from 8.2%. (The percentages do not equal 100% because persons of Hispanic origin can be of any race.)

The change in age patterns of the population reveals a national trend for growth in the number of school-age children (5-19) by 9.8%, the work force (25-64) by 19%, and those over the age of 65 by 21.4% in the year 2000. In Texas the projected percentage of change in population includes an increase of 20.2% for school-age children, 2.3% for traditional-aged college students (15-24), 24.7% in the work force, and 19.8% for those over the age of 65. Overall, there will be a decrease in the number of college-age students (15-34) of 5.4% in Texas (Southern Regional Education Board, 1989, p. 7).

Educational Attainment/Enrollment

Enrollment in U.S. public elementary and secondary schools in the fall of 1981 was 40,099,498. By the fall of 1988, the estimated enrollment only increased to 40,196,263. In Texas, however, the increase was much sharper, 2,935,547 in 1981 to 3,268,605 in 1988 (U.S. Department of Education, 1989, pp. 48-49). The projected increase in public school enrollment in Texas for the next decade is as high as 20% and is second only to that of Florida (28.4%; Southern Regional Education Board, 1989, pp. 8-9).

Non-Hispanic whites made up 51% of the students in Texas schools in 1988-1989, the last year for which statistics are available. Hispanics accounted for 32.2% and blacks for 14.6%, according to Texas Education Agency records ("Ethnic, Racial Diversity," 1990, p. A-7). The agency's statisticians believe the shift to a "minority majority" will occur in the 1992-1993 school year when the public school population will reach 3.5 million, up from 3.3 million in the 1990s.

The number of persons in the age group that accounts for most college enrollments will be smaller across the United States as well as in Texas. Blacks and Hispanics will constitute a slightly larger percentage of total enrollments because they will represent a larger share of the college-age population (Southern Regional Education Board, 1989, p. 10).

Educational attainment has increased nationally but is predicted to lag behind for many groups. The percentage of the population 25 years and older with four years of high school went from 31% in 1970 to 35% in 1980 and is predicted to increase to 41% in 2000 (Southern Regional Education Board, 1989, p. 14). Predictions by racial groups indicate continued disparity (white 42%, black 41%, and Hispanic 30%).

Employment

The National Planning Association predicts the southern states will experience an employment growth rate that will exceed the national rate by 4% by 2000. Between 1986 and 2000, the estimated growth rate for Texas is 31.1% (Southern Regional Education Board, 1989, p. 16).

Of the anticipated 10.6 million new jobs in 15 southern states, 13% are projected to be at the managerial level, 15% in professional occupations, and 6% in "technical" occupations. The managerial and professional occupations generally require

at least a college degree while technical positions require at
least some postsecondary training. Sales and clerical occupations are projected to account for 25% of all new jobs in this
region, and service jobs, another 26%. These data suggest a
greater growth in jobs requiring at least some postsecondary
training. Very few new jobs will appear in the category of unskilled labor. In addition, predicted changes in the patterns of
employment indicated an increase in Texas of 7.9% in manufacturing and 55.1% in services as compared with a decrease
nationally in manufacturing (3.8%) and a 47.3% increase in
services (Southern Regional Education Board, 1989, pp. 16-17).

Poverty

According to a report by the National Center for Children
in Poverty ("Children in Poverty," 1990, p. 6), nearly one out
of every four children in the United States under the age of 6
lives in poverty. The largest group of poor children in the
United States are white (42%); however, minority children
have the greatest chances of being poor. For non-Hispanic
black children under the age of 6 in 1987, the poverty rate was
48%. For Hispanics, the rate was 42%, and for non-Hispanic
whites, 13%.

Statistics relative to Texas illustrate the seriousness of the
problem. Based on a study conducted by the Hogg Foundation for Mental Health at the University of Texas at Austin
(summarized in the Texas Center for Educational Research
Connection, 1991), it was found that

- 1.2 million children from birth to age 17 live in poverty;
- Texas ranks first in the United States in the number of births to
  girls less than 15 and second in the number of births to girls 15
  to 19;
- teenagers receive the least prenatal care of any age group;
- more than half of all poor children have no health insurance
  and families cannot afford regular medical care;

- almost three fourths of the state's low-income women and children eligible for the Supplemental Food Program for Women, Infants, and Children (WIC) are not being served;
- an average of 134 children are victims of abuse or neglect each day (during 1989);
- less than 14% of the state mental health budget was spent on children;
- only 20% of children with severe emotional problems are likely to receive treatment; and
- only 15%-20% of 3- to 5-year-olds eligible for Head Start in Texas were enrolled (in 1988).

State's Response to Changing Demographics

Any discussion of the state's fiscal response to the changing demographics of Texas must begin with the protracted school finance litigation that has buffeted the state's lawmaking apparatus for nearly 25 years. Since 1968 the State of Texas has had to defend in both federal and state courts various school finance plans that perpetuated vast disparities in expenditures per pupil and tax rates among the school districts of the state. It has been the illusive pursuit of fiscal equity by property-poor school districts, which coincidentally have majority Hispanic enrollments, that has driven state school finance policy for two decades.

In July 1968 Demetrio Rodriquez, six other parents, and eight children in the Edgewood Independent School District in San Antonio filed suit in federal district court challenging the constitutionality of the state's school finance law as violating the Fourteenth Amendment's equal protection clause. Yudof and Morgan (1974, p. 391) captured the essence of the plaintiffs' complaints as follows:

The parents complained bitterly of the inadequate education afforded their children in the predominantly (90%) Mexican-American district. The poor facilities, the tremendously overcrowded classrooms, the shortage of classroom teachers, and the lack of basic instructional materials all stemmed from lack of funds. Edgewood, with the highest ad valorem property tax rate in the San Antonio metropolitan area, raised only $26 per student in 1967-68 [footnote omitted]. Edgewood had the lowest property value per student, the lowest per capita income, and the highest proportion of minority students of any district in the San Antonio area [footnote omitted]. Yet, under the Foundation School Program, the state contributed roughly the same amount of money to Edgewood as it did to the wealthiest school district in San Antonio, the Alamo Heights Independent School District [footnote omitted].

After a series of legal maneuvers, the federal court in September 1969 denied the state's motion to dismiss but stayed further legal proceedings to give the legislature time to deal with the school finance problem (Yudof & Morgan, 1974). The state legislature failed to address the school finance problem during the 1971 legislative session, and the trial finally began later in the year. On December 23, 1971, the three-judge district court held that the Texas school finance system violated the plaintiffs' equal protection rights guaranteed by the Fourteenth Amendment (*Rodriquez v. San Antonio Indep. Sch. Dist.*, 1971).

Less than two years later, the U.S. Supreme Court, in a five to four decision, reversed the trial court and held that the system was not unconstitutional (*Rodriquez*, 1973). This ruling came despite the existence of expenditure disparities described by Justice Potter Stewart in his concurring opinion as "chaotic and unjust" (*Rodriquez*, 1973, pp. 33-34).

After the *Rodriguez* decision, the Texas legislature began to increase the state's share of school support and to adjust the Foundation School Program to provide more equalization aid to the poorer school districts. In spite of these efforts to equalize spending, fiscal disparities continued to exist because of extreme variations in local property wealth and substantial reliance on local property taxes to support schools beyond the foundation amount guaranteed by the state.

In May 1984, 11 years after his defeat in the U.S. Supreme Court, Mr. Rodriquez again found himself involved in a lawsuit against the State of Texas as a plaintiff in *Edgewood ISD v. Bynum,* later restyled as *Edgewood ISD v. Kirby.* This time though the plaintiffs filed in state court invoking the state constitution's equivalent of equal protection and the education article.

Just a month after the *Edgewood* case was filed, the state legislature enacted major school reform legislation, including substantial changes in the school finance law. The Second Called Session of the Sixty-Eighth Legislature, which convened on June 4, 1984, enacted House Bill 72. This legislation provided for major school reform initiatives, including a complete restructuring of the school finance system. The legislature committed $2.8 billion in new revenue to education over the next three years (Verstegen, 1985). Property-poor school districts did receive more money under the reform legislation, but because of a number of new state mandates, local school districts found themselves in a position of having to raise property taxes to pay the bill. The unfunded state mandate, coupled with the decline in the state's economy precipitated by the rapid decline of oil prices in the mid-1980s, compounded the financial problems among the state's school districts.

Substantial fiscal disparities remained despite the school finance reform. The extent of the disparities is evident from data for the 1985-1986 school year, the second year of the reform legislation. The wealthiest district in Texas had over $14,000,000 of assessed valuation per child whereas the poorest district had only $20,000—a ratio of 700 to 1. Moreover, the 300,000 students in the poorest districts had less than 3% of the state's property wealth, but the 300,000 students in the highest-wealth districts had nearly 25% of the total taxable wealth. Property wealth in the 100 wealthiest districts was more than 20 times greater than the average property wealth in the poorest 100 districts. Such disparities occurred even when the districts were in the same geographic proximity. Edgewood ISD and Alamo Heights ISD are both located in Bexar County (San Antonio, Texas); yet the per pupil wealth in Edgewood was just under $39,000 while Alamo Heights had just over $570,000 in property wealth per pupil. Per pupil spending disparities persisted and ranged from a low of

$2,112 to $19,330. The wealthier districts averaged spending over $2,000 per pupil more than the poorer districts (Sparkman & Stevens, 1990).

Similar disparities also were evident in local school tax rates. In 1985-1986 local tax rates ranged from $0.09 to $1.55 per $100 assessed valuation. The 100 poorest districts had an average tax rate of $0.745 per $100 valuation and spent an average of $2,978 per pupil. The 100 wealthiest districts, on the other hand, had an average tax rate of $0.47 and spent an average $7,233 per pupil. A person owning an $80,000 house in a low-wealth district in East Texas would pay $1,206 in school taxes, whereas a home owner in a West Texas district with the same $80,000 house would pay only $59. These disparities remained unacceptable to the plaintiffs (Sparkman & Stevens, 1990).

On March 5, 1985, the plaintiffs in *Edgewood* filed an amended petition alleging that the school finance system remained unconstitutional even after the infusion of new funds in the aftermath of the reform legislation the previous year (*Edgewood*, 1985). Nineteen other property-poor districts filed a petition of intervention on September 18, 1986, to join the suit against the state (*Edgewood*, 1986). Ultimately, 67 other school districts would join the original district in the suit. A number of other school districts, primarily wealthy suburban districts, filed as defendant intervenors on the side of the state (*Memorandum to School Superintendents*, 1986).

Nearly three years after *Edgewood* was filed, Judge Harley Clark of the 250th District Court, Travis County, declared the school finance system unconstitutional (*Edgewood*, April 29, 1987). In Judge Clark's final judgment issued on June 1, 1987, he ruled that the school financing system violated the state constitution's guarantees of equal protection, equality under the law, and privileges and immunities. He also declared that the finance law failed to provide an "efficient system of free public schools required by the constitution" (*Edgewood*, June 1, 1987).

As expected, the state appealed the trial court's judgment. The state's Third Court of Appeals, by a vote of two to one, reversed the trial court's decision (*Edgewood*, 1989). The majority rejected Judge Clark's conclusion that education was a fundamental right and that wealth was a suspect classification. Using the most deferential standard of equal protection review, the appeals court held that the use of local property taxes was rationally related to advancing local control of education (*Edgewood*, 1989, p. 864). The court also refused to accept the lower court's judgment that the school finance system was inefficient. Finding that the constitution provided no guidance on how to determine an efficient school, the court concluded that such a determination was "a political question not suitable for judicial review" (*Edgewood*, 1989, p. 867). The court held that the school finance system did not violate the Texas Constitution.

The Texas Supreme Court unanimously reversed the Court of Appeals and affirmed Judge Clark's original opinion with modifications on October 2, 1989 (*Edgewood*, 1989). The court based its decision on the efficiency clause of the state's education article. The education article reads as follows:

A general diffusion of knowledge being essential to the preservation of the liberties and rights of the people, it shall be the duty of the Legislature of the State to establish and make suitable provision for the support and maintenance of an efficient system of public free schools. (Texas Constitution, Art. VII, Sec. 1)

Based on the continuing fiscal disparities, the court concluded that the system was not efficient. The original equal protection claims were not addressed by the supreme court because it resolved the constitutional question on the basis of the education article. The court gave the legislature until May 1, 1990, to come forward with a constitutional school finance plan.

Near the end of February 1990, just prior to the state's political primaries in March, the legislature convened a special session to address school finance reform. It would take four bitterly divided special sessions of the legislature to finally arrive at a bill the governor would sign. Finally, on June 7, 1990, over a month past the court-imposed deadline, Governor

William Clements signed into law S.B. 1 that was to be phased in over the next five years. The law provided an additional $528 million in state funding to districts in the 1990-1991 school year and was to increase total new spending by at least $4.2 billion by the end of 1995 (School Finance Bill, 1990).

Almost immediately the plaintiffs in *Edgewood* returned to the trial court seeking to have the reform law declared unconstitutional. Just after the start of the new school year in 1990, State District Judge Scott McCown (Judge Harley Clark had previously retired from the bench) ruled that the reform law continued to perpetuate the fiscal disparities between the rich and poor districts and ruled that system unconstitutional (*Edgewood*, September 24, 1990). He gave the legislature until September 1, 1991, to enact a constitutional plan. The state naturally appealed to the Texas Supreme Court, which declared the new law unconstitutional, finding that it did not go far enough to remedy the inequities (*Edgewood*, January 22, 1991). The court set a deadline of April 1, 1991, for the legislature to devise a new finance plan and stated that it would enjoin the expenditures of all state education funds if the legislature failed to act by the deadline.

The Texas Legislature convened in its regular session in January 1991, but by the April 1 deadline it had not enacted a school finance plan. The next day Judge McCown held a hearing on several motions to modify the injunction to withhold state education funds. (The next distribution of state aid was scheduled for April 25.) In addition, the judge appointed Deputy State Education Commissioner Lynn Moak to be a court expert to update a school finance plan that had been prepared by court-appointed masters during the previous summer. Judge McCown set a hearing for Monday, April 15, 1991 (*Edgewood*, April 2, 1991).

With a new hearing date set and the possibility of an injunction to halt the distribution of state school funds, coupled with the reality of an alternative school finance plan developed by the court's appointee, the legislature finally approved House Bill 351, a school finance plan, on Thursday, April 11. The bill was signed into law by Governor Ann

Richards just 30 minutes before the court hearing on Monday, April 15.

The district court hearing set for April 15, 1991, was held as scheduled so that Judge McCown could review the status of the legislature's progress toward enacting a school finance law. Judge McCown ruled that he would presume the school finance plan to be constitutional and that he would allow state funds to be distributed to schools later in the month. As if to keep pressure on the legislature, which had not yet approved a revenue bill to fund the new finance plan, he refused to vacate the injunction on state aid and set September 1, 1991, as a deadline to give the respective parties time to review the plan and file appropriate motions if necessary. The school finance plan that had been prepared by Lynn Moak, the court-appointed expert, was not required to be filed with the court, but Judge McCown did order the plan to remain confidential ("McCown Okays School Funding," 1991).

If fully funded, the new law will increase state spending on public education by about $1.3 billion over the next two years. The plan contains two tiers: (a) a basic program and (b) an enrichment, debt-service, and facilities-funding tier. The new law is to be phased in over a four-year period. A key equalizing feature of H.B. 351 is the creation of 188 taxing districts whereby school districts are grouped mainly along county lines so that more students from poorer school districts will have access to a broader tax base ("Legislature Approves," 1991). The only problem is that the legislature has yet to appropriate revenues to fund the new school finance plan. During the 1991-1992 year, Texas faces a $4.7 billion revenue shortfall. It remains to be seen whether the legislature can grapple with the reality of a major tax bill to fund its school finance commitment. State leaders agreed to delay the state budget-writing process until a special legislative session scheduled for early July 1991 ("McCown Okays School Funding," 1991).

Within four days of Judge McCown's ruling that H.B. 351 was facially valid, the Board of Trustees of Carrollton-Farmers Branch Independent School District near Dallas voted to file a

suit against the state challenging the constitutionality of the
law. Apparently, other wealthy districts are likely to join the
suit. The target of the suit will be the 188 taxing districts created by H.B. 351. These units will collect local tax revenue
and redistribute it to school districts within the district,
thereby shifting local property taxes from the wealthy districts to the poorer districts. The attorney for Carrollton-
Farmers Branch ISD asserted that such redistribution of local
taxes violates a 1931 state supreme court decision, which
ruled that the Texas Constitution prohibits taking local tax
funds from one school district and spending them in another.
He questioned as well whether the new law meets the "one-
man, one-vote" requirement. Each school district within the
taxing district will be able to name one member to the govern-
ing board, thereby allowing small districts to have the same representation as larger ones ("Wealthy District," 1991, p. A-7).

Assessment and Conclusions

There are important and difficult issues facing Texas and its
education system. Perhaps the most important question to be
answered by the legislature in 1991 is whether sufficient state
funds will be appropriated to fully fund the new school finance legislation approved in April 1991. Moreover, there is a
serious question as to whether use of the 188 taxing districts
and the requirement that local taxes be redistributed within
those jurisdictions contravenes state constitutional law. The
answer to the first question will be determined in a special
legislative session in July 1991. The answer to the question
will await the inevitable legal strategy that follows the filing
of a lawsuit.

It appears increasingly likely that the student equity issue,
when defined in terms of fiscal disparities, cannot be rectified
without substantial political risks for state leaders. Conventional solutions are fraught with difficulties. Texas has 1,057
school districts and great disparities in local wealth when
measured by the assessed valuation of real property. Some

wealth-related disparity could be reduced by removing oil, gas, and minerals as well as public utility property from the local tax base. In a state that was founded on rugged individualism, such a move would be unthinkable. Furthermore, it would require a constitutional amendment to impose a state property tax on the property. Even if such wealth were removed from the local tax base and taxed by the state, wealth-related disparities would continue to exist because of the concentration of commercial and expensive residential property in many suburban school districts in the Dallas, Houston, and San Antonio metropolitan areas.

Without a doubt, new state revenue will need to be found to fund the finance plan in the face of a $4.6 billion state revenue shortfall for the next fiscal year. Texas could enact a tax on personal and corporate income as a way of generating additional state revenues to support schools as well as reducing reliance on local property taxes. The notion of an income tax is anathema to most traditional state politicians. Since the crash in oil prices in the mid-1980s, however, the idea of a state income tax has gained some credence in political circles and is supported by several political leaders including former Lt. Governor William Hobby and current Lt. Governor Bob Bullock, among others.

School districts could be consolidated to reduce wealth-related disparities, but there are effective limits to consolidation in the sparsely populated school districts in West Texas. School consolidation threatens the hallowed political credo of local control and, in some cases, the very survival of local communities.

The state could explore full-state funding, but that might entail a leveling down of school expenditures in the wealthy districts. Of course this is likely to occur anyway under the revenue limits imposed by H.B. 351 ("Legislature Approves," 1991). It is clear that the state will need bold new approaches to solving the fiscal equity issue.

Frankly, there is no end in sight to the protracted school finance litigation in Texas. School finance reform has been institutionalized in the state. The basic issues have become murky at best. Where the case began as a classic fiscal equity lawsuit, the Texas Supreme Court resolved it under the efficiency clause of the state constitution. It is likely to continue as a case of state versus local taxes and recapture. In the long run, the real issue may not be equity or efficiency or recapture but the adequacy of the educational programs provided the many, diverse students of Texas.

In addition to the sticky political thicket of school finance, the issue of political redistricting, which grows out of population gains in the state and intrastate population shifts, has captured legislators' attention in 1991. It is too early to predict with much certainty the precise configuration of the new legislative and congressional districts that will result from the 1990 census. It remains to be seen whether the new districts will reflect the growth in the minority population in Texas. State political observers are predicting that the three new congressional districts will be in Houston, Dallas, and the Rio Grande Valley, with the possibility that among the three new representatives will be two Hispanics (Houston and the Valley) and one African American (Dallas; G. Hunt, personal communication, April 22, 1991).

A related political boundary issue that is directly related to the increase in minority population is single-member electoral districts for school boards, county commissioner courts, and city government. Single-member districts have the capacity to profoundly change the nature of the political process in Texas school districts, cities, and counties. Minority representation is ensured under the single-member district concept.

The changes in the political landscape brought about by redistricting and single-member districts are not just recent phenomena related to population changes. In fact, what we are observing in Texas, as in many other states, is an expansion of the political gains made by minorities under the "one-man, one-vote" concept that began more than 20 years ago (G. Hunt, personal communication, April 22, 1991).

To a large extent, the election of Ann Richards as governor in 1990 signaled a change in Texas as she pledged to make the state more open to minorities and women. In her first appointment, Governor Richards named Ms. Lena Guerrero to the powerful Texas Railroad Commission that regulates the gas and oil industry in the state (Burka, 1991, p. 132). Ms. Guerrero has the double distinction of being the first woman and the first Hispanic appointed to the Railroad Commission. In April 1991 she was elected the commission's chair.

The voters of Texas in 1990 elected the first Hispanic attorney general, Dan Morales. Hispanic members have been elected to the State Board of Education. Indeed, the state board may be demonstrating an increased sensitivity to the increased bilingual school population by considering on second reading new regulations that would increase the number of bilingual students served by the public schools (Texas State Board of Education minutes, April 13, 1991).

As indicated in the previous section, the state school finance plan provides formula funds for special education, bilingual, and compensatory programs. The state also has increased its special grant funds for targeting at-risk students. Many of the issues cannot be dealt with by the public schools alone. It will take the collaborative and coordinated efforts of all state and local agencies to address the plethora of issues created by the changing demographics and socioeconomics of Texas. At this point, the state lacks a comprehensive and systematic approach to addressing the many issues it faces related to the changing demographics. It is clear to us that the state education system alone should not be expected to respond to the many challenges posed by the changes we described. The responsibility belongs to all the people of Texas through their elected state and local officials as well as to the many private organizations throughout the state.

In conclusion, there are three things that remain certain at the current time: (a) Texas is changing in terms of its population and other socioeconomic characteristics; (b) the education system will be affected by the changes but should not be expected to go it alone; and (c) the state needs leaders with vision and political courage to respond in creative and just ways to the challenges these changes bring.

References

Board approves $10 million plan to modify bilingual/ESL rules. (1991, April 29). *Texas Education News*. Austin.

Burka, P. (1991, May). Ann of a hundred days. *Texas Monthly*, pp. 126-134.

Census figures show state grew 19 percent during decade. (1991, January 26). (Lubbock) *Avalanche-Journal*, p. A7.

Children in poverty. (1990). *Educational Research Service Bulletin*. Arlington, VA: Author.

City posts rise in Hispanic population. (1991, February 6). (Lubbock) *Avalanche-Journal*, p. A1.

Edgewood Indep. School Dist. v. Kirby, No. 362516 (Travis County Dist. Ct., Tex. March 5, 1985; Plaintiffs's first amended petition).

Edgewood Indep. School Dist. v. Kirby, No. 362516 (Travis County Dist. Ct., Tex. Sept. 18, 1986; petition in intervention).

Edgewood Indep. School Dist. v. Kirby, No. 362516 (Travis County Dist. Ct., Tex. April 29, 1987; the court's statement and findings regarding the fundamental right of our citizens to a state-sponsored free public education).

Edgewood Indep. School Dist. v. Kirby, No. 362516 (Travis County Dist. Ct., Tex. June 1, 1987; final judgment).

Edgewood Indep. School Dist. v. Kirby, 777 S.W.2d 391. (Tex. Sup. Ct., 1989).

Edgewood Indep. School Dist. v. Kirby, No. 362516 (Travis County Dist. Ct., Tex. Sept. 24, 1990; judgment and opinion).

Edgewood Indep. School Dist. v. Kirby, No. D-0378 (Tex. Sup. Ct., Jan. 22, 1991; not yet reported), enforced sub nom. Edgewood Indep. School Dist. v. Anderson, No. 362516 (Travis County Dist. Ct., Tex. April 2, 1991).

Ethnic, racial diversity to challenge Texas Schools. (1990, August 27). (Lubbock) *Avalanche-Journal*, p. A7.

Frenship Independent School District. (1990). *1989-1990 annual performance report*. Wolfforth, TX: Author.

Kirby v. Edgewood Indep. School Dist., 761 S.W.2d 859 (Tex. Ct. Appeals, 1989).

Legislature approves funding measures. (1991, April 12). *The Legislative Report*. Austin, TX.

McCown okays school funding plan. (1991, April 19). *The Legislative Report*. Austin, TX.

Memorandum to school superintendents from Don Rogers, Superintendent of Eanes ISD regarding Edgewood v. Kirby. (1986, December 2).

Pay now or pay later to reach at-risk kids, demographer warns. (1990, September 18). *Education Daily*, p. 4.

Rodriguez v. San Antonio Indep. School Dist. 337 F. Supp. 280 (W.D. Tex. 1971).

Rodriguez v. San Antonio Indep. School Dist. 411 U. S. 1, 93 S.Ct. 1278, 36 L.Ed.2d 16 (1973).

School Finance Bill, 71st Leg., 6th C.S. ch.1. (1990). Texas Gen. Laws 1 (To be codified at TEX. EDUC. CODE Ann. 16.01 *et seq.*).

Southern Regional Education Board. (1989). *Trends: Education, employment, population—challenge 2000*. Atlanta: Author.

Sparkman, W. E., & Stevens, M. P. (1990). Commentary: Texas school finance system unconstitutional. *West Education Law Reporter, 57,* 333-339.

Texas Center for Educational Research Connection. (1991). *Growing up isn't easy.* Austin: Author.

Texas public school education: Preparing for the 21st century. (n.d.). A report to the 72nd Texas Legislature from the State Board of Education and the Texas Education Agency, Austin.

Texas State Board of Education Minutes 25-30. (1991, April 13). Agenda item no. 28.

U.S. Department of Education, Office of Educational Research and Improvement (1989). *Digest of educational statistics* (National Center for Educational Statistics). Washington, DC: Author.

Verstegen, D. A. (1985). *The lawmakers respond: Texas education finance reform (Part I) funding formulas—revisions and reviews.* Paper presented at the annual meeting of the American Education Finance Association.

Wealthy district contests school bill. (1991, 23 April). (Lubbock) *Avalanche-Journal,* p. A7.

Yudof, M., & Morgan, D. C. (1974). Texas—Rodriguez v. San Antonio Independent School District: Gathering the ayes of Texas—the politics of school finance reform. *Law and Contemporary Problems, 38*(3), 383-414.

EIGHT

Rapid Growth and Unfulfilled Expectations
PROBLEMS FOR SCHOOL
FINANCE IN FLORIDA

R. CRAIG WOOD

DAVID S. HONEYMAN

If one assumes that America in the future will consist of a
rapidly aging white population, a large but stable black population, a rapidly increasing, diverse and youthful Asian and
Hispanic population, a new blend of service and "high- tech"
jobs, rapid immigration from many nations, a declining base of
middle-class people of working age, transiency and crime,
environmental unreliability, contrasts in wealth, social systems
that cannot keep up with growth, exciting new social and
political innovations and the agony of unfilled expectations,
then Florida is the future of America, more than any other state.

H. L. HODGKINSON, p. 1

Financial support of Florida's 67 public school districts is the
largest single enterprise of the state. In fiscal year 1989-1990
the Florida legislature appropriated $6.63 billion to support
this activity, which accounted for approximately 41% of the

state's total general revenue budget. This amount was 53.8%
of the total $8.5 billion expenditures from all sources for Flor-
ida public school education, with local sources contributing
40% and federal sources slightly exceeding 6%.[1]

Currently Florida ranks as the third fastest growing state in
total population. Florida also has the second largest average
daily membership of public schools in the nation (National
Education Association [NEA], 1990, pp. 6, 11). More specifically, Florida is the eleventh most densely populated state and
seventh in terms of the percentage of the population residing
in metropolitan areas, yet 20% of public education students
reside in rural areas. Only 10 states have fewer school districts (U.S. Bureau of the Census, 1990, p. 21). Florida has
2,432 public school facilities ranking eighth, behind only California, Texas, Illinois, New York, Ohio, Pennsylvania, and
Michigan. Additionally, Florida has the largest elementary
and middle schools in the nation, although only Hawaii
averages more students per high school (NEA, 1990, p. 38). A
closer examination also reveals that Florida ranks last in the
nation in terms of revenue per pupil in average daily attendance and 46th in public school revenues per $1,000 of per-
sonal income. Florida possesses the 16th highest disposable
personal income per capita. Additionally in 1988, the last year
for which data are available, Florida is ninth in personal income per pupil in average daily attendance (NEA, 1990, p. 28).
Florida ranks eighth in total revenue while ranking sixth in
current expenditures (NEA, 1988, p. 7); however, in 1987-1989
Florida ranked 32nd in per capita expenditures for public education at $604 (U.S. Bureau of the Census, 1989, p. 140). His-
torically, various commentators have explained this low
ranking in per capita expenditure by the high percentage
of the elderly and the relatively low number of school-age
children.

In a state that has prided itself on the level of support and
the quality of its public education system, many educators are
beginning to refer to a new "crisis" in Florida education, a crisis that has resulted from excessive centralization of control at

the state level. The current financing plan for Florida's 67 local school districts can be described as restrictive rather than prescriptive. Over the years, political reactions to growth and development of the state's fragile economic base have resulted in decision making and accountability being vested almost entirely at the state level; and the state's school finance plan reflects this highly centralized approach to school control.

The obvious conclusion to be made from studying the relationship between school finance and the demographic changes that are occurring in this state is that, as growth continues and resources become increasingly scarce, decentralization of the decision-making process must be initiated. If resources were unlimited and if sufficient funding were available to support the educational needs of each child, the current system would be adequate. With limited funds, however, school district personnel must be permitted to deal creatively and effectively with the resources that are available. As the recent report of the Governor's Commission on Reforming Education in Florida (1990, p. 1) noted: "Flattening the hierarchial structure and placing greater authority at the local school level must involve both freeing local districts from excessive regulation and providing the incentive for local school management."

Financing Florida's Schools

Florida has a 150-year history of taxation in support of public education. Beginning with the School Law of 1849, control of the common school fund and its apportionment to the counties was vested with the Office of the Register of Public Lands (Shiver, 1982). As Article III, Section 2, of the state constitution specified, the tax was to be levied "in proportion to the quantity and value of taxable property owned by each [taxable inhabitant] ascertained, as far as possible, from the last state assessment role of the county" (Florida Laws of 1849, chap. 229). By 1868 county taxes accounted for 14% of school expenditures. This level grew significantly during the next 15 years until 1884 when the level exceeded 100%

(Shiver, 1982). From 1893 to 1924, the state share dropped from 23% to 5.5%, which placed excessive burdens on property-poor counties and school districts (Shiver, 1982). By 1926 the state share had dropped to 4%, and the inequalities in public education resulting from the decreased state support were noticeable. R. L. Johns (1976, p. 35) wrote:

> Glaring inequalities existed among counties of the state in revenue per pupil, in length of school terms for both white and Negro pupils and for Negro pupils as compared with white pupils in the same county, in female teachers' salaries as compared with male teachers' salaries, in elementary teachers' salaries compared with high school teachers' salaries, and in many other matters.

During the next 20 years, several amendments to the state constitution and several changes in state statutes resulted in minimum school terms, an apportionment scheme based on pupil-teacher ratio and average daily attendance, with an equalization provision based on school size and level (the instructional unit), creation of the Homestead Exemption for property, and reorganization into larger school districts. Through these years, increased funding for transportation, for sparsely populated areas, and for the introduction of instructional units for exceptional students was introduced into the formula (Shiver, 1982).

Major changes occurred in Florida school finance between the years 1945 and 1947. By 1944 the state share of revenue in support of public education had increased to approximately 45%, but the growth and development that occurred following the end of World War II created a surplus in state revenue. In reaction to these factors, the legislature addressed the issues of equal educational opportunity, wealth disparities existing within the state, and the need to increase state assistance to the several counties disadvantaged by the funding formula (Johns, 1976). Rapid growth and inadequate state support were emerging problems for the state. To avert the first statewide financial "crisis," the Minimum Foundation Program (MFP) was enacted in 1947.

The principal factor in the new MFP was an allocation system that determined support on basic instructional units, calculated by school population, the experience level of teachers, and the extent to which services were provided by the local district (Shiver, 1982). Further, conditions of the MFP included "an equalized local effort" requirement wherein "each county's percent of total taxpaying ability of the state was multiplied by the state total yield of a 6 mill tax and the product was the required local effort for the county" (Johns, 1976, p. 56). All formula calculations including teacher salaries by instructional unit for regular education, exceptional education, adult education, summer programs, supervision and administration, allotments for other expenses including art, music, physical education, and guidance, and capital outlay and debt service were included in the determination of the total instructional unit costs. Only the transportation allotment was outside this calculation. By 1948 the state share had grown to 55%.

During the period 1949 to 1968, total revenue from all sources grew from $96 million to $809 million, or from $337 per pupil to $1,562 per pupil in 1976 dollars (Johns, 1976). While the MFP remained basically intact, new revenue sources were developed as allotments increased and new programs, specifically school construction, were added. In 1949 a 3% sales tax was implemented to match the increasing costs of the MFP. In 1952 the automobile license tax proceeds were earmarked for the capital outlay allotment. In 1957, in addition to a special appropriation for school construction, the legislature passed the "County Sales Tax Fund" for school capital outlay. This legislation required the first $18 million in county sales tax collection to be deposited in the fund for school facilities to account for counties with "rapidly growing populations." By 1963 a constitutional amendment allowed the sale of bonds based on utilities' gross receipts tax to finance school construction (Johns, 1976).

This period of growth was also marked by increases in the value of property in the state. As retirees began to move to the Sunbelt, exclusive residential complexes developed, and the tourist industry emerged, property assessments grew and the legislature passed several laws restricting tax increases to certain millage caps. A "rollback" occurred in 1968 when the legislature placed a 10 mill per dollar limit on local taxes, 3 of which were required for participation in the MFP. In addition, the sales tax was raised to 4% to cover the state's share of the program.

The period from 1968 to 1973 was marked by several changes in the financial support for public schools. Although property assessments continued to increase, the millage caps prevented school districts from levying sufficient funds to match the growth in student population. In a special session of the Florida legislature, state support was increased from $341,575,000 in 1967 to $583,914,000 for the 1968-1969 school year (Johns, 1976). During the 1969 legislative session, additional laws were passed that allowed district voters to exceed the millage caps to provide for "district building and bus [needs], required debt service, and millage required for junior college minimum effort" (Florida Laws of 1969, chap. 236-251[31]). By the end of the 1972-1973 school year, the state had increased educational appropriations by almost $90 million and had implemented a state corporate income tax to pay the cost (Johns, 1976).

During the period 1970 to 1973, several studies were conducted on Florida's finance system. Given the changes that were occurring, including growth and development in the southern half of the state, the legislature adopted recommendations to guarantee that students have access to an equal educational program.

The new finance plan was titled the Florida Education Finance Program (FEFP), and several significant changes were enacted. The standard for computing the state allocation was changed from the instructional unit method to a weighted per pupil calculation based on cost calculations, including teacher salaries, for all aspects of the education of a child except transportation and several categorical programs. Weights were determined for 26 student programs in regular, adult, and special education. To address concern about the effect of local economic factors on the rapidly rising costs of educating students in several areas of the state, the sparsity correction factor of the MFP was abolished and a "cost of living differential" was included. This provision allowed for the adjustment of program weights for high-cost districts based on a comparison of living costs by county. Finally, to equalize local leeway funds (7 mills were required to participate in the FEFP with a local discretionary millage allowed such that the total could not exceed 10 mills), a "power equalized" model to guarantee the same dollar yield per mill was applied to funds in excess of the 7 mill requirement not to exceed the 10 mill maximum. By the end of the 1973-1974 school year, total revenue to public schools had exceeded $1.8 billion, almost 33% greater than 1972-1973 (Shiver, 1982).

In 1974 the equalized program for the discretionary millage between 7 and 10 mills was discontinued, and the median per pupil expenditure in the 10 poorest districts was 89.9% as much as that of the 10 wealthiest districts. While approximately $93 million in new money was made available to school districts, rising inflation and rapidly increasing costs in the state resulted in a $78 per pupil increase in constant dollars. In fact, per pupil revenue in constant dollars declined in 1975 as the legislature limited school boards to 8 mills total and included, but never funded, a sparsity adjustment factor (Johns, 1976).

Several social and economic issues emerged during the period 1976 to 1981 that resulted in changes to the FEFP. In 1976 rapid growth in the state stressed existing school facilities in many school districts. As a result, the first specified funds for school construction were allocated to districts lacking sufficient resources to meet immediate needs (Shiver, 1982). In 1977 an increasing number of "disadvantaged" children entering public schools resulted in the funding of compensatory education programs, and cost factors for alternative education and profoundly handicapped programs were added.

During this period, tax relief continued to be a major issue. In 1979 the legislature lowered the required millage rate from 6.4 mills to 5.15 mills and lowered the cap on total millage

allowed to 6.75 mills. In 1980-1981 a constitutional amendment increased the homestead exemption to $25,000 per
household. In both instances, the legislature appropriated
funds to cover anticipated revenue losses. Reacting to the
growth of the student population, however, especially in the
primary grades, where the legislature noted a need for "comprehensive improvement in public education for kindergarten
through grade three" (Florida Stat. of 1989, chap. 230, 2312),
as well as the increasing need for school facilities primarily in
the southern part of the state, the legislature authorized
school boards to levy an additional 2 mills for capital outlay.
Further, the legislature established and funded the Florida
Primary Education Program.

During the period 1981 to 1990, Florida experienced incredible growth and development. To promote educational reform
and assist school districts with increasing pressure for special
populations, several programs were enacted by the legislature. Program cost factors and weights continued as the heart
of the FEFP. By 1989 the number of cost calculations had
grown from the original 26 (in 1973) to 41. The growth in program classifications was the result of increased need to address special education, special need, and at-risk student
populations. For example, in 1983 calculations for full-time-
equivalent community college students also attending high
school was added, and in 1985 the severely emotionally disturbed (SED) handicapped program was expanded to the
multiagency services level. In 1986 the Florida Progress in
Middle Childhood Education Program (PRIME) extended the
programs to make them available to the middle grades.

The Dropout Prevention Act of 1986 was a reaction to
Florida's record number of school dropouts. This act established programs and determined costs for services designed
to meet the growing need for students disillusioned with
school. Programs were detailed to establish alternative educational opportunities specifically for teenage parents, disrup-
tive students, and substance abusers. Other sections of the bill
established youth services and funded in-service training for
teachers.

In addition to the growth of program cost factors in the FEFP, there was a major increase in the number of categorical/incentive programs and grants during this time. In 1981 there were nine categories of funding that were based on entitlements and funded outside of the equalization component of the FEFP. These included transportation, food services, community school programs, health education, bilingual education, and others. In 1981 grants for school volunteers and exemplary programs for gifted education were established as well as additional incentive-based categorical programs supporting writing skills programs in 1982. Grants to fund quality teaching and the state Master Teacher Program, programs of excellence in mathematics, science, and computer education, and science equipment and laboratories were enacted in 1983.

To strengthen both the PRIME—a middle-school program—and the Dropout Prevention Act of 1986, the legislature approved grants to qualified school districts for community-based dropout action programs and "minischool" incentives. These competitive grants were offered to communities with the highest dropout rates to design programs, including the establishment of separate "minischools," to meet the needs of this special student population. In addition, the legislature provided categorical funds for grade-level enhancement activities for middle schools that qualified for participation.

In 1987 the legislature approved categorical funding for the school resource officer program. In this legislation, one third of the start-up costs were provided by the state as matching funds to develop programs for cooperative programs with law enforcement and community agencies. In practice, this program was designed to assist districts to perform law enforcement functions within the school setting.

In 1989 four incentive grant and matching programs were established. The District School Site Restructuring Program was created to facilitate restructuring of Florida's school districts. A trust fund was created and funded by moneys received from the federal government as well as by public and private contributions. Following application to the commissioner of education, grants were awarded to districts based on a prorated share of the total funds available. The district share was calculated as the percentage of full-time-equivalent students in the district to the total number of full-time-equivalent students in the state.

In the same year, the First Start and prekindergarten early intervention programs were established. First Start was developed as a preschool handicapped and at-risk child program. Funding for this program was to be appropriated by the legislature and distributed according to a per child formula that considered the number of live births, the number of handicapped students receiving services, and the number of students eligible for free and reduced-price lunches each year. Likewise, the prekindergarten program was designed to meet the needs of at-risk children to increase a child's chances of achieving future educational success. In the first year of the program, 1990, $1 million was set aside to supplement the school transportation fund for prekindergarten children needing assistance. The general allocation formula for distribution of the remaining funds was as follows:

1/4 (the district percentage of the state 3- and 4-year-old children)
+
3/4 (the district percentage of the state's free lunch students).

Additional funds were available for distribution by the commissioner of education for "exemplary programs."

The fourth categorically funded program passed in 1989 was for accountability program grants. This program was funded from the proceeds of the state lottery. The intent of this legislation was to challenge each high school to develop programs to have students improve productivity as well as to develop measurable outcomes for student productivity. The allocation of funds was determined based on the district's and the school's achievement of statewide indicators. The expressed intent was to improve graduation rates, reduce the dropout rate, and increase enrollment in advanced science and mathematics courses. Funds were distributed according

to a formula that considered the number of goals met and enrollment in the high school. Grants ranged from $10,000 for a
small high school (fewer than 300 students) exceeding in four
state-level indicators to $75,000 for a large high school (more
than 2,000 students) achieving in six indicators.

Demographic and Fiscal Trends

Florida is a state with vast disparities of fiscal resources
and population centers. The state enjoys the uniqueness of
being the fourth largest state in the nation as well as one of
the fastest growing states. Florida's population of 12.7 million
is exceeded only by those of California with 27.6 million, New
York with 17.8 million, and Texas with 16.7 million. Florida is
projected to be the third most populous state by the year
2000.

Florida is truly unique in its development and the state policies that have emerged over the years. Florida has emerged
with this phenomenal growth only since World War II. As an
example of this growth, as late as 1948 there were only three
state-supported institutions of higher learning: Florida A&M
College, Florida Woman's College, and the University of Florida. Wood (1989) has observed that, if air-conditioning and
pesticides had not been invented, there would be serious
doubt whether Florida would have been able to emerge from
Third World status.

Florida's tax structure is based on funding from state sales
tax, corporate income taxes, and a host of user fees. The state
constitution does not allow for an income tax. Since World
War II, the state has embraced a public policy of low taxation.
This policy encouraged corporate development as well as
massive immigration. While low taxation served the state
well for the postwar years, the current picture yields totally
different results. Currently the state tax structure is one of
taxing consumers and users of services. The state derives its
income primarily from the general sales tax, with significant
revenues also coming from selective sales taxes.

Florida is funded, for all practical purposes, from the state's 6% sales tax. In fact, in 1988 Florida ranked fifth in general sales tax revenue per $1,000 of personal income. This elastic tax presents unique results in the absence of a state income tax. In fiscal 1990-1991 the state projected a collection of $7.4 billion in sales tax receipts. Inasmuch that the sales tax is a tax on consumption, in times of recession it will classically decline at a rapid rate. Florida has demonstrated this in that, during the period 1971 to 1990, the sales tax averaged 10.5% growth. Certain industries in Florida, however, most notably construction, have declined significantly in periods of recession, most notably in 1974-1975, suffering a 20.1% decline, and in 1982-1983 a 2.9% decline (Williams, 1990). These figures have a ripple effect on assessed valuations for school districts.

Currently local taxes are rising faster than state taxes. Local per capita taxes have risen 125% since 1980 as compared with state taxes that have risen only 88% during this same period of time. Total state and local taxes average $1,560 per resident. This must be judged in relation to the Florida per capita personal income of $17,694 for 1989.

Currently Florida's public school teachers are relatively average in terms of advanced training with 40% of the teacher work force possessing a master's degree or higher. Further, only 16% of this work force possess more than 20 years of teaching experience. The national average for advanced degrees is 44% with the national average of 21% of teachers having 10 or more years of experience. Florida ranks fourth in the nation as to the total instructional staff in public education for 1989-1990 (NEA, 1990). An examination of these data reveals that Florida ranks 28th in average salaries (NEA, 1990).

Population Growth

Since World War II the state population has grown by 413%, compared with the national growth of 71% (Sly, Serrow, & Calhoun, 1989). Florida's population growth is reflected, by decades, in Table 8.1.

Table 8.1 Florida Population Growth

Year	Population	Percentage of Increase
1950	2,771,000	—
1960	4,951,000	78.7
1970	6,791,000	37.2
1980	9,746,000	43.5
1990	13,264,000	36.1
2000	15,415,000	20.3
2010	17,530,000	13.7

SOURCE: Based on data from the University of Florida, Bureau of Economic and Business Research (1990a, 1990b).

From the fall of 1975 to the fall of 1985, public school enrollment remained relatively steady, with only a .7% increase. More specifically, elementary enrollment increased while secondary enrollment decreased for this period. During this same period of time, the number of classroom teachers increased by slightly over 22%, which resulted in an overall lowering of the student-teacher ratio by 3.7. The enrollment growth rate is projected to increase for public schools, however, as illustrated in Table 8.2. Using this methodology, only Arizona, California, Maryland, and New Mexico are projected to have a greater increase for 1991. In 1992 only Arizona, California, Nevada, New Hampshire, and New Mexico are projected to exceed Florida, while in 1993 only Arizona, Nevada, New Hampshire, and New Mexico are projected to exceed Florida.

Currently the state is receiving an average immigration of nearly 1,000 people per day. This projected growth, as reflected in Table 8.3, reflects growth of nearly 92% from immigration. The normal and net migration figures are shown in Table 8.3. These data reveal that approximately 79% of the population of the state were from outside of the state (Hodgkinson, 1988).

The concentration of the state's population is largely in the 22 standard metropolitan statistical areas, with 91% of the

Table 8.2   Florida Projected K-12 Enrollment Increases

Year	Percentage of Change From 1988
1991	7.1
1992	10.0
1993	13.0

SOURCE: Based on data from the U.S. Department of Education, Office of Educational Research and Improvement (1989, p. 15).

population. Nearly one third of the 67 counties grew by a population increase of more than 20% during the last five years. For example, between the years 1980 and 1989, Brevard County experienced a population increase of 56.4%. In terms of school districts, 14 districts project growth greater than 25% during the next five years.

Population by Age Groups

Florida has the oldest population in the country, with an average age of 36.4 compared with a national median age of 32.3. Florida ranks as the leading state with population over the age of 65 (17.8%). In fact, Florida grew at the seventh fastest rate for individuals over the age of 65. This over-65 category is projected to increase to 19.1% by the year 2000. Contrasted with these data is the projection of the school-aged population for the year 2000 at 16.3%. The school-aged population (5-17) is the seventh largest in the nation. As a percentage of the overall population, however, the school-aged population in Florida ranks 49th (NEA, 1990).

Racial and Ethnic Composition

Due to migration, the population of Florida has changed dramatically this century and in particular since World War II. Florida currently has the fourth largest Hispanic population in

Table 8.3 Florida Population Changes With Projection for Future Years

	1980/1981- 1984/1985	1985/1986- 1989/1990	1990/1991- 1999/2020
Percentage of net natural increase	11.58	13.23	8.25
Percentage of net migration total	88.42	86.72	91.75
Total numerical change	1,532,641	1,805,579	2,838,200

SOURCE: Based on economic and demographic research data from the Joint Legislative Management Committee of the Florida State Legislature (June 1989).

the nation. The Hispanic population is nearly 12% of the state's population. Thirty years ago, only 1.6% of the state's population was Hispanic. Hispanic migration has largely accounted for the increase of this segment of the population. Cuban immigration has occurred in three waves since 1959. Of more recent origin, large immigration from Haiti, Southeast Asia, and Central America has occurred. Since 1980 it is estimated that over 80,000 Nicaraguans, 125,000 Cubans, and 80,000 Haitians have settled in Dade County. Overall, due to immigration from Central and South America, the Hispanic population is projected to be mostly non-Cuban by the year 2000.

Current immigration patterns reveal a composition of more than 90% white. Thus, unlike Texas and California, Florida is not projected to become a "minority-majority" state (Hodgkinson, 1988). Birthrate data are revealing (NEA, 1990). The birthrate for nonwhites is approximately twice that of the white Florida population. Due to the overall numbers of white population, however, the data on current total birth numbers in Florida reflect that 73% of new births are white. Current projections reveal that the current 85% white population will constitute 83% of the population in the year 2000 (Florida Demographic Estimating Conference, 1989). Florida's birthrate data along racial lines are shown in Table 8.4

The state has attracted extremely large populations of individuals who most need state and local services. For example,

Table 8.4   Florida Birthrate by Race (per 1,000 population)

Year	White	Nonwhite
1980	11.5	24.5
1981	11.6	25.2
1982	11.9	25.2
1983	12.1	25.3
1984	12.3	24.7
1985	12.5	25.3
1986	12.5	24.2
1987	12.6	24.7

SOURCE: State of Florida (1986-1987, table E).

Florida has the largest percentage of the population over the age of 65 in the nation and thus the corresponding health care needs follow suit. It is interesting that the attraction of retirees to the state will result in the fact that, by the year 2000, the death rate will exceed the birthrate. Despite this fact, however, the overall rate of population growth is expected to continue.

Florida receives significant numbers of individuals from certain states. For example, Table 8.5 shows migration to Florida from the five states highest in terms of net migration.

School-Aged Populations

Of the massive numbers of immigration between 1975 and 1980, approximately 25% of the immigrants were under the age of 25 according to the U.S. Bureau of the Census. The composition of the Florida school-aged population is shown in Table 8.6.

Florida demographics present a unique situation for state policymakers. The public school population is currently the seventh largest in the nation. As a percentage of the total state population, however, the public school population in Florida is last in the nation. The school-aged population is projected to rise dramatically; however, the total state population is

Table 8.5 Net Migration to Florida From Five Selected States

Source State	1980-1982	1986-1988
New York	44,314	49,187
Michigan	21,112	10,958
Ohio	21,064	11,899
Illinois	20,010	12,774
New Jersey	18,920	22,416

SOURCE: Based on data from Fishkind (1990, p. 11).

projected to increase at a faster rate. The total school-aged population, ages 5-17, was 22.4% of the state population in 1989. It is projected to be 25.6% of the state population for the year 2000. The school-aged population in Florida reflects severe needs, as

> 30 percent of the youngest children in Florida are in poverty . . . 62 percent of children receive no preventive health care, 50 percent have no safe child care, and 90 percent of teenage mothers are not in school. It could be easily argued that half of all the children added to Florida's population are at risk of failure, socially, educationally and occupationally. (Hodgkinson, 1988, p. 9)

Although figures vary from year to year, the dropout rate after the ninth grade for the state averages approximately 40%, the highest in the nation. It has been observed that Florida is "sending one third of its youth into adult life without even the minimum benefits of a high school diploma" (Hodgkinson, 1988, p. 10). Florida has, with its recent efforts to increase educational standards, conceivably raised the dropout rate for the future. On the other hand, this unskilled labor force can be readily absorbed into Florida's service industries to support the state's reliance on the tourist trade.

Based on the latest available data, it is important to note that the State of Florida ranked 47th in current expenditures for public education in 1987-1988 per $1,000 of personal income

Table 8.6   Racial and Ethnic Composition of Florida Population
                Ages 0-17

Race	Florida (%)	United States (%)
White	62.52	70.20
Black	25.63	16.10
Hispanic	9.61	11.60
Other	2.24	2.00

SOURCE: Based on data from the U.S. Department of Health and Human Services (from Herrington et al., 1990).

(NEA, 1990). Despite significant demographic impacts, the state is not making a significant effort to support public education. Thus Florida's educational infrastructure will be severely strained to keep up with the projected increases. In 1987 the state had planned to construct 841 new educational facilities by 1998. The 1987-1988 rate of growth indicated 60,000 net student growth per year. The schools needed will cost an estimated $8 billion while the state has forecast a revenue of only $4 billion (Hodgkinson, 1988, p. 8).

It has been observed by many that the primary infrastructure problem for the future of Florida is the public education system. In Florida the public school system has been turned into a social service agency with all the advantages as well as the disadvantages. The population to be served by the Florida public educational system will continue to increase for the foreseeable future. This will no doubt place severe strains on local and state budgets. This is compounded by several notable pressures including the growing elderly population with the corresponding need for greater health care. This agenda must be viewed with the further need for more prisons and roads as well as the need to protect Florida's fragile environmental structure given the reality of rapid population growth. Perhaps an overall summary of the future was best expressed in an article appearing in *Florida Trend* in which the author wrote:

Today, Florida is arriving at the same point in the state's history that California reached 30 years ago. But Florida does not have the luxury of operating in the same economic and political climate, nor does it possess the same collective vision of its destiny. Florida will try to achieve its economic potential in an era of political and economic limits, and with a political tradition that emphasizes constraints instead of possibilities. . . . Florida sold itself for decades not as a place to build an economic future, but to enjoy the benefits of an economic past. (Fulton, 1990, p. 45)

Note

1. The statistical data in this chapter were derived from a number of sources. Federal sources include the U.S. Bureau of the Census and the U.S. Department of Education. Florida sources include the Florida Legislature, the Office of the Governor of Florida, and the University of Florida.

References

Fishkind, H. H. (1990, August). Population growth takes a new path. *Florida Trend*, p. 11.

Florida Demographic Estimating Conference. (1989, March). *Conference report.* Tallahassee: Office of the Secretary of the Florida Senate.

Florida Laws of 1849, chap. 229.

Florida Laws of 1969, chap. 236-251[31].

Florida Stat. of 1989, chap. 230.2312.

Fulton, W. (1990, September). California, here we come. *Florida Trend, 33,* 39-45.

Governor's Commission on the Reforming Education in Florida. (1990). *Reforming education in Florida.* Tallahassee: Author.

Herrington, C., Cobbe, L., Leslie, D. (1990). *Conditions of education.* Tallahassee: Center for Policy Studies.

Hodgkinson, H. L. (1988). *Florida: The state and its educational system.* Washington, DC: Institute for Educational Leadership.

Johns, R. L. (1976). *The evolution of the equalization of educational opportunity in Florida, 1926 to 1976.* Gainesville: University of Florida, Institute for Educational Finance.

Management Committee of the Florida State Legislature. (1989, June). *Economic and demographic research.*

National Education Association. (1988). *Estimates of school statistics, 1988-89.* Washington, DC: Author.

National Education Association. (1990). *Rankings of the states, 1990*. Washington, DC: Author.

Shiver, L. (1982). *A historical review of the development of Florida's school finance plan and the fiscal equalization effects of the Florida Education Finance Program.* Unpublished doctoral dissertation, University of Florida, Gainesville.

Sly, D. F., Serrow, W. J., & Calhoun, S. (1989). Migration and the political process in Florida. *Florida Public Opinion, 4,* 8-12.

State of Florida. (1986-1987). *Florida vital statistics.* Tallahassee: Author.

University of Florida, Bureau of Economic and Business Research. (1990a). *Florida statistical abstract.* Washington, DC: Government Printing Office.

University of Florida, Bureau of Economic and Business Research. (1990b). *A portrait of America.* Washington, DC: Government Printing Office.

U.S. Bureau of the Census. (1989). *Statistical abstract of the United States.* Washington, DC: Government Printing Office.

U.S. Bureau of the Census. (1990). *Statistical abstract of the United States.* Washington, DC: Government Printing Office.

U.S. Department of Education, Office of Educational Research and Improvement. (1989). *State projections to 1993* (National Center for Education Statistics; CS 89-638). Washington, DC: Government Printing Office.

Williams, D. R. (1990, July). The sales tax roller coaster. *Florida Trend, 33,* 15.

Wood, R. C. (1989, March). *Florida school finance.* Paper presented at the meeting of the American Education Finance Association, San Antonio, TX.

NINE

Demography, Diversity, and Dollars
RETHINKING SCHOOL FINANCE
POLICY IN CALIFORNIA

JULIA E. KOPPICH

California, the nation's most populous state, offers a pan-
orama of breathtaking geography and unparalleled diversity.
It is a state of cosmopolitan cities, sprawling suburbs, desert
expanses, vast tracts of farmland, and rural communities
tucked away in valleys or nestled against mountains. The
state cherishes its time-honored reputation as bold, dy-
namic—and sometimes a little kooky. California's annual
budget of $55 billion is larger than the revenue and expendi-
ture plans of many nations. California is a window on a
changing world. The state's exploding demographics are profoundly affecting public policy. Housing, transportation,
health, and education are all being shaped and reshaped by a
changing and expanding population.

California schools are being called upon to educate a growing
number of children with whom they historically have not been
successful—the poor, minorities, and limited- and non-English

speaking. Moreover, as the eminent sociologist James S. Coleman (1987, p. 32) recently has written,

> Families at all economic levels are becoming increasingly ill-equipped to provide the setting that schools are designed to complement. . . . The implications for schooling are . . . extensive, for school as we conceive of it implies family as we conceive of it.

School finance policy in California is complicated by the sheer size of the school population, the rate at which it is growing, the nature of the incoming students, and the range of "nonschool" problems they bring with them.

This chapter suggests that traditional notions of school finance need to be reconceptualized if students are to be given the best chance to succeed. School finance, in other words, must be viewed through a different policy lens. The funding streams and expenditure categories that conventionally drive kindergarten through grade 12 education need to be rethought in light of the myriad "nonschool" problems students carry with them when they walk through the schoolhouse door. In short, this chapter proposes expanding *school finance* to *education finance,* a broader term designed to encompass a host of issues and conditions that directly affect students' ability to be successful in school. This article is, admittedly, a policy piece. It is likely to disappoint readers searching for neat economic formulas or new econometric designs to improve school financing. The purpose of this chapter is to prompt discussion about and rethinking of the policy parameters of school finance. The context in which this change will be considered is California. It is hoped, however, that the ideas offered and issues raised also will have wider applicability to other states.

The chapter begins with a brief description of California's population. It then proceeds to a more comprehensive statistical exploration of the state's children. Next, school finance policies in California are outlined, and other social services for children, and their funding mechanisms, are described.

The final sections of the chapter attempt to paint a picture of the emerging politics of education finance in California and offer some concluding thoughts about rethinking school finance policy.

Demographic Revolution in the Golden State

California is by far the nation's most populous state. The latest estimates by the state's Department of Finance indicate that California's population of 30 million far exceeds that of its nearest population neighbor, New York, with a population of approximately 17.6 million ("State Says Population Is 30 Million," 1990). Large as these numbers are, population statistics mask the drama of swiftly evolving racial, ethnic, and cultural changes that are transforming the state. Economic expansion may have altered the physical face of California, but by far the greatest social and economic changes in the past decade have been wrought by foreign immigration. California is the entry point for nearly 28% of all immigrant Americans. Large numbers of these individuals settle permanently in the state.

As described in the British journal, *The Economist,* in a lengthy 1990 article on California:

The port city of Long Beach, once known as "Iowa by the sea," is now home to 40,000 Cambodians. Daly City outside San Francisco, once a mostly white, blue collar town, is now called "Little Manila" because of its large Filipino population. Fresno, a farming town in the Central Valley, has become home to 300,000 Hmong, a Laotian hill tribe. A stretch of shops and malls between Garden Grove and Westminster in Orange County [in Southern California] conjures up a vision of what Saigon might look like if it were lucky enough to enjoy American-style influence. Some 80,000 Vietnamese refugees live in the area and thousands more visit it at weekends to shop and socialize. Los Angeles' Hispanic barrio, the destination of a flood of Latin American immigrants, has spread far beyond its traditional core in the east side of the city out to a string of suburban towns. ("American Survey," 1990, p. 27)

A January 1991 lead news story in the *San Francisco Chronicle* proclaimed "breathtaking population changes [which] have spawned an ethnically diverse California in which minorities make up 43 percent of the state's population" (McLeod, 1991). Diversity then is a fact of life in California, and it is reshaping the state's social, political, and economic landscape.

Immigrants bring much with them to their new home. They bring their language, their culture, their hopes and dreams— and they bring their children.

California's Children

More than 7.5 million children currently live in California. More than 8.7 million children are expected to reside in the state by the year 2000. It is not surprising that California's children represent a substantial portion of the nation's minority child population. Recent estimates suggest that Hispanic children in California constitute approximately one in three (35%) of all Hispanic children living in the United States. Children in California of Asian and Pacific Islander descent constitute one in three (30%) of all Asian children nationwide. Within a decade California's child population will be 42% white, 36% Hispanic, 13% Asian, and 9% black (Kirst, 1989). California's public school population mirrors that of the state. Increasing diversity and skyrocketing enrollments are providing the schools with a host of unanticipated challenges.

California Schools, California Students

California maintains 7,358 public schools in 1,010 school districts. Districts range in size from the Fluornoy Elementary District—total enrollment 8—in Tehama County in the northern section of the state, to the giant Los Angeles Unified School District with more than 600,000 students.

More than 4.75 million students—one out of every eight students in the United States—are enrolled in California's public schools. In 1989-1990, 44% more students attended school in California than in Texas. Almost 86% more students were enrolled in California schools than in New York's public schools.

Enrollments are growing by geometric proportions. Nearly 150,000 more students were enrolled in California public schools in 1989-1990 than in the previous year. The state's school enrollment is growing at a rate four times the national average. Stated another way, California's annual public school enrollment growth is equal to the total enrollment of the state of Montana. By 1995 California's school enrollment will equal the total combined enrollments of the nation's 24 smallest states. During the 1990s, 610 new students will be added to California public school rolls every day, including weekends and holidays. Enrollments are now expected to grow each year across all grade levels, kindergarten through grade 12. The average annual growth rate is projected to be 225,000 students. The coming decade's enrollment expansion will total nearly 2.25 million students. In other words, a decade from now, California public schools will be serving nearly 50% (46.7%) more students than they are serving currently. By the year 2000, California public school enrollments are expected to top the 7 million mark.

California schools already are a "majority minority." One out of every six students was born in another country. In 1979-1980, 60% of students enrolled in California public schools were white; one quarter were Hispanic. A decade later, in 1989-1990, fewer than half (46%) of the state's public school students are white, and almost one third are Hispanic. An additional 10% are Asian and Filipino; 8.5% are black. By 1997-1998 Hispanic enrollments are expected to reach or exceed 40% of the total and surpass that of whites. More than 860,000 California students were limited English proficient (LEP) in 1989-1990, an increase of 16% over the previous year.

During the last half decade, the number of LEP students has grown nearly four times as fast as enrollments generally. California's LEP population equals the total school enrollments of 37 other states. In the primary grades (kindergarten through grade 3), one California student in four is limited English proficient; in the middle grades (4-8), one student in six is not facile in English; in high schools (grades 9-12), one student in eight has not mastered English.

Despite valiant efforts on the part of a large cadre of professional educators, California's public schools educationally shortchange significant numbers of both native-born and immigrant students. One third of all students drop out before graduating from high school. Nearly half of all black students (48%), and an equally unacceptably large number of Hispanic students (45%), fail to complete the twelfth grade. Of those students who do graduate, inadequate numbers go on to higher education, and too few sufficiently are prepared to enter an increasingly competitive, technologically demanding world of work.

Completing the Picture of California's Children

In March 1989 Policy Analysis for California Education (PACE), an independent education research center located in the schools of education at the University of California at Berkeley, Stanford University, and the University of Southern California, published an exhaustive research study focusing on the lives of California's children. PACE had come to believe that an improved analysis of education required an enhanced understanding of the environmental factors that affect children's ability to be successful in school. The results of PACE's study, *Conditions of Children in California* (Kirst, 1989), were disturbing.

PACE found that, in the two decades between 1969 and 1989, the number of children in poverty in California had doubled. Nearly one quarter of California's children (23%) live below the federally established poverty level. The state, which once ranked below the national average in terms of the number of children living in poverty, now ranks at about the national average on this dimension. The majority of California's poor (52%) are working poor who receive no public assistance. California has witnessed an alarming increase in the number of extremely vulnerable children. At least 15% of babies born in big city public hospitals are drug or alcohol addicted. While no one knows precisely what the prognosis is for these children, it is certain that their educations will be costly and complicated.

Changing family and work patterns evident on a national scale are reflected in California, where the Ozzie and Harriet family of the 1950s or the Brady Bunch family of the 1960s are more the exception than the rule. Divorce rates in the state have doubled since 1960. One third of all California's children will experience parental divorce before age 16. One in four of California's children is born to an unmarried mother. More than half of all black children are born to single mothers. Almost half of all single mothers and their children live at or below the poverty level. California ranks seventeenth among the states in infant mortality, second in rates of adolescent pregnancy, and first in the rate of juvenile incarceration (Smith, 1989). Many children have inadequate health care, never see a dentist, and are left to care for themselves for long hours while their parents are at work.

More statistics could be recited, but the message conveyed would be the same. For many children in California, life outside school creates pressures and demands so intense that academic achievement in school suffers.

Funding Schools, Financing Children's Services

Conventional discussions of school finance focus on policy levers designed to enhance educational productivity and fiscal measures crafted to improve educational efficiency. Rarely do these conversations include consideration of the non-education services required by increasing numbers of children. Funding schools and financing other social services for children in California are retained as separate fiscal and policy domains.

School Finance in California

California's system of financing its public schools is a complicated amalgam of state-determined general aid limits, categorically funded special needs programs, voter-enacted initiatives, court mandates, and constitutional amendments. The lexicon of California school finance is sprinkled with references to *Serrano,* Proposition 13, Proposition 98, the Gann limit, and the California lottery.

Curiously, a state that prides itself on local control has evolved a system of school finance in which the state calls most of the fiscal shots. Of the $24.9 billion California committed to K-12 public education in 1990-1991, approximately 64% ($15.9 billion) was provided by the state. Local property taxes contributed another 21% ($5.1 billion), federal revenues slightly more than 7% ($1.77 billion), and the state lottery provided somewhat less than 3.5% ($0.8 billion) of the total.

More than $4 billion in earmarked education dollars are spent on categorical programs, the largest of which is special education, carrying a 1990 price tag of $1 billion. Restrictions placed on local generation of new revenues also have shifted the burden of financing new school construction to the state. California currently has a $10 billion backlog in approved school construction projects.

Finally, California is attempting to implement a number of education reform measures. Senate Bill 813, the state's omnibus education reform act of 1983, "pumped" $1 billion a year for each of four years into the state's fiscally sagging school system. Reform measures of lesser magnitude and less cost have followed S.B. 813.

Given current projections of enrollment growth and inflation, California public school revenues will need to increase on average $3 billion each year just to keep even. Yet, despite the seemingly generous dollar investment in education, on most national fiscal comparisons, California ranks below the national average. For example, California's education spending as a percentage of personal income is less than the national average and has been so each year for the last decade. California in 1989-1990 spent 4% of its income on public schools; nationally, the figure was 4.6%.

California's per pupil expenditures also are less than the national average and significantly less than other large, industrialized states. California spends nearly $4,000 less per pupil than New York, $1,600 less per pupil than Pennsylvania, $1,000 less per pupil than Michigan, and $800 less per pupil than Illinois.

A series of court decisions and voter actions have fashioned for California a unique—and perhaps uniquely complicated— school finance system. The first in this series of factors that contribute to California's crazy quilt pattern of school finance is a landmark equity decision, *Serrano v. Priest*.

Serrano v. Priest

The California Supreme Court in 1971 ruled that the state's system of financing its public schools violated the equal protection clause of the California and U.S. constitutions. The court, in the case *Serrano v. Priest* (John Serrano was the plaintiff, Ivy Baker Priest was California's state treasurer), declared that the state school finance system, which relied principally on property taxes, made the quality of a child's education dependent on the wealth of his or her parents and his or her neighbors. This system, decreed the court, discriminated against poor children, was unconstitutional, and would have to be revamped.

The court subsequently ruled that differences in school spending for basic educational services among California's more than 1,000 school districts should be reduced to less than $100 per pupil and could not be wealth related. The legislature was given five years to comply with the court's ruling.

The California legislature's response to the *Serrano* decision was S.B. 90. This statute established state-specified revenue limits that, for each school district, would determine the amount of money available for basic educational programs. Under the state's formula, high-wealth, and therefore high-spending, districts would be entitled to lower annual revenue increases than would low-wealth, low-spending school districts. Over time this system was expected to equalize between-district spending.

S.B. 90 was modified in 1977 by Assembly Bill 65, designed to achieve "substantial compliance" with the *Serrano* decision. The result was a highly equalized school finance system. As of 1990, 95.1% of all students in the state fell within the court-determined per pupil expenditure equalization standard.

Proposition 13

Formally known as the Jarvis-Gann Tax Limitation Initiative, Proposition 13 represented the first major salvo in California's taxpayers' revolt. Approved by voters in 1978, Proposition 13 limited property taxes to 1% of 1975-1976 assessed market value. The initiative also limited assessment increases to no more than 2% each year, allowed property to be reappraised only upon sale or transfer of ownership, prohibited state and local governments (including school districts) from enacting new property taxes, and required a two-thirds vote of the state legislature to increase state taxes.[1]

Proposition 4: The Gann Limit

Californians' appetite for tax reform was not satiated by Proposition 13. In 1979 the citizens enacted Proposition 4, the Gann spending limitation. The Gann limit restricts growth in spending to the rate of increase of the state's population and the lower of the U.S. Consumer Price Index or California Personal Income. In another words, state spending growth is pegged to changes in population and inflation. The measure requires that any unexpended dollars be returned to taxpayers.[2]

The California Lottery

Following the enactment of Proposition 13 and the Gann spending limit, available school revenues were insufficient to meet the demand for education dollars. Tax increases seemed politically out of the question. A new money-raising scheme did not. In 1984 California voters enacted the lottery, whose slogan boasts, "Our schools win, too." A minimum of 34% of the revenue from lottery sales is contributed to public schools and colleges. The lottery, however, has not been the fiscal boon its proponents promised. It contributes barely 3.5% to state education coffers. Moreover, lottery revenues have declined in real terms during the past three years. While the total lottery "take" has remained stable, increasing enrollments have required that the same number of lottery dollars be spread among larger numbers of students. The lottery provided about $171 per pupil in 1988-1989. That amount dropped to $160 per pupil in 1990-1991.

Proposition 98

Four years after the adoption of the lottery, with school budget needs burgeoning and education revenues declining, California school finance politics and policy reached a new crescendo with Proposition 98. Adopted in November 1988, this state constitutional amendment was the brainchild of powerful education interests, led principally by State Superintendent of Instruction Bill Honig and the California Teachers Association (CTA), the state's NEA affiliate.

Proposition 98 guarantees to K-14 education a funding base approximately equal to 40% of state general fund revenues. In other words, before preschool or higher education (except community colleges) receive their share of the state budget, before health care, welfare, or the criminal justice system receive their piece of the state economic pie, K-12 education is awarded its 40%. Advocates of Proposition 98 assured supporters that the constitutional amendment would stabilize school funding and provide a steady and increasing stream of funds for education programs. But Proposition 98 did not solve the schools' fiscal problems. Although spending increased $1.6 billion between 1988-1989 and 1989-1990, real expenditures per pupil declined by 1.5% (Picus, 1990). Nonetheless, however the dollars distributed themselves, Proposition 98 became the ceiling for school funding.

Proposition 98 did not insulate school finance from politics. Rather, this constitutional amendment highlighted education politics. As a subsequent section of this chapter will demonstrate, Proposition 98 became the eye in a storm of controversy surrounding financing public services. Suffice it here to say that the governor, faced with a huge budget deficit, sought legislative concurrence to suspend Proposition 98, reduce education's anticipated revenue, and redistribute some of the earmarked education dollars to other social services.

Confusion over appropriate school finance mechanisms in California is compounded by recent evidence that suggests that the public is of two minds on this matter. A PACE public opinion poll, conducted in January 1991, indicates that a majority of Californians still believe schools are underfinanced. In fact, most are persuaded that lack of proper financial support is the most significant problem facing the schools. The state's citizens are not willing to have their taxes—especially their property taxes—increased, however, so schools can realize more revenue. Less than a third of those polled said they would be willing to have their taxes raised. Less than a fourth responded favorably to the possibility of increasing property taxes for this purpose.

"Nonschool" Social Services for Children

Beginning in the mid-1960s, the federal government enacted a series of new programs designed to address the problems of the nation's poor, including children living in poverty. Many of these new policy thrusts were part of President Lyndon Johnson's Great Society and the War on Poverty. New programs were authorized and established in the areas of health, education, and welfare. Poverty was used as a bench mark for federal financial assistance.

This broad expanse of policy initiatives was part of a new national agenda. In effect, the federal government crafted social goals for the nation through the creation of new federally funded categorical programs. These new policy initiatives also laid a foundation for a new conceptual premise, namely, that the purpose of government was not simply to ensure against economic loss (as had been the thrust of New Deal programs) but to promote social as well as economic gain (Anton, 1989).

California's response to the Great Society programs of the 1960s was to implement services targeted to children and their families. Categorical programs were established in child health, child welfare, protective services, compensatory education, and alcohol and drug abuse prevention. Each program and service was funded and administered separately from any other program and service. California's program-by-program, service-by-service policy approach failed to consider the cumulative effects of these programs on a child's life. Social services were applied to a child much as a Band-Aid to a wound. Diagnosis of a child's overall needs rarely was undertaken. Some children were fortunate enough to receive the appropriate mix of services; some were not. The one "treatment" nearly all children received was education.

California's categorical policy and fiscal approach to children's services has changed little in three decades. The state currently maintains, in addition to education, 169 children- and youth-serving programs that are overseen by 37 state entities located in seven different departments.

Despite the interdependence of children's needs, state-level fiscal and social policy is crafted as if each life situation a child faces is independent of any other. Children's needs are broken down into artificial program boundaries that coincide with major institutions and entities, such as schools, counties, and service agencies, rather than with the overall needs of children. Services are defined by administrative boundaries and conceptions of professional turf (Kirst & McLaughlin, 1990). Monetary incentives for interagency cooperation are nonexistent; disincentives often actively are at work.

Separate funding streams flow to and from this complicated maze of children's services. Some of the Byzantine fiscal arrangements that shape education finance affect the financing of other services. For example, the limited taxing power of local government imposed by Proposition 13 has shifted the burden of financing most local government services—including social services for children—to the state. Financing schools and funding other social services for children in California historically has been a classic case of fiscal and policy dimensions rarely coinciding. The stage may, however, have been set for a shift in direction.

The Emerging Politics of Education Finance in California

By the time Pete Wilson was elected California's governor in November 1990, it had become abundantly clear that the state faced a monumental budget deficit. Revenue shortfall estimates climbed from $6 billion to $8 billion to $10 billion and seemed to continue to increase by another billion dollars each day. Adopting what he called a "share the pain" philosophy, the governor proposed slashing major social service programs, eliminating cost-of-living allowances for remaining programs, and suspending Proposition 98.

The governor also began publicly to broaden the policy and fiscal focus of children's services. The state's chief executive position had been occupied for a quarter of a century in California by a series of governors for whom education policy and children's issues were of minor political importance. Pete Wilson had made children's issues—specifically integrating and coordinating social services for children—a centerpiece of his electoral campaign. Citing swiftly changing demographics and referring often to "non-school" problems that frequently went untended, Wilson pledged that, if elected, he would focus policy attention on ensuring more adequate provision of children's services.

Once elected, Governor Wilson began to make good on this campaign promise. He created a new cabinet-level position, Secretary for Child Development and Education, and appointed the former president of the California School Boards Association to fill it. Despite the state's grim fiscal outlook, the governor also proposed nearly $200 million in new and expanded policy initiatives for children and families in areas such as prenatal care, family planning services for unmarried teens and substance-abusing women, expanded preschool programs, a Healthy Start program to assist local school districts to integrate and coordinate health and social services for children, mental health counseling in elementary schools, and an expanded screening program to detect developmental delays in kindergartners and first graders. The money to pay for these services, under the governor's proposal, was to come partially from the dollars that would not flow directly to education if Proposition 98 were suspended.

The 1991 budget battle in California shaped up largely as a political contest between education interests, who wanted to preserve Proposition 98, and advocates of other children's services, who wanted to ensure that their programs were not gutted. Of course political issues never are quite that simple. The state needed additional revenue. Democrats gingerly proposed increased taxes. The Republican governor suggested minor "revenue enhancement measures." Republican legislators bridled at the possibility of higher taxes. Interested readers of this chapter know, or can learn, the outcome of California's budget drama. At this writing, education financing and funding for other social services for children are at political odds and locked in the state's fiscal vice.

Some Thoughts on
Rethinking School Finance Policy

In California, unlike in many other states, between-district school finance equity is largely a settled issue. California has, however, evolved a system in which the state dominates the financing of public services. Primarily state dollars "buy" education, health, welfare, and other services. Increasingly in California, children require a range of human services. They need this assistance, in part, to be able to take full advantage of the opportunities available to them in school. Yet in California the tradition of maintaining separate policy and funding streams for education and other children's services often produces the unintended consequence of rendering needed services inaccessible or unavailable to children and their families.

California in a sense provides a laboratory for the nation. The state represents a dramatic demonstration of the clash of exploding demographics, mushrooming social needs, faltering economics, and partisan politics. What lessons can be learned from the California experience?

California's situation presents both a challenge and an opportunity. The challenge is to find adequate dollars from all available sources—local, state, and federal—to fund education and other children's services. But there also is an opportunity, namely, to reconsider traditional school policy parameters and conventional school finance boundaries.

This chapter has asserted that the time has come to fashion a new social policy for children. New policy solutions should be crafted to match emerging problems. This entails moving away from rigid, unexamined policy categories and considering conventional and unconventional funding stream linkages. Policy solutions should drive expenditure patterns. In other words, there is a need to find the appropriate policy nexus between school services and other related social services. Within this new set of policies would "nest" appropriate fiscal mechanisms. Beginning to think of *school* finance as *education* finance may be the first crucial step in this process.

Notes

1. While Proposition 13 prevents school districts from levying taxes, taxes can be applied to parcels (square feet of living space) if two thirds of the voters approve. Of 102 parcel tax elections conducted, only 38 have been successful.

2. In 1990 state voters would approve Proposition 111, which increases the Gann limit.

References

American survey: The great society returns. (1990, January 13). *The Economist.*
Anton, T. J. (1989). *American federalism and public policy: How the system works.* Philadelphia: Temple University Press.
Association of California Administrators. (1990). *Student diversity in California's schools* (Report of Student Diversity Task Force). Burlingame, CA: Author.
Categorical aid for California school. (March, 1990). Menlo Park, CA: EdSource.
Coleman, J. S. (1987). Families and schools. *Educational Researcher.*
Goren, P. D., & Kirst, M. W. (1989). An exploration of county expenditures and revenues for children's services. Berkeley: Policy Analysis for California Education (PACE).
The governor's budget for 1991-91. (1991, February). Menlo Park, CA: EdSource.
Guthrie, J. W., Kirst, M. W., Odden, A. R., et al. (in press). *Conditions of education in California 1990.* Berkeley: Policy analysis for California Education (PACE).
Hodgkinson, H. (1989). *The same client: The demographics of education and service delivery systems.* Washington, DC: Institute for Educational Leadership.
Jansan, J. E. (1983). The case of intergovernmental relations: Values and effects. In E. F. Zigler (Ed.), *Children, families, and government: Perspectives on American social policy.* New York: Cambridge University Press.
Kagan, S. (1990). Readiness 2000: Rethinking rhetoric and responsibility. *Phi Delta Kappan, 72,* 372-378.
Kirst, M. W. (1989). *Conditions of children in California.* Berkeley: Policy Analysis for California Education (PACE).
Kirst, M. W., & McLaughlin, M. W. (1990). *Rethinking children's policy: Implications for educational administration.* Bloomington: Indiana University, Consortium on Educational Policy Studies.
Koppich, J. E. (1990, October). *Lines of authority, levels of responsibility: The perspective of the state in children's policy.* Paper presented at the meeting of the American Association for Public Policy Analysis and Management, San Francisco.
McLeod, R. G. (1991, February 26). The challenge posed by state's ethnic mix. *San Francisco Chronicle.*
The melting pot boils over. (1990, October 13). *The Economist.*
Odden, A. R. (1990). *The changing contours of school finance.* San Francisco: Far West Laboratory for Education Research and Development.

Office of the Governor, State of California. (1991, January). *The governor's budget: An agenda for children and families*. Sacramento: Author.

Picus, L. O. (1990). *California school finance*. San Francisco: Far West Laboratory for Education Research and Development.

Powell, D. R. (1990, October). *Parents as the child's first teacher: Opportunities and constraints*. Paper prepared for the U.S. Department of Education, Office of Planning, Budget, and Evaluation.

School finance, 1990-91. (1990, September). Menlo Park, CA: EdSource.

Serrano v. Priest, 96 Cal. Rptr. 601, 437, P.2d. 1241 (1971).

Smith, K. T. (1989). Providing services to children in need. In *California Policy Choices*. Los Angeles: University of Southern California, School of Public Administration.

Smrekar, C. (n.d.). *Governmental organization: The impact on the delivery of children's services*. Unpublished manuscript, Policy Analysis for California Education, Berkeley, CA.

State says population is 30 million tomorrow. (1990, September 8). *San Francisco Chronicle*.

Sundquist, J. L. (1968). *Politics and policy: The Eisenhower, Kennedy, and Johnson years*. Washington, DC: Brookings Institution.

U.S. Department of Education. (1988). *Youth indicators 1988: Trends in the well-being of American youth*. Washington, DC: Author.

Zill, N., & Wolpow, E. (1990, October). *To provide preschool programs for disadvantaged and disabled children to enhance their school readiness: Background paper on a national educational goal*. Paper prepared for U.S. Department of Education, Office of Planning, Budget, and Evaluation, Washington, DC.

TEN

Population Shifts
and Policy Changes
EFFECTS ON SCHOOL
FUNDING IN ILLINOIS

G. ALFRED HESS, JR.

Unlike Florida and California, where enough new students enter the state's schools to establish a new school every week, Illinois is, demographically, in something of a steady state. Following rapid population growth for nearly a century, Illinois has entered a period of very moderate, almost negligible, growth. From 1880 to 1970, decennial census figures showed the population of the state increasing at an average rate of 895,000 per decade, with total population growing from 3.1 million to 11.1 million. Had it not been for the slow growth during the Depression decade (population increased by only 261,000 during the 1930s), decennial growth rates would have averaged more than 1 million. During this period, the population of the state more than tripled. But since 1970 growth has slowed significantly, and projections[1] indicate it will take 40 years to add another million residents. The population of the state as a whole has achieved a virtual "steady state."

It would be a mistake, however, to conclude there was no change occurring in the steady state of Illinois. While the total population numbers are relatively stable, the population within the state is shifting, geographically, racially, and within age brackets. The shifting demographics within a stable total population have important implications for the funding of public schools within the state. These demographic changes have been augmented by state policy changes, however, that have exacerbated the implications for school finance.

Population Changes in Illinois

Illinois, like many other midwestern states, is dominated by one major city, Chicago, and its immediate suburbs. By 1920 the six-county metropolitan area contained more than half (52.4%) of the state's population (see Table 10.1). By 1980 the metropolitan share had increased to 62.2% and is projected to grow slowly until it peaks in 2010 at 65.7%. Historically, the metropolitan area has been dominated by Chicago and Cook County. In 1920 Cook County contained 89.9% of the metropolitan area population. But that domination has been weakening ever since (see Table 10.2). By 1980 the share was down to 74%; it is predicted to continue declining to 67.7% by 2020. From 1930 to 1960, Cook County accounted for more than half of the state's population. This fact influenced reporting formats; many state agencies issued statistics by providing state totals, Cook County totals, and downstate totals. In turn the reports helped condition the terms of political debates, which were often cast in a Cook County (or Chicago) versus downstate context.

But the dynamics of demographics are changing the political scene. Between 1970 and 1980, Cook County lost 250,000 people while the rest of the metropolitan area increased population by 358,000. During that decade, the population of three of the "collar" counties (DuPage, McHenry, and Will)

Table 10.1 Population of Illinois and Changes

Year	State	Downstate	Metro Area	Percentage of State	Metropolitan Counties					
					Cook	DuPage	Kane	Lake	McHenry	Will
Population of Illinois:										
1870	2,540,000	2,046,469	493,531	19.4	349,966	16,685	39,091	21,014	23,762	43,013
1880	3,078,000	2,306,750	771,250	25.1	607,524	19,161	44,939	21,296	24,908	53,422
1890	3,826,000	2,434,110	1,391,890	36.4	1,191,922	22,551	65,061	24,235	26,114	62,007
1900	4,822,000	2,737,749	2,084,251	43.2	1,838,735	28,196	78,792	34,005	29,759	74,764
1910	5,639,000	2,936,535	2,702,465	47.9	2,405,233	33,432	91,862	55,058	32,509	84,371
1920	6,485,000	3,090,004	3,394,996	52.4	3,053,017	42,120	99,499	74,285	33,164	92,911
1930	7,644,000	3,194,354	4,449,646	58.2	3,982,123	91,998	125,327	104,387	35,079	110,732
1940	7,905,000	3,335,357	4,569,643	57.8	4,063,342	103,480	130,206	121,094	37,311	114,210
1950	8,758,000	3,580,132	5,177,868	59.1	4,508,792	154,599	150,388	179,097	50,656	134,336
1960	10,086,000	3,865,087	6,220,913	61.7	5,129,725	313,459	208,246	293,656	84,210	191,617
1970	11,135,000	4,139,645	6,995,355	62.8	5,504,586	493,292	251,788	383,748	111,760	250,181
1980	11,427,000	4,323,376	7,103,624	62.2	5,253,655	658,835	278,405	440,372	147,897	324,460
1990	11,712,000	4,233,639	7,478,361	63.9	5,361,131	781,895	323,814	487,477	171,100	352,944
2000	11,897,000	4,156,728	7,740,272	65.1	5,432,147	863,491	362,205	516,530	186,875	379,024
2010	12,087,000	4,149,970	7,937,030	65.7	5,450,558	905,711	398,611	548,436	207,994	425,720
2020	12,413,000	4,268,857	8,144,143	65.6	5,513,951	937,029	432,315	571,702	224,997	464,149
Change in population:										
1870										
1880	538,000	260,281	277,719	51.6	257,558	2,476	5,848	282	1,146	10,409
1890	748,000	127,360	620,640	83.0	584,398	3,390	20,122	2,939	1,206	8,585
1900	996,000	303,639	692,361	69.5	646,813	5,645	13,731	9,770	3,645	12,757
1910	817,000	198,786	618,214	75.7	566,498	5,236	13,070	21,053	2,750	9,607
1920	846,000	153,469	692,531	81.9	647,784	8,688	7,637	19,227	655	8,540

Year										
1930	17,821	1,915	30,102	25,828	49,878	929,106	91.0	1,054,650	104,350	1,159,000
1940	3,478	2,232	16,707	4,879	11,482	81,219	46.0	119,997	141,003	261,000
1950	20,126	13,345	58,003	20,182	51,119	445,450	71.3	608,225	244,775	853,000
1960	57,281	33,554	114,559	57,858	158,860	620,933	78.5	1,043,045	284,955	1,328,000
1970	58,564	27,550	90,092	43,542	179,833	374,861	73.8	774,442	274,558	1,049,000
1980	74,279	36,137	56,624	26,617	165,543	(250,931)	37.1	108,269	183,731	292,000
1990	28,484	23,203	47,105	45,409	123,060	107,476	131.5	374,737	(89,737)	285,000
2000	26,080	15,775	29,053	38,391	81,596	71,016	141.6	261,911	(76,911)	185,000
2010	46,696	21,119	31,906	36,406	42,220	18,411	103.6	196,758	(6,758)	190,000
2020	38,429	17,003	23,266	33,704	31,318	63,393	63.5	207,113	118,887	326,000

Percentage of change in population:

Year										
1870										
1880	24.2	4.8	1.3	15.0	14.8	73.6		56.3	12.7	21.2
1890	16.1	4.8	13.8	44.8	17.7	96.2		80.5	5.5	24.3
1900	20.6	14.0	40.3	21.1	25.0	54.3		49.7	12.5	26.0
1910	12.8	9.2	61.9	16.6	18.6	30.8		29.7	7.3	16.9
1920	10.1	2.0	34.9	8.3	26.0	26.9		25.6	5.2	15.0
1930	19.2	5.8	40.5	26.0	118.4	30.4		31.1	3.4	17.9
1940	3.1	6.4	16.0	3.9	12.5	2.0		2.7	4.4	3.4
1950	17.6	35.8	47.9	15.5	49.4	11.0		13.3	7.3	10.8
1960	42.6	66.2	64.0	38.5	102.8	13.8		20.1	8.0	15.2
1970	30.6	32.7	30.7	20.9	57.4	7.3		12.4	7.1	10.4
1980	29.7	32.3	14.8	10.6	33.6	-4.6		1.5	4.4	2.6
1990	8.8	15.7	10.7	16.3	18.7	2.0		5.3	-2.1	2.5
2000	7.4	9.2	6.0	11.9	10.4	1.3		3.5	-1.8	1.6
2010	12.3	11.3	6.2	10.1	4.9	0.3		2.5	-0.2	1.6
2020	9.0	8.2	4.2	8.5	3.5	1.2		2.6	2.9	2.7

SOURCE: State of Illinois (1987).

Table 10.2 Percentage of Population in Metropolitan Area by County

Year	Cook (%)	DuPage (%)	Kane (%)	Lake (%)	McHenry (%)	Will (%)
1870	70.9	3.4	7.9	4.3	4.8	8.7
1880	78.8	2.5	5.8	2.8	3.2	6.9
1890	85.6	1.6	4.7	1.7	1.9	4.5
1900	88.2	1.4	3.8	1.6	1.4	3.6
1910	89.0	1.2	3.4	2.0	1.2	3.1
1920	89.9	1.2	2.9	2.2	1.0	2.7
1930	89.5	2.1	2.8	2.3	0.8	2.5
1940	88.9	2.3	2.8	2.6	0.8	2.5
1950	87.1	3.0	2.9	3.5	1.0	2.6
1960	82.5	5.0	3.3	4.7	1.4	3.1
1970	78.7	7.1	3.6	5.5	1.6	3.6
1980	74.0	9.3	3.9	6.2	2.1	4.6
1990	71.7	10.5	4.3	6.5	2.3	4.7
2000	70.2	11.2	4.7	6.7	2.4	4.9

SOURCE: State of Illinois (1987).

jumped by almost a third. It is projected that Cook will gradually recover its lost population, while the collar counties will continue to grow at 10% to 20% per decade for the next several decades. Chicago continues to dominate Cook County, with just under 60% of its total population.

The picture in the rest of the state is more bleak. While population growth was more balanced prior to 1880, for the next nine decades, the metropolitan area provided from 70% to 90% of the state's total population growth, with the single exception of the Depression decade. During the 1970s, the downstate counties gained more population than did the metropolitan area, but they are expected to have lost population during the 1980s and to continue to lose people during the next two decades. The population loss is about equally divided between the 12 counties with sizable urban centers and the other 84 more rural counties.

While the total population of Illinois is expected to grow very slowly during the next four decades, the white popula-

Table 10.3   Minority Population Projections: State of Illinois

	Nonwhite 1980	Nonwhite 1990	Nonwhite 2000	Nonwhite 2010	Nonwhite 2020	Nonwhite 2025	Increase by 2020 (%)
Statewide total	2,514,812	2,993,380	3,465,179	3,962,912	4,436,573	4,680,464	76.4
Black	1,661,785	1,822,747	1,956,115	2,087,382	2,204,905	2,261,270	32.7
Hispanic	635,589	878,563	1,137,561	1,409,473	1,673,554	1,810,183	163.3
Other	217,438	292,070	371,503	466,057	558,114	609,011	156.7
Black	66.1%	60.9%	56.5%	52.7%	49.7%	48.3%	−17.8
Hispanic	25.3%	29.4%	32.8%	35.6%	37.7%	38.7%	13.4
Other	8.6%	9.8%	10.7%	11.8%	12.6%	13.0%	4.4

SOURCE: State of Illinois (1987).

tion is expected to decrease. The white population is projected to fall from 8.9 million in 1980 to just under 8 million in 2020. About 600,000 of that decrease will be experienced in the six-county Chicago metropolitan area, and about 300,000 will occur downstate. During the same period, the nonwhite population will grow by 76%, increasing from 2.5 million in 1980 to 4.4 million in 2020 (see Tables 10.3 and 10.4). The white population declines reflect an expected net out-migration of whites totaling about 550,000 during the 1990s and 386,000 in the first decade of the new century. White out-migration will dwindle during the second decade (193,000) and reverse after 2020. In-migration of nonwhites is expected to increase from 54,000 in the 1990s to 72,000 in the 2000s and 102,000 in the teens. In-migration of Hispanics and Asians will more than balance a small out-migration by blacks. Higher fertility rates for blacks and Hispanics will provide an additional growth component.

The racial composition differs significantly in different parts of Illinois. In 1980 nonwhites made up 22% of the population, a figure that will grow to 35.7% by 2020. Most nonwhites (86.8%) live in the Chicago metropolitan area. Most of those nonwhites (90.9%) lived in Cook County in 1980. Expected

Table 10.4 Minority Population Projections by Areas of Illinois

Region/County No. & Name	Type of County	Nonwhite 1980	Nonwhite 1990	Nonwhite 2000	Nonwhite 2010	Nonwhite 2020	Nonwhite 2025	Increase by 2020 (%)
Chicago metro		2,181,620	2,607,988	3,024,187	3,428,342	3,843,871	4,043,735	76.2
Downstate urban		249,832	290,292	328,868	378,922	433,907	464,659	73.7
Downstate rural		83,360	95,100	112,124	155,648	158,795	172,070	90.5
Chicago metro:								
16 Cook	M	1,982,176	2,322,741	2,655,277	2,971,997	3,266,720	3,414,574	64.8
22 DuPage	M	46,229	70,829	94,864	101,159	147,034	161,118	218.1
45 Kane	M	42,696	64,074	86,140	113,163	139,422	152,736	226.5
49 Lake	M	57,002	74,906	91,480	114,172	134,974	145,816	136.8
63 McHenry	M	4,105	5,882	7,928	10,954	14,078	15,663	242.9
99 Will	M	49,412	69,556	88,498	116,897	141,643	153,828	186.7
Downstate urban:								
10 Champaign	U	21,422	25,056	28,337	34,030	39,784	43,413	85.7
46 Kankakee	U	16,890	18,724	20,882	23,761	27,079	28,886	60.3
50 LaSalle	U	3,705	4,480	5,285	6,316	7,391	7,936	99.5
55 Macon	U	15,106	18,512	21,879	25,478	29,416	31,478	94.7
57 Madison	U	18,319	20,522	22,607	25,354	28,483	30,324	55.5
64 McLean	U	6,927	9,123	10,281	12,429	14,892	16,342	115.0
72 Peoria	U	25,880	34,123	41,307	49,420	58,757	63,854	127.0
81 Rock Island	U	18,575	24,016	29,952	36,759	44,027	47,901	137.0
82 St. Clair	U	78,759	84,797	90,499	98,789	108,618	114,221	37.9
84 Sangamon	U	13,827	16,738	19,717	23,227	26,894	28,841	94.5
90 Tazewell	U	1,672	2,049	2,602	3,262	3,957	4,279	136.7
101 Winnebago	U	28,750	32,152	35,520	40,097	44,609	47,184	55.2

SOURCE: State of Illinois (1987).

growth rates for nonwhites in the metropolitan area and downstate are similar (76.2 and 77.9%, respectively) but submerge widely different growth dynamics in individual counties. In Cook County, where minorities made up 37.7% of the population, nonwhites are expected to increase by 1,285,000, up 64.8%. By 2020 nonwhites will make up 59.2% of the Cook County population. Except for St. Clair County (across the Mississippi River from St. Louis), all other counties had fewer than 16% of residents who were nonwhite in 1980. By 2020, however, two suburban counties (Kane and Will) will be nearly a third nonwhite, while downstate Peoria will have joined St. Clair in that category. Taken together, nonwhites will make up 47.2% of the metropolitan area population, 20.9% of the downstate urban counties, and 7.2% of the population of the more rural counties.

In 1980 blacks represented 66.1% of the nonwhite population in Illinois; Hispanics accounted for 25.3%, while Asians and "Others" were 8.6%. By 2020 the black share is expected to fall to 49.7%, even though black residents will increase by more than half a million (up 32.7% over 40 years). Due to different migration patterns and higher fertility rates, Hispanics and "Others" will more than double during the next four decades, with Hispanics increasing by a million and "Others" by 230,000. In 2020 Hispanics will make up 37.7% of the minority population and "Others" will constitute 12.6%. If the current trends continue, Hispanics should outnumber blacks in Illinois about the middle of the next century.

In addition to changes in the racial composition of the population, there will be some changes in the population of various age brackets during the next 40 years. The major effect will be the passage of the baby boom generation through the various adult age cohorts. Table 10.5 shows the bulge in the Illinois population age groups reflecting this cohort of post-world war babies. The preschool population was largest in 1960, resulting in a larger school-age population in 1970 and young adult group in 1980. This group swells the ranks of the mature adults for the next three decades and joins the retirees in 2020. A second miniboom follows three decades later for each age group.

Table 10.5 Population by Age Group

| | Age Groups | | | | | 5-17 (%) | Age Group Proportions 0-17 (%) | Workers (%) | 65+ (%) | Ratio Workers/ Retiree |
	0-4	5-17	18-29	30-64	65+	Total					
1950	843,000	1,565,000	1,579,000	3,971,000	754,000	8,712,000	18.0	27.6	63.7	8.7	7.4
1960	1,130,000	2,309,000	1,440,000	4,227,000	975,000	10,081,000	22.9	34.1	56.2	9.7	5.8
1970	937,000	2,859,000	1,977,000	4,248,000	1,094,000	11,115,000	25.7	34.2	56.0	9.8	5.7
1980	842,000	2,401,000	2,492,000	4,428,000	1,262,000	11,425,000	21.0	28.4	60.6	11.0	5.5
1990	946,000	2,156,000	2,208,000	4,951,000	1,451,000	11,712,000	18.4	26.5	61.1	12.4	4.9
2000	812,000	2,223,000	1,890,000	5,460,000	1,512,000	11,897,000	18.7	25.5	61.8	12.7	4.9
2010	788,000	2,028,000	2,025,000	5,640,000	1,606,000	12,087,000	16.8	23.3	63.4	13.3	4.8
2020	794,000	2,011,000	1,934,000	5,656,000	2,018,000	12,413,000	16.2	22.6	61.1	16.3	3.8

SOURCE: State of Illinois (1987).

Aside from the obvious implications of these numbers for school enrollments, the shifting proportion of the population in different age categories puts different kinds of economic pressure on the state. The growing elderly population adds pressures for both income maintenance and health care. It also raises significant questions about the adequacy of funding levels for pension funds. The declining share of the population who are children, together with the increasing share who are over 65, means the focus of public policy will inevitably move away from children's issues to those of retirees. The ratio of workers to retirees was relatively constant at a little over 5.5:1 from 1960 to 1980; from 1990 to 2010 it is expected to hover just under 5:1. The ratio is expected to fall to under 4:1 by 2020 and will fall rapidly thereafter.

Looking at the school-age group specifically, the bulge of the baby boomers is clearly evident in 1970, with significant decreases in 1980 and 1990. The miniboom hits in 2000 but recedes thereafter. The population patterns hold fairly well for the Chicago metropolitan area, but downstate the decline is more linear, and the miniboom does not appear, suggesting an out-migration of female baby boomers during their child-bearing years.

Corresponding to general changes in the racial composition across the state, the proportion of white school-age children is expected to decline significantly during the next four decades, from 72.5% in 1980 to 58.2% in 2020. The black school-age population will stay fairly stable, increasing slowly from 18.5% of the age group to 20.5%. Hispanics will increase from 7.1% to 16.7%, while "Others" will increase from 1.9% to 4.5%. Thus the school-age population will become more heavily minority during the next four decades.

School Enrollment Changes

Public school enrollments generally follow the broad population trends just described; however, some 16% of Illinois school-age children do not attend public schools. Thus actual enrollments are somewhat lower than the population figures.

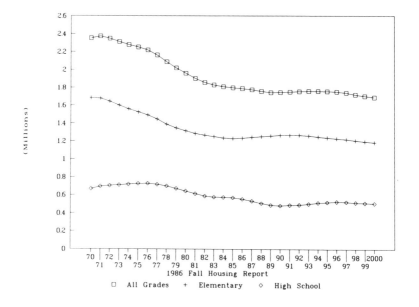

Figure 10.1. Illinois Enrollment Trends
SOURCE: Illinois State Board of Education (1986)

But school enrollments are recorded annually and therefore present a more detailed record statewide. Figure 10.1 shows the actual fall enrollments from 1970 through 1985 for all Illinois public schools and projections for those schools through the end of the century.

The baby boom forced the building of numerous schools across the state during the 1960s. By 1970 elementary grade enrollments were already beginning to fall and continued to do so until 1985, when they reached their low point of 1,227,510 students. As the baby boomers graduated from elementary school, in the late 1960s and early 1970s, high school enrollments continued to rise, reaching a high point in the fall of 1976 at 728,048. High school enrollments have been falling since then. The miniboomer effect is expected to peak in the elementary schools in the fall of 1992 (at 1,266,417) and in high schools in 1996 (at 525,693) (see Table 10.6). Individual

Table 10.6   Illinois Public School Enrollment

Year (Fall)	K-8 & Special Education	High School & Special Education	Total Enrollment
1970	1,684,132	668,654	2,352,786
1971	1,678,517	695,142	2,373,659
1972	1,643,486	704,311	2,347,797
1973	1,600,486	711,311	2,311,797
1974	1,559,386	719,170	2,278,556
1975	1,525,152	726,991	2,252,143
1976	1,491,456	728,048	2,219,504
1977	1,444,888	717,656	2,162,544
1978	1,388,151	700,580	2,088,731
1979	1,347,128	671,779	2,018,907
1980	1,314,862	644,636	1,959,498
1981	1,284,867	614,919	1,899,786
1982	1,267,175	588,912	1,856,087
1983	1,250,165	577,520	1,827,685
1984	1,233,519	575,142	1,808,661
1985	1,227,510	569,972	1,797,482
1986	1,232,057	555,491	1,787,548
1987	1,242,701	534,072	1,776,773
1988	1,250,041	506,700	1,756,741
1989	1,257,323	487,125	1,744,448
1990	1,264,197	480,980	1,745,177
1991	1,264,735	486,280	1,751,015
1992	1,266,417	489,768	1,756,185
1993	1,259,444	500,108	1,759,552
1994	1,246,950	513,929	1,760,879
1995	1,237,351	519,291	1,756,642
1996	1,227,252	525,693	1,752,945
1997	1,219,275	521,834	1,741,109
1998	1,206,550	514,099	1,720,649
1999	1,194,793	510,137	1,704,930
2000	1,185,685	506,169	1,691,854

SOURCE: Illinois State Board of Education (1986).

school districts have experienced these demographic changes as cycles of expansion-contraction-expansion-contraction. Some overbuilt, then sold unneeded facilities, only to find themselves desperately searching for space again.

A more specific analysis is available by looking at enrollment data for three specific years during this time sequence. District-level enrollment data, by race and by income level, were secured from the electronic files of the Illinois State Board of Education's Fall Housing Reports for 1973, 1981, and 1989. Due to data limitations, it was not possible to match these data with census data and projections. They do, however, match some other finance-related data to be presented later.

For 1973 the Fall Housing Report presents data on 1,056 districts across the state. Together these districts enrolled 2,318,641 students. Of this number, 23.1% were nonwhite while 13.8% were categorized as low income. By 1981 the number of districts had fallen to 1,048, and the number of students had fallen to 1,923,863. As could be expected from the previously presented demographic data, the number of minority students increased by more than 36,000 and the percentage of nonwhites increased to 29.8%. There were some 430,000 fewer white students in 1981. What could not be anticipated from the census numbers was that the percentage of low-income students also increased, to 22.5%.

Eight years later, in 1989, with 1,000 districts, there were 1,796,864 students in public schools. This was some 40,000 more students than the State Board of Education had projected in its 1986 report, portrayed in Figure 10.1. Nonwhite enrollment continued to increase, by nearly 42,000 students, while white enrollment dropped by 170,000. The percentage of low-income students also rose to 27.8%. Thus the number of low-income students enrolled in Illinois public schools grew from 319,000 in 1973 to over 500,000 in 1989, while minority enrollments were increasing by 78,000, and total enrollments plummeted by 600,000 students. The public schools of Illinois have become progressively more nonwhite, and their students include many more who live in poverty (see Table 10.7).

Table 10.7 Enrollment Changes in Illinois Schools (in thousands)

Year	White	Nonwhite	Total	Minority (%)	Low Income	Low Income (%)
1973	1,783	536	2,319	23.1	319	13.8
1981	1,351	572	1,924	29.8	434	22.5
1989	1,182	614	1,797	34.2	500	27.8

NOTE: Some numbers do not total due to rounding.

A surface examination of these data would tempt the reader to assume that Illinois schools were enrolling more poor minority students now than 18 years ago. While that may be true, to some small extent, a closer examination shows that such a conclusion would be misleading, particularly for the past decade. Correlations between the percentage of students who were nonwhite and the percentage of low-income students in each district were relatively high in 1973 ($r = .54$) and in 1981 ($r = .51$), but dropped significantly for 1989 ($r = .34$; data were not available at the individual student level).

District statistics were aggregated to the county level to allow for district consolidation. At the county level, the percentage of low-income students and the percentage of minority students were frequently closely related in 1973, with a few notable exceptions. Brown County, served by a single school district of only 1,140 students, had no nonwhite students but a 38.9% low-income enrollment. On a larger scale, among the 21 counties in the southernmost portion of the state (basically south of U.S. 50, for those who know Illinois), there were two counties, Alexander and Pulaski, at the tip of the state, with high minority enrollments (52.7% and 46.8%) and a high percentage low income (46.9% and 66.9%). But across the southern tier area, only 5.9% of the students were nonwhite while 18.9% were from poverty homes.

By 1989 the picture had become much more striking. When districts were aggregated into eight areas of the state, combining between 6 and 21 counties into areas, the percentage of low income significantly exceeded the percentage of minority enrollment in every area except the Chicago suburban collar counties, where the percentage of minorities doubled that of low-income students. What accounts for these changes?

Minority enrollments increased dramatically in some districts across the state. The number of districts with at least 10% nonwhite enrollment grew from 90 in 1973 to 262 in 1989. Of the 90 in 1973, 46 were from the six-county metropolitan area with most of the rest in the southern tier counties or near cities like St. Louis, Peoria, and Springfield. In 1989, 170 districts of 309 in the metropolitan area had at least 10% minority students while 92 districts downstate had similar proportions—a third in the southern tier, 20 near St. Louis, and the rest near the state's smaller urban areas.

In terms of higher concentrations of minority students, the picture was similar. In 1973 there were 17 districts with majority nonwhite enrollments, 8 of them downstate. In 1989 there were 46 majority minority districts, only 10 of which were downstate. From 1973 to 1989 the number of minority students increased by 78,671, with the suburban districts growing by 85,564 and downstate districts by 15,351, while Chicago lost 22,244 minority students (blacks down 72,075, Native Americans down 285, Asians up 6,537, and Hispanics up 43,579).

Meanwhile, as we have already seen, the number of low-income students rose even more dramatically, by 180,000. And these low-income students were dispersed far more widely across the state. In 1973 there were 322 districts with at least 10% of their students classified as low income (the statewide proportion was 13.8%). In 1989, when 27.8% of the state's students came from low-income homes, there were 609 districts with at least 10% economically disadvantaged. In 1973, 10 districts had more than half of their students living in poverty, with another 37 with low-income enrollments over 25%. By 1989, 33 districts had half of their enrollments composed of economically disadvantaged students, and 194 others had a quarter of their students in that condition.

These districts serving high proportions of low-income students were spread much more widely across the state. Only

36 of the 322 districts with 10% low income in 1973 were located in the Chicago metropolitan area; in 1989, of 609 districts, 83 were in the metropolitan area. That means 526 of 691 downstate districts had at least 10% of their students who are economically disadvantaged.

While Black, Asian, and Hispanic students may require some cultural sensitivity on the part of their teachers, and might benefit from some curricular adaptations, economically disadvantaged students have been more closely associated with educational need. Since the Coleman Report (1966) onward, lack of achievement has been more closely associated with economic disadvantage than any other educational indicator. It was for that reason that a poverty effect factor was included in the Illinois school aid formula adopted in 1973. School districts with high proportions of economically disadvantaged students were to receive extra revenue to support their efforts to overcome the effects of poverty on their students. It is now appropriate to examine the actual record of student support in Illinois.

Educational Revenues and the Needs of Students

During the 1980s, total revenues for Illinois schools from all sources rose by 40.8% (from $5.6 billion to $7.9 billion). This increase slightly exceeded the increase in the Consumer Price Index for the period (up 31.8% from January 1982 to January 1989). The State of Illinois played a minor role in this revenue increase. General Distributive Aid accounted for only 14.1% of the increase; categorical support and funding for special initiatives included in the 1985 state reform package accounted for a similar amount, 13.7%. Federal government support made up 6.2% of the increase. Local property taxes and other local resources provided the majority (70.0%) of the increase in revenues to school districts across the state (see Table 10.8). This means that the state share of the costs of education dropped from 33.0% of all revenues to 31.5%. Because of proportionately larger increases in categorical funds,

Table 10.8 Education Revenues by Areas of Illinois, 1981-1982 Versus 1988-1989

	Property Taxes	Percent of Total	Other Local	Percent of Total	General State Aid	Percent of Total	Other State Revenues	Percent of Total	Federal Revenues	Percent of Total	Total Revenue
Statewide:											
state totals—1982	2,836,798,053	50.4	619,878,728	11.0	1,513,713,640	26.9	343,848,086	6.1	312,637,062	5.6	5,626,675,569
state totals—1989	4,384,889,592	55.4	584,860,452	7.4	1,837,365,706	23.2	658,358,958	8.3	455,065,218	5.7	7,920,539,926
change 1982-1989	1,548,091,539		(35,018,276)		323,652,066		314,510,872		142,428,156		2,293,864,357
change from 1982 (%)	54.6		-5.6		21.4		91.5		45.6		40.8
Metropolitan area suburbs:											
metro area totals—1982	1,461,887,227	60.9	355,309,900	14.8	398,705,602	16.6	128,102,351	5.3	55,493,887	2.3	2,399,498,967
metro area totals—1989	2,382,760,132	70.1	316,261,645	9.3	426,967,749	12.6	190,086,810	5.6	84,113,934	2.5	3,400,191,948
change 1982-1989	920,872,905		(39,048,255)		28,262,147		61,984,459		28,620,047		1,000,692,981
change from 1982 (%)	63.0		-11.0		7.1		48.4		51.6		41.7
Chicago public schools:											
Chicago totals—1982	443,346,945	34.5	40,510,664	3.2	558,194,865	43.5	79,194,829	6.2	162,104,101	12.6	1,283,351,404
Chicago totals—1989	836,898,788	42.1	65,299,305	3.3	587,481,721	29.6	263,665,091	13.3	233,822,200	11.8	1,987,167,105
change 1982-1989	393,551,843		24,788,641		29,286,856		184,470,262		71,718,099		703,815,701
change from 1982 (%)	88.8		61.2		5.2		232.9		44.2		54.8
Downstate districts:											
downstate totals—1982	931,563,881	47.9	224,058,164	11.5	556,813,173	28.6	136,550,906	7.0	95,039,074	4.9	1,943,825,198
downstate totals—1989	1,165,230,672	46.0	203,299,502	8.0	822,916,236	32.5	204,607,057	8.1	137,129,084	5.4	2,533,180,873
change 1982-1989	233,666,791		(20,758,662)		266,103,063		68,056,151		42,090,010		589,355,675
change from 1982 (%)	25.1		-9.3		47.8		49.8		44.3		30.3
Share of change:											
metro suburbs	59.5		111.5		8.7		19.7		20.1		43.6
Chicago	25.4		-70.8		9.0		58.7		50.4		30.7
downstate	15.1		59.3		82.2		21.6		29.6		25.7

SOURCE: Chicago Panel on Public School Policy and Finance (1989).

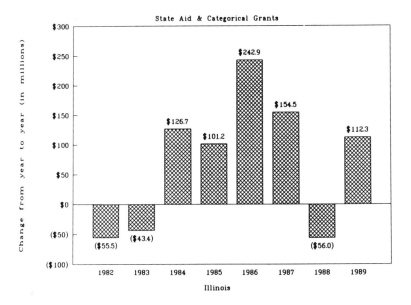

Figure 10.2. Change in State Funding of Education

however, the state funds devoted to equalizing distributive
aid provided a smaller proportion of all education revenues
(23.2%) in 1989 than they had in 1982 (26.9%).

An important factor in the state increases that have occurred is that they have been inconsistent. Douglas Whitley,
president of the Taxpayers Federation of Illinois, has suggested that Illinois schools have been on a "revenue roller-
coaster" in terms of state support (see Figure 10.2).

In three years of the 1980s decade, combined state funds for
education have actually decreased from the preceding year.
In another year, total elementary and secondary education
funding increased by nearly a quarter billion dollars. In a remaining year, increases have been a little over $100 million—
a 4% to 5% increase. This inconsistent funding by the state,
usually not decided until the end of June after the end of the
preceding school year, creates havoc with local district financial planning and contract negotiations.

In urban counties like Cook, with a program of quadrennial (recently changed to triennial) property reassessment, the inconsistency of state funding is accentuated. In one year out of four, a school district can receive a big jump in local tax revenues without changing its tax rate, resulting simply from an increase in the assessed valuation of local property (half of Chicago is reassessed during each of two years in the cycle). The increased property value will decrease the proportion of state aid in the succeeding years, however. For districts that receive little state aid, this is not important. For property-poor districts, which receive a large portion of their revenues from the state, property assessment practices create boom and bust cycles in school district budgeting.

Increased property tax revenues played a far more important role in Chicago and its suburban neighbors than in downstate communities outside the six-county metropolitan area. Revenues from property taxes for operating purposes increased by 63% in the metropolitan area suburbs and by 88.8% in Chicago. State distributive aid in those areas increased by only 7.1% and 5.2%, respectively, reflecting the small increases in state aid during the period and the increased property wealth in each area. By contrast, other state funds (categorical aid and reform program support) increased by 48.4% in the suburbs and by 232.9% (more than tripling) in Chicago.

The picture was much more grim downstate. In these 96 counties, which enrolled more students than either the suburbs or the city, the total revenue increase from 1982 to 1989 was $489 million, a 30.3% increase, slightly under the rate of inflation. This increase was a little over half (58.9%) the $1 billion increase in the suburbs and 83.7% of the increase for Chicago, which had less than two thirds as many students. The primary reason for this more dismal performance was the inability of downstate property taxes to support large revenue increases as had happened in the metropolitan area. Downstate property taxes increased only 25.1%. Even with the predominant part (82.2%) of the increase in state aid going to downstate districts, the slower than inflation growth in

Table 10.9   Changes in Equalized Assessed Value of Property

| | *(in billions of dollars)* | | |
	1981	1987	*Change*
Metropolitan counties	46.9	65.9	18.5
Downstate counties	29.1	27.6	-1.5

property tax revenues created financial problems for down-state districts, three quarters of which had at least 10% of their students coming from low-income homes.

What explains this slower property tax revenue growth downstate? In the mid-1980s, the General Assembly made a simple policy decision called "farmland reassessment." By simply decreeing a different method of assessing the value of farmland, hundreds of school districts were turned from being relatively wealthy (in terms of the property tax base) districts into being very poor districts. A comparison of equalized assessed value (EAV) of property shows the problem faced by downstate districts (see Table 10.9).

Illinois differentiates between types of property to be assessed. One county, Cook, assesses different categories of property at different proportions of true market value. Downstate counties use a common measure, one third of market value, on all categories of property. Farmland reassessment changed this practice, giving farmers a huge break on their property tax liability and reducing property tax revenues for rural school districts. Thus about 8% of the value of the property tax base of downstate school districts was removed at one stroke of the legislative pen. In individual counties, the effect was far more severe and it was even more severe in individual districts within those counties. Only 18 of the 96 downstate counties showed an increase in property value between 1981 and 1987. Some counties, like Fulton, lost more than a third of their EAV during this period. Property values in the 96 downstate counties declined from 38.3% of the state's total EAV to 29.7%. It was this declining property

Table 10.10   Changes in Assessed Value of Types of Property

| | 96 Downstate Counties (in billions of dollars) | | |
	1981	1987	Change
Residential	12.6	12.5	-0.1
Farm	8.9	6.5	-2.4
Commercial	3.9	4.2	0.3
Industrial	3.3	4.1	0.8
Railroads	0.1	0.2	0.1
Minerals	0.2	0.2	0.0
Total	29.1	27.6	-1.5

value that shifted the bulk of state distributive aid to the downstate area during the 1980s. But the state invested so little in distributive aid that it could not offset the decline in property values resulting from farmland reassessment (see Table 10.10).

An examination of a subset of school districts with more than half of their students coming from low-income homes is also instructive. In 1989 there were 227 school districts in the state with at least a quarter of their students in the low-income category. Chicago is the largest of these districts, and it alone enrolled 53.7% of all low-income pupils in the state. Chicago's share of the state's low-income students was virtually the same in 1981. As we have already seen, however, during the 1980s, Chicago was in a somewhat unique position. While its internal proportion of low-income students increased from 50.4% to 65.8%, matching the statewide increase, property values expanded from $13.2 billion to $21.7 billion—64.4%. This increase in the district's EAV resulted both from new building in the Loop, the city's downtown area, and from rising market values of property in the metropolitan area, reflected in reassessments. Together with legislatively restored high tax rate limits as the district recovered from virtual bankruptcy in 1979-1980, these higher property values allowed higher than normal budget growth during the 1980s. Chicago's budget expanded by 54.8% during this period,

compared with an average increase in the suburbs of 41.7%
and in downstate districts of 30.3%. Thus Chicago is somewhat of an anomaly. Its tax revenue growth allowed it more
flexibility in the face of an inadequate state effort to meet the
increasing poverty levels of the state's students. But what of
other school districts with high levels of low-income children? It has already become clear that the state's effort in the
downstate area was inadequate in light of the state's debilitat-
ing action in farmland reassessment.

Of the remaining poverty-impacted districts, 26 are located
in the suburban metropolitan area, most of them in southern
Cook County and neighboring Will County. Together these 26
districts enrolled 74,487 students in 1988-1989, the last year
for which finance data were available. Of that number, 42.1%,
or 31,359, were from low-income homes. In 1981-1982 these
districts had enrolled 37.1% who were considered low-income
students. Among these school districts, the average per pupil
revenue in 1981-1982 was $2,931; that figure increased to
$4,086 in 1988-1989. Among all districts in the suburban area,
the comparable figures were $3,388 and $5,125; the figures for
Chicago were $2,898 and $4,865. Thus Chicago, thanks to its
huge increases in property tax revenues, slightly closed the
gap between it and its suburban neighbors, in aggregate. By
contrast, the poverty-impacted suburban districts, while increasing their per pupil revenues by 39.4%, fell further behind
both their neighbors and Chicago.

When the specific sources of revenue are examined, the
greater ability of Chicago and most suburban districts to use
increased property tax revenues becomes clear (see Table
10.11). The selected poverty-impacted districts averaged a
$666 per pupil increase in property tax revenues while losing
$228 per pupil in other local revenues. By comparison, the
suburban districts as a whole were increasing per pupil property tax revenue by $1,528 while Chicago was increasing the
same revenues by $1,048. Other local revenues varied only
slightly in both cases.[2] State revenue increases were greater
for the poverty-impacted districts than for their suburban
counterparts as an aggregate but, due to high categorical and

Table 10.11   Per Pupil Revenues by Areas of Illinois

| | | | 1981-1982 Versus 1988-1989 | | | | |
| | | Property Tax | Other Local | State Aid | Other State | Federal | Total |
	Enrolled				(per pupil)		
Statewide:							
state totals							
1982	1,923,863	1,475	322	787	179	163	2,925
1989	1,766,324	2,482	331	1,040	373	258	4,484
change 1982-1989	(157,539)	1,008	9	253	194	95	1,560
change (%)	−8.2	68.4	2.8	32.2	108.5	58.5	53.3
Poverty-impacted suburban districts:							
selected districts							
1982	77,703	1,285	501	723	207	214	2,931
1989	74,487	1,951	273	1,209	364	289	4,086
change 1982-1989	(3,216)	666	(228)	486	157	75	1,156
change (%)	−4.1	51.8	−45.6	67.3	76.2	34.8	39.4
Metropolitan area suburbs:							
metro area totals							
1982	708,320	2,064	502	563	181	78	3,388
1989	663,434	3,592	477	644	287	127	5,125
change 1982-1989	(44,886)	1,528	(25)	81	106	48	1,738
change (%)	−6.3	74.0	−5.0	14.3	58.4	61.8	51.3
Chicago public schools:							
Chicago totals							
1982	442,889	1,001	91	1,260	179	366	2,898
1989	408,442	2,049	160	1,438	646	572	4,865
change 1982-1989	(34,447)	1,048	68	178	467	206	1,968
change (%)	−7.8	104.7	74.8	14.1	261.0	56.4	67.9
Downstate districts:							
downstate totals							
1982	772,654	1,206	290	721	177	123	2,516
1989	694,448	1,678	293	1,185	295	197	3,648
change 1982-1989	(78,206)	472	3	464	118	74	1,132
change (%)	−10.1	39.2	1.0	64.4	66.7	60.5	45.0
Change (%) compared with state average:							
metro suburbs	28.5	151.6	−279.6	31.8	54.5	50.9	111.4
Chicago	21.9	104.0	767.6	70.2	240.6	217.0	126.2
downstate	49.6	46.9	31.0	183.2	60.8	78.3	72.6

SOURCE: Chicago Panel on Public School Policy and Finance (1989).

reform program revenues in Chicago, were about equal to the city's state revenues per pupil. Thus the huge differential in property tax revenues between these poverty-impacted districts and their suburban and city neighbors meant they had relatively fewer new dollars to meet the needs of their slowly increasing low-income population.

As might be expected, lower property revenues are related to more slowly increasing property values. Total EAV increased by $16.4 billion for all metropolitan suburbs between 1981 and 1988, the relevant years for school years being examined here. The change in Chicago was $8.5 billion. These increases represented a 49% and 64.3% increase, respectively. For the selected poverty-impacted districts, EAV growth, in aggregate, was $549 million, a 14.6% growth rate. More relevant for revenue growth patterns, the EAV per pupil (a component of the school aid formula) figures are also instructive (see Table 10.12). These changes are so extreme and so stark that even the resulting higher proportional share of distributive state aid, given the state's meager effort in increasing state aid revenues, is simply overwhelmed. Thus the districts with the most disadvantaged students skimp by on resources that only slightly exceed the rate of inflation while districts with few needy children throughout the rest of the suburbs have experienced per pupil revenue increases exceeding 50%. The school aid formula, at its current level of funding, is inadequate to compensate for such problems.

Alan Hickrod (Hickrod et al., 1988), in his MacArthur/ Spencer Project Report *Guilty Governments*, has outlined more extensively the decline in equity in school funding in Illinois. He has reviewed the changes in the formula that have weakened the state's efforts since a resource equalizer formula was adopted in 1973. He has also examined the meager level of state funding for elementary and secondary schools. This chapter has attempted to add to Hickrod's analysis the effects of rapid property value changes, both those resulting from market forces in the metropolitan area and from changes in assessment practices originating in the state legislature. The combination of negligible state support and escalating property

Table 10.12   Changes in Property Values in Metro Chicago

	EAV/Pupil 1981-1982 ($)	EAV/Pupil 1988-1989 ($)	Change ($)	Percentage of Change
Poverty impacted:				
elementary	46,870	54,549	9,443	20.1
high school	102,484	137,369	34,885	34.0
unit	28,961	31,946	2,985	10.3
Metro suburbs (aggregate):				
elementary	77,012	113,781	36,768	47.7
high school	138,666	246,735	108,068	77.9
unit	40,251	65,404	25,152	62.5
Chicago (unit)	29,819	53,763	23,944	80.3

values in the more affluent parts of the state has dramatically increased the inequity between property-rich and property-poor districts. It has similarly had a disastrous impact upon school districts enrolling an increasing number of low-income students. Only in Chicago, where the increases in property values across some parts of the city are equally accessible to schools with increasing numbers (as well as proportions) of low-income students, have resources expanded as the need has expanded.

Alternatives to the Current Revenue Generating Pattern in Illinois

There are essentially four alternative approaches under consideration in Illinois to correct the current inequity in school revenues in the state. Some advocates are concerned with improving taxpayer equity as well as equity in revenues per pupil. All are concerned with addressing the added burdens of students with special needs. On November 13, 1990, the Committee for Educational Rights, an intergovernmental compact between some 49 Illinois school districts, brought suit against the governor, the State Board of Education, and the state superintendent of schools, asserting that the current funding pattern is unconstitutionally inequitable. The suit has avoided proposing alternative solutions, but advocates across the state are urging various solutions upon the General Assembly, hoping that the suit will prompt a more speedy legislative resolution.

The first alternative is simply to increase state support for public schools, moving from the current low foundation program to a high foundation program. If the formula were altered slightly so that the funds were focused more clearly on low-spending districts, and if low tax effort districts were forced to increase their tax rates, advocates suggest that the foundation level could be increased to about $5,000 per pupil. Some estimates have suggested that an additional $800 million in state aid could accomplish this goal; other more pessimistic estimates are three times that amount, requiring an increase in the state income tax rate from 3% to 5.25%. Such a proposal would reduce the variance in per pupil revenues to a little more than 2 to 1 at the 5th and 95th percentile levels but would do little for taxpayer inequities, which currently exceed 2 to 1 in elementary districts.

A second proposal is a variant on this high foundation theme. It involves a tax swap with a small tax increase. A bill proposing an increase of 1 percentage point on the state income tax, part of the revenues of which would be used to rebate property taxes in high tax rate school districts, was proposed in the last session of the General Assembly but it never got out of committee for floor debate. While attractive on its face for its property tax rebate feature, the rebates would disproportionately benefit commercial, industrial, and farm interests, which represent 52% of the state's EAV but pay less than 20% of state income taxes. Thus a bill that purports to create greater taxpayer equity does so among individual residents by increasing their share of taxes to support education while reducing further the tax burden of farmers as well as commercial and industrial interests. Per pupil revenue equity is virtually unchanged, except to the extent that the income tax increase exceeds the funds necessary for the property tax rebates. To the extent that additional funds are raised, this swap proposal works like a higher foundation proposal.

A third alternative emulates the Chicago effect by seeking greater access to the property wealth of some parts of a county for all residents in the county. For finance purposes, counties would be treated as if they were a single school district. All property within a county would be taxed at the same rate, with receipts distributed to school districts on a per pupil basis. Differences between counties would be equalized through the state aid formula, now applied to counties instead of districts. In some versions of this proposal, Cook County would be divided into four parts—the city and three suburban areas (north, west, and south, following current lines for the state's Educational Service Centers). Another variant would divide Cook into the city and 27 townships, treating each township as it treats counties in other parts of the state. This county-based proposal would significantly improve per pupil revenue equity, reducing the ratio at the 5th and 95th percentiles under 2 to 1, and would create total taxpayer equity across each county, though not necessarily between counties. With relatively few additional dollars, mostly derived from more equitable tax rates on currently undertaxed properties, this proposal moves significantly in the direction of both pupil and taxpayer equity. It does so at the cost of reducing spending levels in some of the most affluent school districts.

A fourth proposal also would widen the access of the state's citizens to the property wealth of the entire state. Under this proposal, all nonresidential property would be the subject of a state education property tax. The receipts from this statewide tax would be deposited in the common school fund for distribution through the equalizing aid formula. School districts as they currently exist would continue to levy property taxes but only on residential property. Thus there would continue to be some differences in property wealth between districts, and different districts would continue to be able to levy taxes at different rates to increase or minimize education spending. But the predominance of funding would now shift to the state's distributive aid fund, with its equalizing effect. Under this proposal, per pupil revenue ratios would fall to under 1.5 to 1. Taxpayer equity for commercial, industrial, and farm property would be total across the state, with a tax rate set to produce some additional funding to take advantage of formerly undertaxed property. Taxpayer equity for individual residences would also improve as low-wealth districts would receive more support from the state and could afford to reduce their high rates; low-rate districts will be pressured to increase their rates to sustain previous levels of school services.

In any of these alternatives, if the basic inequity of overreliance upon the property tax to fund public schools can be eliminated, the poverty-impact element of the school aid formula should provide extra assistance to districts with higher numbers of low-income students. Over the years, the legislature has restricted the number of such students a district can use in the formula. To adequately meet the needs of these low-income students, the formula should allow all low-income students to be counted and should provide added assistance to school districts to meet their needs. If a more equitable funding scheme is adopted and full weighting is given to low-income students, the state will begin to align its school funding with changes in demographics within this "steady state" state.

Notes

1. Population figures and projections in this chapter are drawn from State of Illinois, Bureau of the Budget data contained in the publication *Illinois Population Trends from 1980 to 2025* (State of Illinois, 1987).

2. Per pupil percentage increases are greater than the percentage increase of gross revenues due to declining enrollment across the state. State legislators often used declining enrollments as justification for minimizing state funding for education. Because property tax revenues are not related to pupil counts, declining enrollments will increase per pupil property tax receipts.

References

Chicago Panel on Public School Policy and Finance. (1989). *1989 Metrostat databook: Vol. 2. Education finance*. Chicago: Author.

Coleman, J. S. (1966). *Report of the Commission on Equal Educational Opportunity*. Washington, DC: Government Printing Office.

Hickrod, G. A., Franklin, D. L., Hubbard, B. C., Hines, E. R., Polite, M. M., & Pruyne, G. B. (1988). *Guilty governments: The problem of inadequate educational funding in Illinois and other states*. Normal: Illinois State University, Center for the Study of Educational Finance.

Illinois State Board of Education. (1986). *Fall housing and enrollment report*. Springfield: Author.

State of Illinois, Bureau of the Budget. (1987). *Illinois Population Trends from 1980 to 2025*. Springfield: Author.

ELEVEN

Tipping the Scales From Inequality to Inequity

WILLIAM EDWARD EATON

This chapter is influenced by three books and 20 years of personal reflection about the history of U.S. education. The books are Kevin Phillips's *The Politics of Rich and Poor* (1990), C. Wright Mills's *The Sociological Imagination* (1959), and E. E. Schattsneider's *Semisovereign People* (1960). The Phillips's book I read only recently. The Mills's book was a book I managed to read while a graduate student (probably because it is a thin book, a requirement I held for books during that era). Schattsneider was read a few year ago when I was pressed into service to teach a course in the politics of education. Each book presented an idea or two that stuck with me, and these ideas influenced me as I wrote this chapter.

Kevin Phillips was a political strategist for the Nixon presidential campaign of 1968. His earlier book, *The Emerging Republican Majority* (1969), was an analysis of sectional politics and contained the prediction that a Republican hegemony over the White House was about to begin. As time passed, the prediction became prophecy and Phillips's status was transformed from political staffer to political pundit.

Phillips's 1990 book, *The Politics of Rich and Poor*, develops the central thesis that the growing disparity in personal wealth in this nation will eventuate in a revolt of the taxpaying masses. This will end the Republican hegemony and give the Democratic party an opportunity to seize the initiative—if it is bold enough to do so. The book is replete with charts, tables, and graphs that illustrate how the decade of the 1980s favored the economic "haves" at the expense of the "have-nots." I am also reminded of Ravi Batra's 1987 book titled *The Great Depression of 1990*. Batra's book is more economic than political, but its analysis pivots on the reality of financial disparity.

As I read Phillips's book, I could not help comparing his descriptions of the wide variance in personal wealth with the wide variance in school district wealth. Phillips points out that in 1979 the difference between the salary of corporate chief executive officers and their manufacturing employees was a multiple of 29. By 1985 the multiple stood at 40, and by 1988 *Business Week* reported that it had reached 93 (Phillips, 1990, pp. 179-180). The Congressional Budget Office reported that the average after-tax family income of the lowest 10% fell from $3,528 to $3,157 between 1977 and 1987, while, during the same period, the average family income of the top 10% increased from $70,459 to $89,783 (Phillips, 1990, p. 14). In my home state of Illinois, data collected by the State Board of Education for 1987-1988 showed that the poorest school district spent just $2,085 per child while the richest spent $12,866. But these numerical facts deserve to be placed in a broader context. Phillips, realizing that as well, quoted journalist William Greider, who wrote:

> Concentration of wealth was the fulcrum on which the most basic political questions pivoted, a dividing line deeper than region or religion, race or sex. In the nature of things, government might choose to enhance the economic prospects for the many or to safeguard the accumulated wealth

held by the few, but frequently the two purposes were in irreconcilable conflict. The continuing political struggle across this line, though unseen and rarely mentioned, was the central narrative of American political history, especially in the politics of money. (Phillips, 1990, p. xix)

Phillips also includes an interesting quotation taken from Will and Ariel Durant's *The Lessons of History*:

Since practical ability differs from person to person, the majority of such abilities, in nearly all societies, is gathered in a minority of men. The concentration of wealth is a natural result of this concentration of ability and regularly recurs in history. The rate of concentration varies . . . with the economic freedom permitted by morals and the laws. Despotism may for a time retard the concentration; democracy, allowing the most liberty, accelerates it. (Phillips, 1990, p. 73, the editing of this quotation was done by Phillips)

The quantitative "facts" and qualitative judgments mustered by Phillips get us back to an old question frequently posed by those who study school finance, "When does inequality become inequity?" That is, when does the difference in per pupil expenditure between districts stop becoming a measure of positive effort and start becoming an index for measuring the declining state of an educational underclass?

In *The Sociological Imagination*, C. Wright Mills draws a distinction between what he termed "the personal troubles of milieu" and "the public issues of social structure." I was reminded of this dichotomy while reading an article by John J. Rodger (1985) titled: "On the Degeneration of the Public Sphere," where Rodger uses this idea as well. In Mills's words:

Troubles occur within the character of the individual and within the range of his immediate relations with others; they have to do with his self and those limited areas of social life of which he is directly and personally aware. Accordingly, the statement and the resolution of troubles properly lie within the individual as a biographical entity and within the scope of his immediate milieu—the social setting that is directly open to this personal experience and to some extent his willful activity. A trouble is a private matter: values cherished by an individual are felt by him to be threatened.

Issues have to do with matters that transcend these local environments of the individual and the range of his inner life. They have to do with the organization of many such milieux into the institutions of an historical society as a whole, with the ways in which various milieux overlap and interpenetrate to form the larger structure of social and historical life. An issue is a public matter: some value cherished by publics is felt to be threatened. (Mills, 1959, p. 8)

I believe that this distinction is useful when considering the contemporary issue of school finance equity. School finance issues are nearing, I believe, the stage where they are being recognized as being beyond private matters and are vying to become the subject of widespread public policy debate.

I lean upon Schattsneider for his fascinating ideas about how individual concerns pass into policy options and eventually into specific policies. Schattsneider provides us with a process model that meets the test of common sense. His basic ideas are worth restating.

Ideology lies at the base of the policy formulation process. It is the ideology of our culture, borne of history and tradition and blended into custom and law, that determines what issues will emerge and how they will be treated. Our belief in democratic forms of government requires, for example, that any topic that enhances freedom be discussed and that discussion processes be open and inclusive. Thus policy options that result in the restriction of freedom or the restriction of participation are not likely to be popular and will probably be criticized by the judgment of the voters, the courts, or history. Despite their immense personal popularity, for example, President Abraham Lincoln's restriction of habeas corpus and President Franklin Roosevelt's internment of Japanese Americans escaped contemporary political agitation and the courts but not the focused hindsight of U.S. historians.

As ideology determines the general values inherent in any discussion of policy options and guides the processes by which discussion will take place, power politics will determine whether the issue even makes it to the table for discussion. Once policy options enter the stage of discussion, the conflict of the participants, or lack of conflict, will determine the shaping of the final policy. Radical change in policy requires radical conflict, or at least the potential for radical conflict.

So we have several threads: the disparity of per pupil expenditure, the conditions necessary for transforming personal problems into public issues, and the process by which public policy might emerge. What remains for me is the formidable task of weaving a fabric from these threads and looking backward into U.S. history for a usable pattern.

As a historian who has concentrated on the social history of U.S. education in the nineteenth and twentieth centuries, I have been influenced by three dramatic examples where private matters of milieu have become public issues. The first was the era of the common school, which began in the 1820s and lasted, in its final stages of completion, into the 1870s. The second was the era of progressive school reform, which was under way by the 1890s and extended into the 1920s. The third was the reform era of 1954 to 1975, where the issue of "equality of educational opportunity" forced the U.S. public school to think about its mission in terms of thousands of children previously underserved: ethnic minorities, the physically handicapped, and the mentally disadvantaged. To make my point, I will need to review these three periods briefly.

Education before the common school movement was essentially a private matter. To be sure, there were schools, and these schools took various shapes and forms and varied in quality from the excellent to the absurd. One need only point to Boston Latin Grammar School and Harvard College as examples of the excellent, which were on a par with anything offered by more refined societies in Europe. One needs also to be reminded of the sort of schooling available on the frontiers of the new nation or even its largest cities, which ranged from nonexistent to haphazard. Abraham Lincoln's education in

Pigeon Creek, Indiana, which was conducted only in the coldest of winter months so as not to interfere with anything important, is illustrative.

The common school movement was a movement precisely because it raised public questions about the desirability of keeping education a private matter. Horace Mann, Henry Barnard, and all of the men and women who became the greater and lesser known lights of the movement were catalytic agents who framed the issues of schooling as public policy concerns. Their arguments followed two basic lines: that, borrowing from Thomas Jefferson and other architects of the emerging republic, democracy required an educated populace; and, recognizing the economic horizons, that the incipient stages of the industrial revolution needed schools for the promotion of commerce. Clearly, the ideological elements were favorable.

We should not underestimate the political power or sophistication of either Horace Mann or Henry Barnard. Mann began his personal crusade for common schools only after becoming president of the Massachusetts Senate and having a legion of loyal followers among the reform Whigs throughout the Commonwealth and throughout New England. He was to go on to become a U.S. congressman and his name was frequently mentioned as a gubernatorial candidate.

Barnard led the movement for schools from Hartford, Connecticut, and was on a first name basis with every president of the United States from the 1840s onward. It was his constant harangue of these gentlemen of the White House that led every president from Franklin Pierce to Andrew Johnson to advocate the establishment of a U.S. Bureau of Education. He was finally successful and was given the appointment as the bureau's first director in 1867 (Warren, 1974, p. 110). But the times were also ripe for extending educational opportunity. The common school movement occurred during what historians were later to label the Jacksonian Era—an era where commonness itself was lauded, where there was a determined purpose to build new institutions and extend the scope of old institutions to populations previously unserved.

We should not underestimate the force that spawned de-
mocratization during the Jacksonian Era. The resolve to
change the fundamental nature of U.S. society was unwaver-
ing; the threat to use force to do so never far from the surface.
Schooling had left the "personal troubles of milieu" to become a public issue that affected basic social structure.

The progressive reform era that was well under way by the
1890s concerned itself with the form and substance of public
schooling. The consequences were several: the greater training and professionalization of teachers, child-centered pedagogy,
curricular innovations, and new ideas about what schools
ought to look like physically. The ideas themselves have long
roots extending back into the early nineteenth century. But
these issues moved from the dreams of reformers into the
consciousness of the practitioners and finally into the public
policy arena. It is interesting that there was a considerable
time lag between the point at which these ideas became the
conventional wisdom of the educators—largely realized in
the 1920s—and the 1940s when they became identifiable public policy concerns. In large part, the explanation for this time
lag is associated with the effects of the economic depression
and World War II. To a lesser extent, resistance came from a
fundamental belief that public institutions ought to practice
vigorous economy (sometimes bitter frugality, a tradition that
continues to haunt public schooling). Opponents of the progressive ideas bought time by associating the progressive
ideas as frills or as "soft pedagogy" based upon gadgets and
gimmicks. Progressive pedagogy is impossible, after all, with
the large classes that characterized the burgeoning city
schools of the late nineteenth and early twentieth centuries
that sought to serve the immigrant hordes.

The political allies of the educational progressives were the
political progressives. Their interest in reforming public institutions in general gradually spilled over into reforming the
schools. At first their concerns were structural rather than
curricular. They sought to depoliticize school boards by insist-
ing upon the replacement of large ward-based school boards
with the appointment of "blue-ribbon" boards of education.

With the successful completion of the progressive philosophy, we had moved from educational opportunity to the opportunity for educational quality. Left to be realized in the new century was equality of educational opportunity.

The Supreme Court's *Brown v. Board of Education* and the U.S. Congress's approval of the Elementary and Secondary Education Act and the Education for All Handicapped Act became the cornerstones of the reform era, which had as its purpose the extension of educational opportunity to African Americans, non-English-speaking ethnic minorities, the physically handicapped, the economically disadvantaged, and the mentally deficient. These cornerstones were laid only after a prolonged period of national debate that followed the realization by the parents of the black child, or the handicapped child, or the recent immigrant child, or the poor child that the schools were not helping that child realize the American dream of opportunity and the possibility of self-success. As with other historical instances, reality fell far short of rhetoric.

The *Brown v. Board of Education* decision came as no particular shock to followers of the court. Throughout the 1940s, the federal courts had decided a number of cases that chipped away at the "separate, but equal" idea of *Plessy v. Ferguson.* In the early 1950s, the U.S. Supreme Court had several cases similar to *Brown* waiting for consideration. In the Congress, Representative Adam Clayton Powell, Jr., as chair of the House Committee on Education and Labor, had held up every piece of legislation for federal aid to education that failed to promise racial integration. President Truman's executive order that desegregated the armed forces is yet another example that racial segregation, so carefully nourished for hundreds of years, was melting due to the small fires lit under its icy mass.

The Elementary and Secondary Education Act of 1965 was an extension of the War on Poverty. Its central provisions provided an influx of welcomed financial support for inner-city poverty areas. The research that it sponsored provided insight into the problems of educating the children of the subculture of poverty. The construct of "culturally deprived" (happily later changed to "culturally different") explained the problems of ethnic minorities and the difficulties of children who did not have English as their mother tongue or who lived in conditions destructive to personal growth.

The passage of the Education for All Handicapped Act was, I believe, an ideological extension of the concept of extending educational opportunity. In this case, the affected groups were children in wheelchairs or on crutches or children who could not learn under the normal conditions of schools, rather than children with brown faces or children with Spanish accents.

We have seen in our past then three movements that I have characterized as (a) the move for basic educational opportunity, (b) the move for educational quality, and (c) the move for equality of opportunity. This gradual evolution of ideas about schooling will shape our approach to the problem of school finance equity.

Imagine, if you will, a parent in the community of East St. Louis, Illinois. This parent has a child who has just graduated in the upper third of his high school class. Yet the child is informed that his score on the American College Testing (ACT) examination is a 12. This score, when compared with a national average that hovers around 18 from year to year, will disqualify the child from attending a four-year college, at least as a regular student. The parent is puzzled because the child was always thought to possess above-average intelligence and attended school faithfully and regularly across the grades.

The parent is distraught as he ponders the future of this child now seemingly condemned to a life of minimum wage jobs. There would be, of course, a period of self-doubt about his capability as a parent and probably doubts about the capacity of the child. But let us assume that this parent can move beyond these normal reactions and eventually conclude that these rationalizations are insufficient. In speaking with friends, the parent finds that several of these friends have children in a similar situation. These interactions soon become a topic for telephone conversations. Then a group meeting is organized. This group meeting becomes a scheduled public forum. Once expressed, a consensus bred of despair turns to righteous indignation. What if the school failed the child rather than the child failing the school?

The school district, by way of response, produces reams and boxes of computer printouts that show that the district taxed its citizens to their capacity, that the district's equalized assessed valuation per student was the lowest in the state (Illinois State Board of Education, 1989; $5,620), and that its failures lay with a system of state financing that is out of their hands (Hall & Smith-Dickson, 1990).

Assume further that this public forum becomes a public outcry and the citizenry conclude that their children have been victimized. Local politicians, never too far from the fray, assure the parents that they will argue this issue in the state capital. Thus unleashed, this grass-roots political movement gains momentum as parents throughout the state begin to see their own children similarly disadvantaged by a public school system that is underfinanced. Problems of the personal milieu have been transformed into a public issue.

Potential critics of the movement are largely silenced by the ideology. Can they argue that poor children deserve less? Can they blame the child for whatever the social or economic status of his or her parent might be? They are forced instead to rail against the higher taxes that significant improvements in education would require. Supply-side economists, Friedman free marketers, parental choice advocates, and tax watch groups form coalitions. But these coalitions lack an important ingredient in their struggle—moral conviction. Meanwhile, the issue bogs down in a state legislature caught in the morass of expediency, harangue, and deficit spending.

At this juncture, a test case is organized in which an individual parent files suit in the circuit court on behalf of his minor child contesting that the child's right to a constitutionally guaranteed efficient and effective education has been violated. A parade of academic witnesses, testing companies, and civil rights advocates testify before the court arguing that, when within-district analyses are made, African Americans suffer a form of subtle discrimination—they are unprepared by reasons of instruction to score at median levels on national standardized tests. But this is not true when small numbers of African American students are enrolled in primarily Caucasian schools. The latter fact militates against any interpretation that calls intellectual capacities based upon race into question.

After due deliberation, the court finds the system of financing that allows such disparity with concomitant negative educational outcomes to be "inherently unequal and inequitable." The state is ordered to redesign its financing structure with "due deliberate speed."

This hypothetical example may seem far-fetched, but it is not without some plausibility. To begin with, some of its plausibility is borne of history. The historical vignettes that were presented earlier lend credence, I think, to the case. I am confident that those who argued initially for a system of tax-supported public schools in the early 1800s were thought to be a bit cranky and out of step. But they did prevail.

Second, our traditions of looking to the public schools to redress grievances of the larger social order are well established. The decision of *Brown v. Board* and the passage of the Elementary and Secondary Education Act and the Education for All Handicapped Act bear that out. We have come to expect the schools to do what we as citizens refuse to do: racially integrate, provide encouragement and sustenance for the downtrodden, and offer compensatory experiences for those whose social and economic means have diluted the full richness of life—especially if those persons are children.

Third, although our courts are a long way from accepting the sort of legal challenge I have outlined, they are meandering in that general direction. The language of the Supreme Court of Kentucky (*Council for Better Education v. Wilkerson*) in its 1989 ruling, which rendered that state's system of school financing unconstitutional, stated that

> *education is perhaps the most important function of state and local governments.* Compulsory school attendance laws and the great expenditures for education both demonstrate

our recognition of the importance of education to our democratic society. It is required in the performance of our most basic public responsibilities, even service in the armed forces. It is the very foundation of good citizenship. Today it is a principal instrument in awakening the child to cultural values, in preparing him to adjust normally to his environment. In these days, it is doubtful that any child may reasonably be expected to succeed in life if he is denied the opportunity of an education. *Such an opportunity, where the state has undertaken to provide it, is a right which must be made available to all on equal terms.* (p. 190)

The state trial court proceedings, which the Kentucky Supreme Court was reviewing, had accepted a very broad definition of "efficient schools." This included the usual concerns for standard uniformity and prudent management but went on to accept testimony that determined that "the achievement test scores in the poorer districts are lower than those in the richer districts. Expert opinion clearly established that there is a correlation between those scores and the wealth of the district" (*Council for Better Education v. Wilkerson*, p. 197). Increasingly then relationships between wealth and achievement will become fodder for the courts to digest.

On Tuesday, November 12, 1990, a suit was filed in the Circuit Court of Cook County, Illinois, by 47 school districts that challenged the system of state school finance (*Committee for Educational Rights v. Thompson, et al.*). The complaint alleged, similar to the Kentucky case, that the state constitution promises "an efficient system of high quality public educational institutions and services." It was further charged that the disparity in school district financing violated the "Equal Protection Clause" of the Illinois Constitution as well as its promise of efficiency.

The Illinois case (*Committee for Educational Rights*) cites a lot of data comparing the richest 10% of the school districts with the poorest 10%. In so doing, it was pointed out that the wealthier districts have a 29% better pupil-teacher ratio, that 55% more teachers had master's degrees, and that teacher salaries were 26% higher. Unlike Kentucky, where the state assembly was the defendant, the Illinois plaintiffs named the governor, the state superintendent of education, and the State Board of Education. These two cases go a long way in substantiating the possibility of my argument.

Finally, we are a culture in which children are held in high esteem. The late anthropologist Margaret Mead lost no opportunity in her writings to remind us of that. And yet the poorest segment in U.S. society today are children. As John Naisbitt and Patricia Aburdene (1980, p. 46) point out in their otherwise upbeat book, *Megatrends 2000,*

> In the early seventies 1 family in 9 was headed by a woman, but beginning in the early 1980's, there were huge increases in the number of unwed mothers. Today 1 family in 6 is headed by a single mother. There are 5.5 million poor families with children, contrasted with 4.1 million in 1979. That means that the poor are overwhelmingly children.

No system that sorts out children in order to cast some upon the garbage heap will be allowed to endure.

This final point—the future of children—holds the key, I believe. Welfare programs have had only moderate success because they have concentrated upon the adult populations. Habits of heart, mind, and body are difficult to undo, especially when the mandates to do so flow through layers of faceless bureaucrats into the stark reality of being. Food stamp programs, adult reeducation programs, and subsidized housing reach children only indirectly.

I am more optimistic about the effects of schooling upon poor children. Breakfast and lunch programs, Head Start and all-day kindergarten programs, and special reading programs help these children. And these programs foster hope, a quality that the child of poverty may not experience anywhere else.

We are, I believe, in the beginning stages of a new dialogue. What may emerge is a movement that will discuss the relationships between schooling, learning, school finance, poverty, and educational opportunity. This dialogue has the chance of leading to a major movement if the scales are tipped from the fact of inequality to a sensitivity about equity. If this comes to fruition, we may in the future refer to it as "education for equity."

References

Batra, R. (1987). *The great depression of 1990.* New York: Simon & Schuster.
Committee for Educational Rights v. Thompson, et al. (filed in the Circuit Court of Cook County, Illinois, Chancery Division, November 1990).
Council for Better Education v. Wilkerson. Kentucky Supreme Court (1989).
Hall, R. F., & Smith-Dickson, B. (Eds.). (1990). *Financing Illinois schools in the 1990s: Reaching a consensus.* Macomb: Western Illinois University, Institute for Rural Affairs.
Illinois State Board of Education. (1989). *Illinois public school financial statistics, 1987-88 school year.* Springfield: Illinois State Board of Education.
Mills, C. W. (1959). *The sociological imagination.* New York: Oxford.
Naisbitt, J., & Aburdene, P. (1980). *Megatrends 2000.* New York: William.
Phillips, K. P. (1969). *The emerging Republican majority.* New Rochelle, NY: Arlington House.
Phillips, K. P. (1990). *The politics of rich and poor.* New York: Random House.
Rodger, J. J. (1985). On the degeneration of the public sphere. *Political Studies, 33,* 203-217.
Schattsneider, E. E. (1960). *Semisovereign people: A realist's view of democracy in America.* New York: Holt, Rinehart & Winston.
Warren, D. (1974). *To enforce education: A history of the founding years of the United States Office of Education.* Detroit: Wayne State University Press.

TWELVE

Schools and the Struggle for Democracy
THEMES FOR SCHOOL
FINANCE POLICY

JAMES GORDON WARD

The foregoing chapters present a complex and somewhat bleak picture of the future of U.S. public schools and public school finance. Some common themes run through the chapters in this book. U.S. schools are becoming more racially and culturally diverse. Another way of saying this is that the differences among children are increasing, raising issues of pedagogy, community building, and financing as well as issues relating to governance and political support. Many of these differences relate to different experiences prior to formal schooling. U.S. public schools will see more children whose home language is not English, more children who were not born or whose parents were not born in the United States, more children who were born and are growing up in poverty, and more children who have home lives that differ significantly from the traditional American dream.

Many of these children will live and go to school in communities that are geographically and socially isolated from "middle-class America." Poverty and culturally diverse populations are not evenly spread across the landscape and tend to be concentrated in urban enclaves as well as in certain self-contained suburban and rural communities.

At the same time, economic and political power in the United States is more and more concentrated in an elite that has seceded from the rest of society in much of their daily lives (Reich, 1991). This elite is well educated, affluent, and not likely to live near those different from themselves. This elite uses private transportation to travel between a home in an urban high-rise building, trendy town house, or lush suburban community to a secure and opulent office building in the city center or suburban office park, rarely seeing the rest of the world along the way. Class and race have a lot to do with the cultural differences that exist in the United States, and these factors all have a major impact on education and school finance. The quality of schooling received and the amount of money spent on that schooling differ greatly depending on where one lives and in what social strata one's parents reside. This has provided an enduring dilemma for public school finance specialists and for public policymakers, and demographic changes are likely to worsen the situation. What is emerging is a situation where, more than ever before in the history of our nation, the acquisition of economic and political power is dependent on access to high-quality education. As a scarce resource, high-quality education is carefully allocated, and it is no accident that those who have economic and political power allocate it to their own children, either through private schools or excellent public schools, and the rest of society makes do with the leftovers. Demographic trends in the United States set the stage for a situation where economic and political power will be held by a maturing, affluent middle class who will tend to live in the suburbs, while the greatest educational needs will be among poor and often minority children in the inner city or in rural ghettoes. Will the former pay higher taxes to properly educate the latter?

Schools and Democracy

This question raises the question of what schools are likely to be like as organizations. Greenfield (1984, p. 145) has written that "organizations are manifestations of culture and we may understand them with only so much ease or difficulty as we can understand the culture in which they are embedded." Recent social and economic analysis has indicated that the rich are getting richer and the poor are getting poorer in the United States, and the implication is that two distinctly different cultures can be associated with the affluent and the needy in this country (Phillips, 1990; Reich, 1991). Reich (1991) argues that the affluent are part of a global culture, based on information and the ability to engage in symbolic analysis. Those performing routine production services or in-person services are less mobile, have fewer life opportunities, and earn much less money. This social analysis would suggest that these two different cultures will produce two different kinds of school organizations, which will in turn produce educational experiences that will vary greatly in nature and quality through the process of cultural reproduction (Bowles & Gintis, 1989).

The nature and quality of schooling not only are important for economic reasons, such as career preparation, but are politically important as well. The political aspects of education may have been stated best by Cremin (1990, p. 85) when he wrote that "education has always served political functions insofar as it affects, or at least is believed or intended to affect, the future character of the community and the state." Giroux and McLaren (1989, p. xxi) remind us that "American schooling becomes a vital sphere for extending civil rights, fighting for cultural justice, and developing new forms of democratic public life within a life-affirming public culture." These issues suggest the development of a community with common cultural values and argue for an approach to public schooling that prepares children for living through common experiences. Values form the basis for public policy decisions about schooling and for school finance policy decisions (Guthrie,

Garms, & Pierce, 1988; Ward, 1987). It is fundamental to a democracy that public institutions will represent democratic values. Gutman (1987, p. 14) argues that

> a democratic theory of education recognizes the importance of empowering citizens to make educational policy and also of constraining their choices among policies in accordance with these principles—of nonrepression and nondiscrimination—that preserve the intellectual and social foundations of democratic deliberations.

The issue of nondiscrimination must be raised concerning the differing nature and quality of education among different schools and school districts. When different cultures produce different school organizations that support very different kinds of educational services, questions of discrimination arise because of the economic, social, and political consequences of those educational services. This is the essence of the issue of student equity in school finance. The question is not fundamentally one of finance, however, but one of governance and control. Gutman (1987, p. 16) goes on to say that "the central question posed by democratic education is: Who should have authority to shape the education of future citizens?"

The Control and Financing of Schools

The traditional view of public education in the United States is that it is the responsibility of the states but is delivered through local agencies under state supervision. Therefore the systems of governance and finance for U.S. public schools have been mixed state-local systems. This very fact has produced much discontent, because different individuals and groups have had different views on what the relative responsibilities of each party should be in differing circumstances. Much of this has had to do with differences in values and interests. This poses a dilemma, which has been described as follows:

> Education for citizenship and self-government . . . affir-
> matively obligates the state to provide all citizens with
> the quality and character of education appropriate for
> participation in political and community affairs. The state
> must provide an education that conforms to the level of
> participation self-governing communities expect from the
> citizenry. (Hubsch, 1989, p. 99)

The precise nature of the dilemma concerns what constitutes a
community for purposes of self-governing. The implication in
much of the school governance and school finance literature is
that the community is a local community, such as a city, town,
or village and its hinterlands. This is embodied in the traditional
idea of local control, which has had a long and healthy life in
public education in the United States. While not predicting its
demise, Alexander (1990) makes a powerful argument that local
control is a powerful mechanism for fostering discrimination
and perpetuating privilege in public schooling. What then might
constitute the proper community?

In his classic work, Morrison (1930) argues that the state is
the community. After careful and exhaustive analysis of the
history and functions of the U.S. public school system, he concluded that

> the several states themselves are the appropriate fiscal
> and administrative units in the support and conduct of
> the citizenship school which has long been held to be the
> cornerstone of our polity as a self-governing State. (Mor-
> rison, 1930, p. 214)

To the extent that the affluent and the less than affluent live
in the same state, although not in the same local community,
by regarding the self-governing community as the state, we
can move toward removing some of the repression and discrimination that may now exist in public schooling. If the
"quality and character" of education is determined at the
state level, and that quality and character are assured for all
children, then progress is being made. The critical issues become the definition of the quality and character of public

education and the enforcement of that definition across school districts. Local community control, just as parental or family control, will undermine attempts to ensure a high level of quality and character for all children. Local communities will lose much of their ability to be enclaves for the protection of privilege or as places to which the "successful have seceded" from the rest of society (Reich, 1991).

Policy Mechanisms for Attaining Equality of Opportunity

Following the early intellectual leadership of Cubberley (1905), school finance policymakers have used state equalization formulas as one mechanism for providing some standardization of education quality among communities. There is a broad literature in this area, and there is no need to examine it here. State equalization formulas, however, have generally failed to accomplish their purposes for two reasons: They are seldom funded at a high enough level by the state to be effective, and they continue to allow local communities discretion in setting local property tax rates for school purposes. The politics of privilege and exclusion prevent either of these from being changed. Affluent local school districts can support a high level of education without a great deal of assistance from the state. Any increase in state taxes to assure this level of education for all children in the state would produce a heavy tax burden on the residents of these affluent districts with the economic benefit flowing to other districts in the state. Affluent communities also want no restrictions on their tax levying ability because they fear that state controls may reduce their ability to maintain their position of privilege. In many states, the growing political power of suburban legislators, representing areas where most of the affluent districts are located, prevent any resolution of this problem.

Another policy mechanism that has been used to address this problem is petition to the courts for redress for alleged discrimination or failure to provide quality education. This approach has had varying popularity with particularly heavy periods of judicial activity in the early 1970s and since 1989 (Thro, 1990). While there is ample evidence that such legal suits have altered state school finance formulas in states where the plaintiffs have been successful in court, the evidence is much less clear on whether there have been any significant gains in overall funding levels as a result of school finance reform suits, and there is scant evidence that the quality and character of the education of children of the poor have been significantly improved (Salmon & Alexander, 1990; Ward, 1990).

Outside of the realm of school finance policy, a variety of policy interventions have been attempted to solve the problem through attempts at the alleviation of poverty, income distribution, and local community economic development. Williams (1989) has documented the extreme difficulties inherent in indigenous neighborhood organizing for urban school reform, while Wilson (1987) has analyzed the persistence of urban poverty and the difficulties of maintaining high-quality social institutions and services in the midst of urban decay. The problems of rural poverty and maintaining viable social institutions under conditions of rural decline have been well established by Davidson (1990). Finally, the classic work of Ogbu (1978) has discussed the issues of race and education and documented the castelike rigidity of race-based barriers to educational and economic success. The politics of redistribution have also met with little success in alleviating urban poverty and the low quality of social services in declining urban areas (Peterson, 1981). These all call into question the effectiveness of various social policy interventions in moving our society toward quality education for all children.

What can be some avenues for freeing U.S. public schools from being antidemocratic instruments of social reproduction that support the perpetuation of privilege among our political and economic elite and fail to properly serve many of our children?

Some Themes for Policy
Research and Development

I do not propose that I have the answer to the question I just posed, but I do want to suggest some areas for the redirection of our current policy research and development activities in education finance and governance that I think will move us toward answering the question.

The connections between educational outcomes and results and spending and governance patterns need additional exploration. The weak link in much of the educational research and in the factual base for school finance reform cases is the relationship among governance systems, expenditures per pupil, and educational outcomes. Traditional production function studies are limited methodologically and present few useful outcomes. Their error factors are too large to be of any explanatory value. Many of the school finance reform lawsuit complaints claim a direct relationship between spending per pupil and educational results, but upon careful scrutiny, they fail to prove the case. We need more studies that show the relationship between the way schools are organized and the way they are financed and the results they produce. Outcome variables are needed to make these studies useful; process variables are of much less value. If commentators like Reich and Phillips are correct, we should be able to discern the relationship between the dollars spent on education and the qualitative outcomes of that education.

We need to rethink the state's role in specifying educational outcomes and results for local schools. While states have constitutional responsibility for public education, they allow tremendous latitude in what they permit local school districts to do in the name of curriculum and instructional programs. As a result, the quality of education varies greatly across districts according to patterns described in this chapter. We need to give greater consideration to state standards and state expectations without constraining local districts in their ability to innovate and experiment. Accountability measures need to focus on outcomes and results rather than processes.

The federal role in education also needs reexamination. If some consistency of quality and character of education within states is important, then a similar degree of consistency among states is also a critical issue. The traditional federal role of funding programs for special needs students will require expansion. States do not have the fiscal resources, in many cases, to provide sufficient funding for programs for those with special needs. In a global economy, based on information and symbolic analysis, there is sufficient national interest in high-quality educational services for all children to justify a much larger federal role in education.

We need to rethink the program content and curriculum of our public schools. Some schools offer the kind of curriculum that allows students to succeed in an information-based society; many do not. One of the problems of local control is that the preferences of many communities do not include the quality and character of education that is needed for success in contemporary society. While parents have a responsibility to do what is best for their children, they should not have the right to intellectually handicap their children for life. In these instances, the responsibility of the state should take precedence over the rights of the parents. Local control is often a stalking-horse for educational mediocrity.

We need to institute systems of full-state funding and statewide school systems to protect the rights of all children. The current state-local system of public schools fails many children. Only a system where the state assumes responsibility for the quality and character of education for all children will ensure equal educational opportunities. It has been known for more than 60 years that current systems of school finance and school governance are inadequate to the task, but we are not willing to change. Until we are willing to do so, little if any progress will be made.

We need to engage in a public dialogue about why all these innovations are necessary. We cannot underestimate the power of public discourse in convincing the citizens of our states that major systemic changes need to take place to ensure the equal educational opportunity for all children for the future of our society. Public conversations can be a powerful device to arrive at social consensus.

All of these ideas require additional research and development work. They should help set the research agenda for school finance specialists for the next decade or so. We have a moral imperative to make sure that they do.

References

Alexander, K. (1990). Equitable financing, local control, and self-interest. In J. K. Underwood & D. A. Verstegen (Eds.), *The impacts of litigation and legislation on public school finance: Adequacy, equity, and excellence* (pp. 293-309). New York: Harper & Row.

Bowles, S., & Gintis, H. (1989). Can there be a liberal philosophy of education in a democratic society? In H. A. Giroux & P. McLaren (Eds.), *Critical pedagogy, the state, and cultural struggle* (pp. 24-31). Albany: State University of New York Press.

Cremin, L. A. (1990). *Popular education and its discontents.* New York: Harper & Row.

Cubberley, E. P. (1905). *School funds and their apportionment.* New York: Columbia University, Teachers College.

Davidson, O. G. (1990). *Broken heartland: The rise of America's rural ghetto.* New York: Free Press.

Giroux, H. A., & McLaren, P. (1989). Introduction: Schooling, cultural politics, and the struggle for democracy. In H. A. Giroux & P. McLaren (Eds.), *Critical pedagogy, the state, and cultural struggle* (pp. xi-xxxv). Albany: State University of New York Press.

Greenfield, T. B. (1984). Leaders and schools: Willfulness and nonnatural order in organizations. In T. J. Sergiovanni & J. E. Corbally (Eds.), *Leadership and organizational culture* (pp. 142-169). Urbana: University of Illinois Press.

Guthrie, J. W., Garms, W. I., & Pierce, L. C. (1988). *School finance and education policy: Financing educational efficiency, equality, and choice.* Englewood Cliffs, NJ: Prentice-Hall.

Gutman, A. (1987). *Democratic education.* Princeton, NJ: Princeton University Press.

Hubsch, A. W. (1989). Education and self-government: The right to education under state constitutional law. *Journal of Law and Education, 18,* 93-140.

Morrison, H. C. (1930). *School revenue.* Chicago: University of Chicago Press.
Ogbu, J. U. (1978). *Minority education and caste: The American system in cross-cultural perspective.* New York: Academic Press.
Peterson, P. E. (1981). *City limits.* Chicago: University of Chicago Press.
Phillips, K. (1990). *The politics of rich and poor.* New York: Random House.
Reich, R. B. (1991). *The work of nations: Preparing ourselves for 21st-century capitalism.* New York: Knopf.
Salmon, R. G., & Alexander, M. D. (1990). State legislative responses. In J. K. Underwood & D. A. Verstegen (Eds.), *The impacts of litigation and legislation on public school finance: Adequacy, equity, and excellence* (pp. 249-271). New York: Harper & Row.
Thro, W. E. (1990). The third wave: The impact of the Montana, Kentucky, and Texas decisions on the future of public school finance reform litigation. *Journal of Law and Education, 19,* 219-250.
Ward, J. G. (1987). An inquiry into the normative foundations of American public school finance. *Journal of Education Finance, 12,* 463-477.
Ward, J. G. (1990). Implementation and monitoring of judicial mandates: An interpretive analysis. In J. K. Underwood & D. A. Verstegen (Eds.), *The impacts of litigation and legislation on public school finance: Adequacy, equity, and excellence* (pp. 225-248). New York: Harper & Row.
Williams, M. R. (1989). *Neighborhood organizing for urban school reform.* New York: Teachers College Press.
Wilson, W. J. (1987). *The truly disadvantaged: The inner city, the underclass, and public policy.* Chicago: University of Chicago Press.

A P P E N D I X

American Education Finance Association Board of Directors, 1991-1992

OFFICERS

Van D. Mueller, *President*
David H. Monk, *President-Elect*
George R. Babigian, *Executive Director and Secretary/Treasurer*
Margaret E. Goertz, *Immediate Past President*

DIRECTORS

1992 Term

Stephen M. Barro
Terry G. Geske
William F. Hughes, Jr.
C. Phillip Kearney
Cyril Kent McGuire

1993 Term

Patricia Anthony
Debra S. Haas
David Honeyman
Anne L. Jefferson
Joel D. Sherman

1994 Term

James N. Fox
G. Alfred Hess, Jr.
Stephen B. Lawton
Mary T. Moore
Lawrence O. Picus

Index

Achievement: blacks and, 38, 42; class size and, 36-37; dropouts and, 108; federal programs and, 90; Hispanics and, 127, 130-131, 132; minorities and, 35, 37-38; poverty and, 35; school expenditures and, 35-36; socioeconomic status and, 52, 213; tracking and, 134
Administration for Children, Youth, and Families, 112
Africa: average incomes, 80; poverty in, 79, 81
African Americans, *See* Blacks
Aid to Families With Dependent Children, 41, 78
Alaska, per pupil expenditures, 84
American Federation of Teachers, 5
American schooling, trends in, 4-6
Asia, poverty in, 79
Asian/Pacific Islanders, 5, 174; California and, 10, 115, 116, 183, 184; Florida and, 113; Illinois and, 203, 205, 212; population percentages, 6, 100; Texas population, 144
Attention deficit disorder, 107
Average daily attendance, current expenditure per, 3

Baby boom generation: "echo effect" of, 7; maturation of, 3, 7-8, 205
Balance-of-payments crises, 81-82
Baltimore, state financing systems and, 32
Basic skills problem, 117
Behavior disorders, 107
Bilingual education, 110, 129, 135
Birthrates: minorities and, 127-128; public school enrollments and, 12; public policy and, 126; *See also specific populations*
Black culture, teaching, 22
Blacks, 4; achievement and, 38, 42; average age, 128; birthrates, 99, 128; California and, 115, 116, 184; caste system and, 22; dropouts, 84, 86, 103; female-headed households and, 25, 75, 101; Florida and, 113; high school population, 7; homeless, 77; Illinois and, 203, 205, 212; population growth and, 6, 7, 100; poverty and, 11, 24-25, 40, 75, 101; Texas population, 144, 145; urban schools and, 5, 22-24
Boston, financial mismanagement and, 30
Brazil, infant mortality rate, 80-81

Guerrero, Lena, 157

Handicapped children, 4; federal
    funds for, 111; urban schools
    and, 26-27
Head Start, 89, 109, 111, 147
Health care, 92; California and, 186;
    federal support of, 90; poor
    families and, 78; poorest na-
    tions, 82; prenatal and postna-
    tal, 27, 101, 146; quality of, 13;
    Texas and, 146; urban areas
    and, 40; World Bank and, 87
High school diploma, 3; extrinsic
    value of, 137; income and, 9;
    jobs requiring, 142
High school dropouts, *see* Dropouts
Hispanics, 5; achievement and, 127,
    130-131, 132; average age, 128;
    birthrate, 99, 127-128; Califor-
    nia and, 10-11, 115, 116, 183,
    184, 185; college preparatory
    classes and, 131; dropouts, 84,
    86, 103, 126, 130, 133, 136; edu-
    cational attainment, 130-131;
    family income, 132; female-
    headed households and, 25,
    101; Florida and, 113, 173-174;
    gifted programs and, 129;
    homeless, 77; Illinois and, 203,
    205, 212; immigration trends,
    127; intracultural diversity, 131-
    133; isolation of, 128-129; lim-
    ited English proficiency and,
    129; political representation
    and, 156; population growth
    and, 6-7; poverty and, 11, 24-
    25, 40, 75, 132; public policy
    and, 127; rising enrollments,
    125-139; school finance and
    funding and, 138; school re-
    sponses to changing popula-
    tion, 133-139; segregation and,
    128-129; southwestern states
    and, 10-11; special education
    and, 129; Texas and, 145; track-
    ing and, 127, 134; un-
    dereducated, 126-127, 128;

urban areas and, 128; voca-
    tional programs and, 129, 131
Hispanos, 132
HIV positive mothers, 27
Hmong immigrants, 182
Homelessness, 40, 77, 105
Homicides, urban areas and, 40
Household size, population trends
    and, 8-9
Housing, 92; lack of affordable, 77;
    poor families and, 78; urban
    areas and, 40, 41
Housing and Urban Development as-
    sistance, 78
Human capital theory, 88

Illegal aliens, 115, 132
Illinois: alternatives to current reve-
    nue generating pattern in, 222-
    225; educational expenditures,
    129, 198-225, 238-239; elderly
    and, 207; Hispanic enroll-
    ments, 129; minorities in, 129,
    203, 205, 210-212; population
    changes in, 199-207; poverty
    and, 212-213; property reassess-
    ment and, 216-221; school en-
    rollment changes, 207-213;
    spending for elementary educa-
    tion, 83; whites in, 202-203; *See
    also* Chicago
Illiteracy, 82, 83, 89
Immigration to U.S., 7, 88, 99, 100;
    California and, 182-183; Florida
    and, 113, 174; Hispanics, 127;
    public school enrollments and,
    12; service jobs and, 8; urban
    schools and, 21
Immigration Control and Reform
    Act (1986), 107
Income: education level and, 10, 12-
    13; median family, 73; sym-
    bolic analysts and, 13
Income distribution, 9-10, 12, 74, 80,
    247
India, income distribution in, 79, 80
Indianapolis, school expenditures
    and, 34

Industrial countries, economic performance in, 71
Infant mortality, 76, 80-81, 89, 116, 186
Inflation, 1980s, 73, 74
Information Age, 72, 249
Interest rates, developing countries
and, 81
Isolation: curriculum and, 53; Hispanics and, 128-129; limited English
proficiency classes and, 129; student migration and, 58-59

Job training, 89
Juvenile incarceration, California
and, 186

Kindergarten, historical enrollments
in, 3

Labor, unskilled, 98, 146, 176
Labor force, population trends and, 8
Labor unions, 5. See also Collective
bargaining
Latchkey children, 116, 186
Latin America, poverty in, 79, 80. See
also Central/South American
immigrants
Latinos, 132
Learning disabilities, growth in, 107
Life expectancy, 89
Limited English proficiency, 4, 12,
105-106; California and, 184-
185; Hispanics and, 129, 133;
Mexican Americans and, 133;
urban schools and, 28
Local control: California and, 187;
curriculum and, 249; policy decisions and, 15, 98; property
taxes and, 150, 246
Local government, school revenues
and, 3-4, 29, 98
Local support systems, for teachers,
106
Los Angeles: bilingual teachers and,
106; Hispanic barrios, 182-183;
limited-English proficients in,

28; public school enrollments,
184; steady deterioration in, 39
Lunches, free and reduced-priced, 78

Malnutrition, 80, 89
Mann, Horace, 232
McCown, Scott, 152, 153
Medicaid, 90
Mexican Americans: birthrates and,
128; limited English profi-
ciency and, 133; subgroups,
131-133; See also Hispanics
Migrant children, 106-107
Migrants, 105
Migration, from rural areas, see
Rural outmigration
Military expansion, 77-78, 79
Military service, rural outmigration
and, 57, 59, 60, 62, 63
Milwaukee: limited-English proficiency and, 28; misallocation of
resources, 36; property taxes
and, 29; pupil poverty rate, 32;
school districts, 30-31; school
expenditures and, 32, 34
Minorities, 6; achievement and, 35,
37-38; birthrates and, 127-128;
California and, 115, 116; college attendance and, 109; dropping out, 38, 142; increasing
numbers of, 86; in workplace,
8; political power and, 14; population percentage, 99-100; poverty and, 24-26; public policy
and, 7; special education and,
27; Texas and, 144; See also
Asian/Pacific Islanders;
Blacks; Hispanics
Minority-majority state: California
as, 184; Texas as, 145
Mississippi, per pupil expenditures
in, 84
Moak, Lynn, 152
Monetary policy, 1980s, 73
Morales, Dan, 157
Mothers, drug dependent, 27
Mothers, single, see Female-headed households; Single-parent families

equity and, 230-240; school size
and, 61; social trends and, 2;
special populations and, 98;
states and, 5, 15; urban underclass and, 12; values and, 243-
244; welfare and, 41
Public school system: local control
of, 15; rapid expansion of, 7
Puerto Ricans, 131, 132, 133

"Quality problem," 35

Racial change, urban schools and, 22-
24
Racial differences, education level
and, 4
Reading ability, 90, 108
Reagan administration, 72; education cuts and, 29; poverty increasing during, 79; Title XX
and, 112; urban policies and, 41
Recession, 33; 1974-1975, 171; 1980s,
73, 75, 82-83
Reform era, 231
Restructuring movement, 137
Retirement, 8
Richards, Ann, 152-153, 156-157
*Rodriguez v. San Antonio Indep. Sch.
Dist.*, 148
Rural areas: ability test scores, 59;
college attendance and, 62; curriculum and, 49, 51-68; economic opportunity in, 50, 52;
loss of intelligent youth and,
50; poverty in, 24, 75, 80; socioeconomic status and, 63; vocational courses and, 68; *See also*
Rural outmigration
Rural economic activity, vocational
training and, 56-57
Rural outmigration, 48-68; college attendance and, 57, 59-60, 62;
common routes, 57; curriculum
effects on, 51-68; military service and, 57, 59, 60, 62, 63;
school effects on, 51; school
size and, 66

Rustbelt: teacher salaries and, 37;
urban decline in, 29

San Antonio, Texas, education expenditures in, 148
San Francisco, education expenditures in, 28
Savings rate, 73
Scholastic Aptitude Test: central city
schools and, 38; Hispanics students and, 130
School(s): construction, 4; control of,
244-246; democracy and, 243-
244
School districts: property-poor, 147-
150; size of, 16
School expenditures, *see* Education
expenditures
School finance and funding, 181; California and, 180-195; Florida
and, 160-178; Hispanics and,
138; historical sources for, 3-4;
Illinois and, 198-225, 238-239;
public policy and, 230-240; reform, 4, 14, 18; states and, 18-19
School governance, teachers and, 5
School push-outs, 109
School reform, *see* Education reform
School size, 59; curriculum and, 52,
61-62; public policy and, 61;
rural outmigration and, 66; vocational courses and, 60
School structure, experimentation
and, 16-17
Secondary schools: black population
and, 7; curriculum and, 54-68;
federal funds for, 110; historical enrollment, 3; revenues for,
3, 78, 110; school district size
and, 16
Segregation: economic stratification
and, 98; Hispanics and, 128-
129; private schools and, 16;
urban schools and, 22-24
Seriously Emotionally Disturbed,
107-108
Serrano v. Priest, 188-189
Service jobs, 8, 146, 176, 243

Unemployment: 1960s, 89; 1980s, 73;
     World Bank's strategy and, 87
Unemployment insurance, 78
Unions, *see* Labor unions
United Kingdom, poverty in, 79
Unwed parents, 85, 100-101
Urban areas: decaying, 247; dropout
     rates, 86; drug use and, 40; fed-
     eral grants and, 41; Hispanics
     in, 128; homicides and, 40; mi-
     gration to, 50; 1960s crises, 7;
     poverty and, 24-26, 39-42, 75;
     stagnating, 10; tax base and, 29
Urban schools: art and music cut-
     backs and, 33; blacks and, 5, 22-
     24; bureaucratic dysfunction
     of, 35-36; changes in racial com-
     position, 22-23; class size and,
     31, 33, 37; cultural diversity in,
     21-45; desegregation problems,
     24; educational costs and, 33;
     equity perspective, 31-34; ex-
     penditures and, 31-34; financial
     resources of, 28-31; handi-
     capped and, 26-27; immigrants
     and, 21; indicators of pupil
     need and, 24-28; limited-En-
     glish proficiency and, 28; pov-
     erty and, 24-26; productivity
     perspective, 35-38; racial
     change and segregation in, 22-
     24; state revenues and, 30;
     steady deterioration in, 39; stu-
     dent migration and, 58; teacher
     salaries and, 37; urban ecology
     perspective, 38-42
Urban superintendencies, vacancies
     in, 31
Urban underclass, 12, 39
United States, economic and demo-
     graphic changes in, 72-79

U.S. culture, Mexican Americans re-
     sisting, 133

Values, public policy and, 243-244
Vietnamese refugees, 182
Vocational courses/training, 56-57;
     college attendance and, 63; His-
     panics and, 129, 131; rural areas
     and, 68; school size and, 60

War on Poverty, 88, 101, 110, 192
Wealth, disparities in, 9, 74, 149-150,
     243
Welfare, 101; dropouts and, 84; poor
     families on, 77; public policy
     and, 41
Western states: political conserva-
     tives in, 14; population trends
     and, 10-11
Whites: average age, 128; birthrates,
     99, 128; dropouts, 103, 126; Illi-
     nois and, 202-203; population
     percentage, 99; poverty and,
     11, 24-26, 75; Texas population,
     144; urban schools and, 23
Whitley, Douglas, 215
Wilson, Pete, 193-194
Women: education versus income
     and, 10; income distribution
     and, 9; *See also* Female-headed
     households; Teenage mothers
Work ethic, 88
World Bank, 87

Youth at risk, 11

Zambia, poverty in, 80

About the Editors:

James Gordon Ward is Associate Dean of Education, and Associate Professor of Educational Administration, Curriculum and Instruction, and of Government and Public Affairs at the University of Illinois at Urbana-Champaign. He is a past president of the American Educational Finance Association. He is a former teacher, educational policy analyst, and served eight years as Director of Research for the American Federation of Teachers. He received his Ed.D. from Virginia Polytechnic Institute and State University. His research interests include the political and legal aspects of state school finance policy, school organization and leadership, and political theory. He has an emerging interest in the institutional relationships among school finance, curriculum, and school quality.

Patricia Anthony is Assistant Professor of Educational Administration at the University of Massachusetts at Amherst. Prior to entering higher education, she was a special education teacher and curriculum specialist. From 1985 to 1989, she was editor of the *Journal of Educational Finance*, which she now serves as a member of the editorial advisory board. She received her doctorate from the University of Florida. Her primary research interests are in the interrelationship of law and finance in producing public policy relevant to the use of public funds for private schools, and in the funding of programs for special needs students. She has published widely in the fields of school law and school finance.

Biographical statements for contributors are contained in the text.